6/28	DATE DUE		

OVERDUE FINE
$0.10 PER DAY

THE

RED

CAT

COOKBOOK

THE

125 RECIPES FROM NEW YORK CITY'S

RED

FAVORITE NEIGHBORHOOD RESTAURANT

CAT

COOKBOOK

JIMMY BRADLEY & ANDREW FRIEDMAN

Photographs by David Sawyer

Clarkson Potter/Publishers
New York

Published in the United States by Clarkson Potter/
Publishers, an imprint of the Crown Publishing Group,
a division of Random House, Inc., New York.
www.crownpublishing.com
www.clarksonpotter.com

Clarkson N. Potter is a trademark and Potter and colophon
are registered trademarks of Random House, Inc.

Library of Congress Cataloging-in-Publication Data
Bradley, Jimmy.
    The Red Cat cookbook : 125 recipes from New York City's
favorite neighborhood restaurant / Jimmy Bradley and
Andrew Friedman.
    1. Cookery.   2. Red Cat (Restaurant)   I. Friedman,
Andrew.   II. Red Cat (Restaurant)   III. Title.
TX714.B67   2006
641.5—dc22   2006011054

ISBN-13: 978-1-4000-8281-0
ISBN-10: 1-4000-8281-1

Printed in China

Design by 3+Co.

10   9   8   7   6   5   4   3   2   1

First Edition

To all The Red Cat patrons . . .

CONTENTS

INTRODUCTION

Let me get this out of the way right up front, just so there's no confusion: This is not—I repeat *not*—a restaurant cookbook. Yes, it happens to be named after one of my restaurants, and, yes, a fair amount of the food hails from the menu there, but that's where it ends. Apart from this introduction, in which I'll explain where I'm coming from and how it all began, we're going to be talking food in these pages, not taking a behind-the-scenes peek at the industry in general or my places of business in particular. More to the point, this is a cookbook, not a souvenir, and it's meant for the kitchen, not the coffee table.

In this book, I'm going to share recipes for the food I love—my idiosyncratic synthesis of the Italian-American classics I grew up on, crossed with the down-to-earth sensibility of my native New England, and filtered through the no-holds-barred mentality of the New York City chef I've become. As you graze through it, you'll find a fondue that's broiled right in a skillet; hors d'oeuvres plucked from my fish-house memories of Rhode Island; a quick sauté of zucchini and slivered almonds topped with Pecorino cheese; a deconstructed tomato and bread soup; ravioli filled with mashed potatoes (you heard right); a new way to roast chicken without trussing or weighting it down; grilled fish; braised meats; a whole range of vegetables that you can dispatch as appetizers, sides, or garnishes; and desserts that beg, borrow, and steal from France, Italy, and America.

So why is this thing called *The Red Cat*? For the same reasons my restaurant is.

And why is that, you ask?

Well, that's a slightly longer story. Here you go . . .

WHAT'S IN A NAME?

A Brief History of The Red Cat

No matter where I've lived, worked, or traveled—coast to coast basically, with the occasional detour to Europe—there's always been a special little restaurant. I bet there's one like it near you: a can-do joint that is, in hospitality terms, all things to all people—a gathering place where you can drop in for a drink or a snack at the bar, or sit down in a dining room that's perfect for just about any occasion. Basically, a come-as-you-are destination for young and old, singles and families, respectable citizens and harmless hooligans alike—a place that exudes camaraderie, where you can gather with friends to end the day, or begin an evening.

You feel at home in a restaurant like this. In fact, a place like this *could* be your home, if your living quarters were big enough to seat about 100 people.

The food at these places is critical to their success; you go for the good vibe, but it's the food that really keeps you coming back. A great chicken and steak are *de rigueur*—the barometers that tell you whether or not the kitchen has a firm grasp of the fundamentals. But they are also just the beginning. The menu has to hit a lot of marks. There have to be some irresistible hors d'oeuvres, finger foods that you see described on the specials board, hear verbally, or watch the person next to you devouring, and think, "Let's have that. *Now.* Let's have that and then figure out the rest of the meal." There have to be a few great salads, some creative seafood and meat dishes, a handful of killer vegetables, and desserts that more than get the job done.

I love places like that, but when I came to New York City in 1989, they were the last thing on my mind. I more or less thought I was leaving them behind for something bigger, something better.

New York is called the Big Apple because that's how jazz musicians used to refer to it. An "apple" was a town on their touring itinerary. When they'd talk shop with their buddies, they'd say, "I'm going to this apple, and that apple, and then I'm going to the Big Apple." Manhattan is that way for a lot of industries, including the restaurant biz. There's no more exciting restaurant city in the world—I'd say in the *history* of the world—than New York. The allure of the city for an aspiring chef is virtually endless—a food world to be explored and conquered, both as a diner and as a creator of new ideas. So when I showed up here, I was looking forward to eating my way through all of Manhattan's great restaurants and being blown away and inspired.

I was blown away, all right, because I arrived in New York at the height of the movement widely referred to as New American Cuisine, a time of unprecedented experimentation in American restaurant kitchens. There was a lot of brilliant stuff going on—much of it having to do with weaving world ingredients and minimalist techniques into our food—but there was also a lot of freakiness afoot. It's almost impossible to spoof what was being served in some places: If you could turn something into a jelly, then someone was doing it. Tomatoes were served for dessert for no reason other than, technically speaking, they're a fruit. Neon-tinged sauces were squirted from squeeze bottles with abandon. Oh, and let's not forget vegetable juices and waters. I always think of that scene in *2001: A Space Odyssey* when the businessman is served an in-flight lunch that includes peas he sucks through a straw. I thought that that scene might become *real* in my new hometown by the time 2001 actually rolled along.

It's true what they say: Absence does make the heart grow fonder. Who would've thought that I could be living in New York City and find myself homesick for the kind of foods I grew up on? Then I realized that the dishes that I was weaned on, personally and professionally, have been around forever . . . but for a very good, reason: They press all the right buttons to leave you feeling satisfied. Like New England clam chowder, which for my money is sheer perfection: smoky bacon, clams, and veggies, all infusing a creamy soup. Or fish-house fare, like crab imperial and shrimp fritters. I get hungry just thinking about that stuff. On the Italian side, tomato bread soup is pretty perfect. Same goes for osso buco. Broccoli rabe with garlic and crushed red pepper flakes? No two ways about it: all great food.

Daydreaming about those dishes, I resolved to one day open my own kind of restaurant in New York, the one that I was dying to visit myself but which, at the time, was out of date, or out of vogue . . . but whose time I knew would come again. There was just one catch: The menu wouldn't simply be an auto-pilot one of classics, because if there was a silver lining to my late-1980s and early-1990s dining experiences, it was that freedom was being extended to every chef in the country. I was still honing my palate, and I felt liberated to bring a certain whimsy to my tradition-based cooking—to tweak those standards enough that they were recognizable but fresh. That habit has stayed with me and defined my style to this day.

When the time came and I was able to put together the right team, I opened my own place, with my business partner Danny Abrams; put those dishes on the menu; and called it The Red Cat. I thought the name had a nice ring to it. I still do. The Red Cat. It's kind of a blank canvas. There's no chef's moniker in there. There's no "bar" or "grill." It promises nothing of particular ethnicity. It just sounds like a place you'd go for some dinner, a nice hot meal at the end of a long day. I designed The Red Cat to be the ultimate neighborhood joint, a casual food hall with wainscoting and huge lanterns and abstract art on the walls, and a menu that doesn't take itself too seriously. Don't get me wrong. I take flavor seriously. I take satisfaction seriously. But once you clear those hurdles, I just want people to be comfortable and have a good time.

So Red Cat food is food that takes Western classics, primarily from Europe and the Eastern seaboard of the United States, plus a smattering of stuff I've discovered in my travels, and spins them just enough to make them different-—a little more fun to eat and a little more fun to cook, but never more of a hassle to prepare.

THE RED CAT COOKBOOK

Like The Red Cat, the restaurant, this book reflects the two food-obsessed cultures that coughed me up into the world: my personal home region of New England and my ancestral home country of Italy. As far as food is concerned, those communities have a lot in common, with an emphasis on simple, big-flavored dishes that can be prepared with relative ease. Neither is particularly concerned with labor-intensive methods, shock value, or what I call the BBD—the bigger, better deal that a lot of big-city restaurants and chefs seem to be pursuing, the way I was before I saw the light and returned to my good-food roots.

Like the cooks who populate New England and Italy, I like to prepare food in a straightforward manner, and stay true to the seasons. I'm not looking to put ingredients through a procession of complicated techniques. What I do falls smack in the center of the current movement back toward simplicity, but it isn't a response to a trend; it's just the way I like to cook.

The distinction between my dishes and the classics that inspired so many of them is, to borrow a phrase from John Travolta in *Pulp Fiction*, "the little differences," which, when it comes to food, can make a big impact. For example, in many of the recipes that follow, I take traditional American, Italian, or Mediterranean food, and put my own little spin on it, often employing French technique. The introduction of just one high-impact ingredient can reinvigorate a staple, like the shot of alcohol that adds a cool undercurrent to Split Pea Soup with Rum or the unexpected citrus in Halibut with Grapefruit, Parsley, Red Onion, and Shiitake. By the same token, I also love combining components in a new but very thoughtful way, like Spaghetti with a Salad on Top which is just that—a tangle of spaghetti dressed with a spicy red seafood sauce, with a simple arugula and scallion salad piled on top of it. I try to bring this food to life for an American sensibility, combining ingredients from different origins on occasion, but always staying true to the spirit of the original dishes. You won't find any so-called "fusion" in my food; for my money, fusion belongs in jazz, not cooking.

Red Cat food breaks a few rules. For example, there's a lot of sense behind the classic formula of including a protein, a starch, a vegetable, and a sauce in main courses. But I find that checklist a bit confining and feel that it often leads to extraneous elements on the plate. Over the years I've made some adjustments to it. One is that, in order to keep the focus squarely on the central combination of a dish, I usually serve a protein with a starch *or* a vegetable. As a happy consequence of this approach, many of my recipes ask the cook (this means you) to do less work than usual.

Then there's the variety of temperatures present on the plates. One of the challenges for the home cook in years gone by was getting everything to come out piping hot at the same time. I've devised a way to avoid worrying about that too much, because I like to serve different elements at different temperatures: usually the fish or meat is hot, but the starch or vegetable might be hot, just warm, or room temperature. For you at home, this means that you can make some dishes ahead and not stress about having several pans going at once just to get dinner on the table for family or friends. I wouldn't do that to you; there's just no reason.

I hope this book becomes for you what The Red Cat has become for the residents of Chelsea and their extended family of New Yorkers and visitors to our fair city: a reliable standby promising comfort and company. When you're not looking to spend the whole day in the kitchen—after work, say, or on a sunny summer afternoon—when you have the radio turned up loud, and a few beers cracked open, and just want to make something yummy and accessible that can be on the table in maybe an hour or two, I hope this is the book you'll pull off the shelf—or maybe keep on your kitchen counter at all times—for the quick fix, the dish you're craving, the stuff we all love to cook and eat.

GO-TO INGREDIENTS, DRESSINGS, AND SAUCES

Over the years, I've come to rely on a few key ingredients and preparations that show up over and over in my cooking. They're rarely the center of attention, but I love their flavor and effect so much that I couldn't cook without them. If they didn't exist, I'd probably be a guy still knocking around from job to job, trying to figure out what I wanted to do with my life. Here's what they are and why I use them so much.

GO-TO INGREDIENTS

Oils (Canola Oil, Olive Oil, and Extra-Virgin Olive Oil)

When to use which oil seems to be a source of confusion among home cooks. Let me break it down as simply as possible: I use the relatively neutral-flavored canola oil (you can substitute peanut or vegetable oil if you like) for high-heat cooking such as searing and sautéing. I also sometimes use it in dressings and vinaigrettes when I'm not looking to taste the oil itself.

As for olive oil, in my kitchens (home and work), I use three types: olive oil, virgin olive oil, and extra-virgin olive oil. For this book, I've confined myself to what you can find in most supermarkets, which is olive oil and extra-virgin olive oil.

Extra-virgin olive oil is the product of the first pressing of the olives, and it's by far the most flavorful, distinct, and expensive type of olive oil. Each extra-virgin olive oil has its own taste profile, ranging from fruity to almost harsh. Conventional wisdom is that extra-virgin olive oil doesn't stand up to high heat and should only be used in uncooked dishes, such as salads, or to finish soups and pastas. While I do use it for those things, I also often use extra-virgin olive oil on meats bound for the oven because I find that, while it's wasted on dishes cooked in a pan where it comes into direct contact with the heat, its flavor survives the ambient heat of the oven very well. That said, I will occasionally sauté quick-cooking ingredients in extra-virgin olive oil because it can impart tremendous flavor.

Olive oil is a catch-all category that encompasses the second press of the olives, and beyond. It's less expensive and less flavorful than extra-virgin olive oil, but a more flavorful option than canola or peanut oils. I use it for cooking, and in vinaigrettes that I don't want to be too rich or fruity. A big difference in use between olive oil and extra-virgin olive oil is that I *never* use olive oil as finishing oil.

Lemons

I use lemons in everything: The juice goes into vinaigrettes and sauces; the zest into marinades; slices get fried along with fish and poultry, then munched on like chips; and I serve wedges next to fried foods and rich sauces. I love lemons for their acidity, for their unique power to lift the other flavors in a dish, for their brightness, and for their singular energy. Once you've cooked a handful of my dishes, you might find yourself buying more lemons as part of your weekly shopping. I hope you do. They'll make your food better.

Parmigiano-Reggiano and Pecorino Romano Cheeses

It'd be tough to exaggerate how much home cooks in general, and Italian-Americans in particular, use Parmigiano-Reggiano and Pecorino Romano cheese. And with good reason: I melt them grated into sauces, pasta dishes, and risottos, where they bind the other ingredients together and add crucial saltiness. I also often top finished dishes with cheese shards.

In my opinion, these two cheeses should not be used interchangeably: Parmesan is meant for lighter ingredients, such as vegetable and fish preparations; Romano for larger, lustier flavors, such as braised meats and game. I also sometimes call on cheese in unusual places, such as the Pecorino Romano I blend into the Lemon-Coriander Aïoli served with fried clams on page 33; it helps bind the aïoli and make it creamy.

Olives

There are a wide variety of olives on the market—a lot of supermarkets these days have olive bars that are bigger than entire *salad* bars used to be. I primarily use black olives (such as Gaeta, Niçoise, kalamata, and oil-cured), and I call on them to add a subtle salinity and extra texture to all kinds of dishes, but especially salads, pastas, and seafood. I also like pureeing them into a sauce. To always have the flavor of olives on tap, keep some tapenade (olive paste) in the fridge.

Pepperoncini

You might not know their name, but you've definitely seen pepperoncini. They're those little pale green peppers often sold at salad bars. They're sweet and full of slightly spicy juice, and for that reason are a popular ingredient among Italian-American home cooks, of which I am one. You can buy them stored in a briny solution, in jars in supermarkets. I use them a lot in salads and pastas. If you or someone you love doesn't dig the heat, you can cut it by half by rinsing out the seeds after slicing the peppers.

(Crushed) Red Pepper Flakes

You've seen these at every pizza parlor you've ever been to, right next to the shakers of garlic powder and dried oregano. Unlike those other ingredients, which have few uses outside of a pizza place, crushed red pepper flakes can be used to add heat to everything from marinades to sauces to finished dishes. One neat trick is to grind your flakes in a spice mill for a hotter alternative to cayenne. Keep track of when you buy your pepper (writing the date on the label is the easiest way to do this), store it in a cool, dark, dry place, and replace it every twelve months to ensure that your supply packs some punch.

GO-TO DRESSINGS AND SAUCES

There are a handful of dressings and sauces that I use repeatedly throughout this book, and I want to explain why. In many dishes, there's a protein (fish, meat, or poultry), which has been seasoned, marinated, and/or cooked in some way that imparts flavor. Then, there's an accompaniment, such as a potato or vegetable side, featured to complement the protein. The combination of those two elements is usually the core idea of the dish, after which a sauce or dressing is only necessary to act as a bridge, pulling all the flavors together.

So, if you notice that I use olive oil and lemon juice to dress greens a lot, or a balsamic vinegar reduction or veal demi-glace as a sauce, it's just because that's all I think you really need. In instances where a more unique sauce is required, I make one, but in many cases, I find that there's simply nothing like a go-to dressing or sauce to finish things off.

HOW TO USE THIS BOOK

This book doesn't require much explanation. The recipes are organized pretty conventionally, running through starters, soups, pastas and risottos, main courses, vegetables, and desserts. Each recipe is kicked off with a headnote that tells you a little about the dish, its backstory, and what you might need to know to cook it well.

Notes on Ingredients

As for the recipes themselves, I've tried to keep things as simple as possible. Where ingredients need to be measured exactly, exact quantities are given. Where possible, however, I try to keep things casual, as befits home cooking. I often call for a medium onion, or the juice of a lemon, without specific cup or tablespoon measurements. I also use ½ tablespoon as a measurement although it's something you'll need to eyeball because there's no half-tablespoon measuring spoon on the market. I just find it easier than the official way of expressing a half tablespoon, which is 1½ teaspoons.

Unless otherwise stated, I use the following shorthand in my ingredient lists:

Butter is unsalted butter

Cream is heavy cream, aka whipping cream

Eggs are large eggs

Flour is all-purpose flour

Herbs are fresh and I'm talking about the leaves. In the case of parsley,
     I'm talking about flat-leaf parsley, also called Italian parsley.

Lemon juice is freshly squeezed and seed-free

Milk is whole milk

Onions are Spanish onions

Pasta is dried pasta

Salt is coarse kosher salt

Sugar is granulated white sugar

What I Mean When I Ask You to "Slice" Herbs (or Leafy Greens)

With very few exceptions, I use the word *sliced* in ingredient lists to describe how to prepare herbs and the occasional leafy green (and one leafy "red"—radicchio). It's a very deliberate word choice, selected over the more widely used *chopped*. When I say to slice an herb, I mean to slice the individual leaves no more than one time in any one place. A parsley leaf, for example, may be sliced in one or two places, *max*. Same goes for tarragon, cilantro, chervil, and leafy greens such as spinach and escarole. In the case of those greens, and of larger-leafed herbs, such as basil, you can stack and roll the leaves, then slice the roll crosswise, resulting in ribbons, which French cooks call *chiffonnade*. The reason for this is simple: When you chop a mound of herbs or leaves, repetitively bringing your knife down on it, you inevitably bruise them, robbing them of color and flavor. The three exceptions to this rule are oregano, rosemary, and thyme leaves, which are so small that—when you don't want entire leaves in the dish— they simply have to be chopped.

Note to the Cook

Some recipes are followed by Note (or Notes) to the Cook. This is where I offer advice that makes the recipe even more user-friendly, such as how to shop for an ingredient, possible substitutions, items that can be left out, and simpler presentations, or share kitchen tips such as notes on grilling and frying, and interesting tidbits.

FINGER FOODS, APPETIZERS & SALADS

FRIED GREEN BEANS *with Sweet Hot Mustard*

FRIED ZUCCHINI BLOSSOMS

ENGLISH SHELL PEAS *with Olive Oil and Salt*

FISH-HOUSE SPECIALTIES

SHRIMP CAKES

FRIED OYSTERS *with Spicy Salsa Fresca*

CRISPY FRIED CLAMS *with Lemon-Coriander Aïoli*

BAKED FONTINA *with Garlic, Olive Oil, and Thyme*

CHOPPED AIRPORT SALAD

CUCUMBER, WATERMELON, AND FENNEL SALAD *with Ricotta Salata*

SUNFLOWER SALAD

SLICED HEIRLOOM TOMATOES *with Blue Cheese Puffs*

QUICK SAUTÉ OF ZUCCHINI *with Toasted Almonds and Pecorino*

SHAVED MUSHROOM AND FENNEL SALAD *with Dry Jack Cheese*

ASPARAGUS AND EGGS *with Bacon Tempura*

FIG TART *with Caramelized Onions and Blue Cheese*

GRILLED HEN-OF-THE-WOODS MUSHROOMS *on Soppressata*

PEACH, RED ONION, AND PECAN SALAD *with Goat Cheese*

BITTER GREENS SALAD *with Gruyère Fondue*

PAN-FRIED ARTICHOKES *with Lemon and Parmesan*

WARM JERSEY CORN SALAD

BAKED SEAFOOD IMPERIAL

VITELLO TONNATO *with Anchovy-Caper Mayonnaise*

SQUASH SALAD *with Soft Lettuce and Parmesan*

GRILLED BELGIAN ENDIVE *with Gorgonzola Gratineé and Balsamic Vinegar*

SEARED TUNA CROSTINI

CLAMS OREGANATA

SEARED LAMB CARPACCIO *with Chopped Egg and Scallions*

I like to start get-togethers off with a bang, in the truest sense of the word—something attention-grabbing that makes you stop and appreciate it the moment you put it in your mouth. The recipes in this chapter basically fall into two categories: finger foods (my term for hors d'oeuvres) and plated first courses. They are diverse and, I think, interesting, and many of them are built for speed, with a few more intricate ones thrown in for those occasions when you want to pull out the jams.

I suggest selecting starters not just based on compatibility with the main course, but also to take advantage of what you're cooking and how you're cooking it. For example, if you're making an entrée with zucchini, you might think about starting things off by breading and frying the blossoms, as we do on page 25. Or, if you're grilling the main course, then you should probably select a starter that's cooked on the grill as well. These efficiencies can make cooking, even for a full-blown dinner party, a lot easier. There's another way to make cooking more fun and less work: Enlist your guests as kitchen helpers. When I entertain, unless it's a formal occasion, I have everybody help out, and I serve the finger foods in this chapter to keep them going when we're all hanging and cooking together.

The hors d'oeuvres that follow can be passed around when everyone shows up, the perfect thing to wash down with a glass of wine or a cold beer. They're also good snacks in their own right

that you can make and munch on whenever you feel like it—in the middle of the afternoon, or late at night. These are some of the shortest recipes in the book because I believe you're more likely to make your own if they're fast.

Something a lot of them have in common is that I often rely on a high-impact cooking technique to do most of the work—adding to the ingredients' natural flavor and texture—such as the char provided by grilling, or the crunch of frying. There's also a lot of dunking here: whether it's scooping up melted cheese with a hunk of bread or dipping fried shellfish into a sauce. Dunking is fun, and it loosens people up right off the bat.

As for the first courses, a friend of mine once noted that most of the dining public wants a salad as an appetizer, and after a lot of consideration and observation, I decided she was right, so most of the plated dishes here are salads, which I loosely define as a vegetable-heavy preparation. Outside of that standard, there are really no rules: hot shares the plate with cold, watermelon with fennel and ricotta salata, melted cheese with greens, and eggs with something we created on a dare one night: bacon tempura.

One last piece of advice: Don't be bound by categories. If you're looking for a quick meal some time, and aren't too rigid about how you define it, a lot of these recipes, especially the salads, will do just fine for dinner, and especially for lunch.

FRIED GREEN BEANS

with Sweet Hot Mustard

SERVES 4

A fresh look at a taken-for-granted ingredient. Rather than serving green beans only as a side dish, I like to batter and fry them for a communal finger food. The batter is light and airy—just enough to provide the desired crunch and keep the beans themselves from frying—and the mustard sauce is surprisingly nuanced, thanks to the balance struck between hot sauce, honey, and soy. This dish knows no fixed place on the menu: At The Red Cat, customers eat these as a bar snack and starter, as well as a side dish.

1¼ cups Dijon mustard

⅛ teaspoon dry mustard

1 tablespoon plus 1 teaspoon hot sauce

3 tablespoons light soy sauce

¾ cup honey

Canola oil, for frying

4 egg whites

3 cups flour

2¾ cups plus 2 tablespoons club soda or seltzer

1 pound green beans, trimmed

Salt

Put the Dijon, dry mustard, hot sauce, soy, and honey in a saucepan and set over low heat. Whisk until all ingredients are incorporated and the sauce is warm, approximately 5 minutes. Transfer to a small serving bowl and set aside to cool.

Line a plate or platter with paper towels. Pour the oil into a large pot to a depth of 4 inches and heat over medium-high heat to a temperature of 350°F.

Meanwhile, in a large bowl, whisk the egg whites until soft peaks form. Whisk in the flour and club soda. Dip the beans into the batter, letting any excess batter run off, and carefully lower the beans into the oil in small batches, so they do not stick together. (Do not overcrowd, or the oil can over-flow, and the beans will not cook evenly.) Cook the beans, stirring periodically to keep them from sticking together, until lightly golden brown, approximately 3 minutes. Remove the beans from the oil using a slotted spoon and transfer to the paper-towel-lined plate. Season immediately with salt.

Let the oil return to a temperature of 350°F and repeat with another batch of beans. Continue to repeat until all of the beans have been battered and fried.

Serve the beans hot in a bowl or on a platter, passing the mustard sauce alongside for dipping.

NOTES TO THE COOK You can also serve this, or most fried foods in this book, with a lemon wedge for squirting on top instead of the dipping sauce.

A couple of tips on frying: Whenever frying, the temperature of the oil is very important. (If you don't have a clip-on thermometer for checking the temperature of frying oil, use this tried-and-true test:

recipe continues

Wet your fingers and flick a drop of water, or in this case a drop of batter, into the oil. If it sizzles on contact, you're good to go.) The oil needs to be hot when the food goes in, and stay hot while it cooks. That's why all my recipes say not to overcrowd the pot; add too many solids and the temperature will plummet and never recover, and your food will be flabby and pale instead of crisp and lightly browned. As for doneness, all the recipes in this book have cooking times, but a general rule of thumb for frying is that if it floats and is golden, it's probably done. Finally, when I have them around, I like to toss some herbs or thin lemon slices into the pot with whatever's being fried—you get more flavor, and something else to munch on. Add them during the final minute of cooking time.

While frying generally calls for a relatively large quantity of oil, the good news is that you can reuse it. Let it cool, then strain it into an airtight container (I use a Mason jar) and keep it in a cool, dark place. You can generally reuse oil two or three times, or until it becomes dirty or cloudy. If you're frying fish or bacon, though, the oil should be discarded after the first use; those flavors are just too powerful and will take over the next thing you fry.

To discard oil, let the oil cool, fill a used container such as a milk carton or large aluminum can with paper towels, and pour the cold oil into the container. The paper towels will absorb the oil and then you simply throw away the container.

FRIED ZUCCHINI BLOSSOMS

SERVES 4

I'm a music lover, and I have a personal rule about whether or not an artist or band should cover a classic: If they can't improve on the original, then they've got no business messing with it. The most successful cover of all time was probably Jimi Hendrix's version of Bob Dylan's "All Along the Watchtower." When Dylan heard it, he said (I'm paraphrasing): "That's the way that song was always meant to sound; that's how I'm gonna play it from now on."

Which brings me to what I call the Watchtower Test: Even with my predilection to tinker with classic recipes, there are times when there's just no reason to. Unless I feel my version could pass the Watchtower Test, pleasing the creator of the original if he or she happened to show up for dinner one night, I just let it ride. Case in point: fried zucchini blossoms, a summertime favorite in Piedmont, where I've been known to pass a summer's day with my cousin Pio Boffa, proprietor of Pio Cesare Winery in Alba, snacking on these with some ice-cold prosecco before dinner.

2 cups fine bread crumbs (preferably Japanese panko), crushed or ground to a powder

1 cup finely grated Parmigiano-Reggiano

2 tablespoons sliced parsley

1 teaspoon salt, plus more for serving

1/2 teaspoon freshly ground black pepper

About 2 cups flour, for dredging

3 eggs

16 zucchini blossoms, with the stems attached

3/4 cup canola oil

3/4 cup extra-virgin olive oil

Put the bread crumbs, Parmigiano-Reggiano, and parsley in a bowl and season with the salt and pepper. Stir to incorporate the seasoning.

Spread the flour out on a plate. Crack the eggs into a bowl and beat them with 1 tablespoon cold water.

Press the blossoms into the flour, then dip in the egg, then dredge in the bread-crumb mixture, pressing gently to make sure it adheres.

Line a large plate with paper towels.

Heat 1/4 cup of the canola oil and 1/4 cup of the extra-virgin olive oil in a wide, deep, heavy-bottomed sauté pan set over medium-high heat. Add 5 blossoms and sauté, turning once, until lightly golden brown, approximately 3 minutes per side. Transfer to the paper-towel-lined plate to drain and season immediately with salt. Repeat twice to use the remaining oil and blossoms, using 6 blossoms in the last batch.

Arrange the blossoms on a plate or platter and serve hot.

NOTE TO THE COOK For fine-grating cheese into a snowy white powder that will disappear into a bread-crumb mixture or melt right into soups and sauces, use a Microplane zester. This implement features hundreds of tiny, razor-sharp blades that grate hard cheeses with minimal exertion.

ENGLISH SHELL PEAS
with Olive Oil and Salt

SERVES 4

If you love *edamame*, the Japanese hors d'oeuvre of steamed soybeans, then you'll go nuts for this new American variation made by grilling peas in the pod, then drizzling them with extra-virgin olive oil and seasoning them with salt. It's the ultimate user-friendly starter: focused on one primary ingredient, super-easy for the cook, fun for the guests (who get to suck out the peas), and loaded with flavor. They're so quick and easy that you can make them to order, grilling up fresh batches as you run out, though in my experience you'll go through as many peas as you have in the house, so you may as well cook 'em all up from the get-go.

2 pounds largest available peas in the pod, at least 4 inches in length

⅓ cup canola oil

Salt

Extra-virgin olive oil, for serving

Freshly ground black pepper

Preheat a gas grill to high, or prepare a charcoal grill for grilling, letting the coals burn until covered with white ash.

Put the pea pods in a large bowl. Drizzle with the canola oil, and season with salt. Grill, turning with tongs every 2 minutes, until the skins blacken and blister and the peas feel soft through the pod, approximately 8 minutes. Use the tongs to transfer the pea pods to a large plate or platter. Drizzle with extra-virgin olive oil, and season generously with salt and pepper.

Serve hot, passing an empty bowl or two alongside for trashing spent pods.

NOTES TO THE COOK If you can't find pea pods large enough that they won't fall through your grill grate, lay a wire cooling rack, top side down (so the legs are facing upward), on top of the grate and grill on that.

When grilling, trust your eyes more than your stopwatch. All the grilling recipes in this book feature cooking times, but these should be taken as a guideline, not as gospel. Unlike using an oven, where you can control the exact temperature at all times, and the temperature is the same on all sides of the food being cooked, using a grill is not an exact science. The grilling time will be influenced by whether you're using charcoal or gas, how hot the fire is, how close your grill grate is to the heat source, and even how strong the wind is blowing across your backyard. Plus, the food is only cooked from below; even if you cover the grill, the heat under the grate will be more intense than the ambient temperature. Bottom line: Keep a watchful eye on whatever you're grilling.

FISH-HOUSE SPECIALTIES

Even if you've never been to New England, you probably know what a fish house, or clam shack, is: a seaside structure, usually made of wooden planks that look like they were slapped together in a few hours' time and somehow have been standing for the past forty years in the same spot. There's a window and a handwritten or stenciled menu on the wall behind the counter person, who is either a grizzled old dude who's owned the place for decades, or one of the town's finest teenagers, on break from the local high school. There are paper cups for soda, plastic ones for beer, and paper plates or little cardstock baskets for the food. There's always a line, and if you ask for a tray on which to carry your food away, it will look suspiciously like the cardboard bottom of a case of beer.

And the food itself? Well, it isn't going to win any awards from the American Heart Association, but nobody cares because it's so damn good: fried oysters and clams, seafood cakes (fritters to you), lobster rolls, chowder, and stuffies, which are basically a giant version of clams casino, minus the bacon on top, made with quahog clams that have been steamed open, chopped, tossed with bread crumbs, onion, and celery, then *stuffed* back into the shell. You know the kind of food I'm talking about—the food you love to grab on a hot summer day when you're taking a break from the beach to cool off and devour some sustenance before getting back out there for the rest of the afternoon.

These three recipes for fried shellfish preparations to which I've added a sauce or topping are inspired by my fish-house memories of New England. You'll notice that each one has its own batter or breading: In my ongoing effort to create compelling contrasts wherever possible, I use lighter, airier batters (along the lines of a tempura) with sturdier shellfish, and crunchier batters (featuring, say, cornmeal) with more delicate shellfish.

SHRIMP CAKES

SERVES 4

"Cakes" is the New England word for "fritters," and shellfish cakes are New England street food at its finest, the kind of thing I grew up eating everywhere, from the beach to carnivals to roadside stands. I remember them with clams, but shrimp are just as popular, and less work, so that's what I call for here. That said, you can make these with clams, or with anything from oysters to scallops.

This is one frying recipe that really requires a thermometer; the temperature of the oil needs to stay within a very specific range throughout the cooking time.

½ cup flour

½ cup semolina flour, or fine yellow cornmeal

2 teaspoons baking powder

Salt

Freshly ground black pepper

2 eggs, beaten

5 ounces peeled, deveined large shrimp, coarsely chopped

½ cup finely chopped scallions, white and green parts

¼ cup finely chopped red onion

¼ cup Shellfish Stock (page 247), or bottled clam juice

¼ cup light-style beer, such as pilsner

1½ teaspoons finely chopped jalapeño pepper, with its seeds

Canola oil, for frying

Rémoulade (recipe follows)

Lemon wedges

Put the flour, semolina flour, and baking powder in a bowl, season with salt and pepper, and stir to incorporate. Add the eggs, shrimp, scallions, red onion, stock, beer, and jalapeño, and stir gently but thoroughly with a rubber spatula. (This is your dough. It can be covered and refrigerated for up to 2 days. Be sure to let it come to room temperature before frying.)

Line a cookie sheet with paper towels. Pour the oil into a heavy-bottomed pot to a depth of 4 inches and set over medium-high heat. Heat to a temperature of 350°F.

Meanwhile, shape the dough into rounded-teaspoon-size cakes.

Carefully lower the cakes into the oil in small batches. (Do not overcrowd, or the oil can overflow, and the cakes will not cook evenly.) Cook the cakes, stirring periodically to keep them from sticking together, and maintaining the temperature at no lower than 325°F, until the cakes are puffed, deep golden brown, and cooked through, approximately 6 minutes. Remove the cakes from the oil using a slotted spoon and transfer to the paper-towel-lined cookie sheet. Season immediately with salt.

Let the oil return to a temperature of 350°F and repeat with another batch of cakes. Continue to repeat until all of the cakes have been fried.

Transfer the cakes to a platter or bowl and serve with rémoulade and lemon wedges alongside.

Rémoulade

MAKES ABOUT 2 CUPS

Rémoulade is a fancy tartar sauce that's gussied up with mustard and herbs. It can also be served with other fried foods—I especially like it with fried oysters—as well as with chicken, cold poached fish, veal, or raw vegetables.

1 cup mayonnaise

¼ cup coarsely chopped capers

3 tablespoons finely diced red onion

2 tablespoons Dijon mustard

2 tablespoons sliced tarragon

2 tablespoons sliced parsley

1 tablespoon red wine vinegar

1 tablespoon thinly sliced scallion

½ teaspoon lemon juice

¼ teaspoon hot sauce

Salt

Freshly ground black pepper

Put the mayonnaise, capers, onion, mustard, tarragon, parsley, vinegar, scallion, lemon juice, and hot sauce in a bowl. Season with salt and pepper, and stir well to incorporate.

The rémoulade can be covered and refrigerated for 2 to 3 days. Try to make it at least a day in advance, because it's always better the next day.

NOTE TO THE COOK To make a conventional tartar sauce, a fine condiment for any of these fish-house recipes, leave out the mustard and herbs.

FRIED OYSTERS
with Spicy Salsa Fresca

SERVES 4

Some people object to frying oysters, and I understand where they're coming from: There's nothing much better than a pristine, icy cold oyster. But, let's be honest: Everything's great fried. To make the flavor of these pop, I add a little curry powder to the otherwise conventional breading.

Canola oil, for frying

2 cups flour

½ tablespoon curry powder

½ teaspoon salt, plus more for seasoning

¼ teaspoon freshly ground black pepper

¼ teaspoon cayenne

1 pound freshly shucked oysters (about 20 oysters)

Spicy Salsa Fresca (recipe follows)

Line a plate or platter with paper towels. Pour the oil into a large heavy-bottomed pot to a depth of 4 inches, and heat over medium-high heat to a temperature of 350°F.

Meanwhile, put the flour, curry powder, salt, pepper, and cayenne in a bowl and stir together. Roll the oysters in the seasoned flour, pressing down to make sure it adheres.

Carefully lower the oysters into the oil, in small batches. (Do not overcrowd, or the oil can over-flow, and the oysters will not cook evenly.) Cook the oysters, stirring periodically to keep them from sticking together, until lightly golden brown, 3 to 4 minutes. Remove the oysters from the oil using a slotted spoon and transfer to the paper-towel-lined plate. Season immediately with salt.

Let the oil return to a temperature of 350°F and repeat with another batch of oysters. Continue to repeat until all of the oysters have been battered and fried, letting the oil reheat between each batch.

Arrange 20 tablespoons on plates, or a large platter, and set 1 fried oyster in the well of each spoon. Top with a little salsa fresca and serve.

Spicy Salsa Fresca

MAKES ABOUT 1¼ CUPS

Salsa fresca is Italian for "fresh sauce," and it generally refers to an uncooked mixture of chopped vegetables and herbs. This one is a simple, clean, and spicy variation on that theme. All of the ingredients need to be diced or chopped as fine as possible so the sauce can fit atop a tiny fried oyster. If you make the sauce a bit chunkier, it's a perfect accompaniment to crab cakes and grilled or fried fish. It can also be tossed with tuna fish for a mayo-less tuna salad, or spooned onto grilled or toasted country bread for a vegetable *crostini*.

¾ cup finely diced ripe red tomato

⅓ cup peeled, seeded, and finely diced cucumber

1 tablespoon seeded, finely diced red bell pepper

1 tablespoon seeded, finely diced yellow bell pepper

1 tablespoon finely diced red onion

1 teaspoon finely chopped garlic

1 tablespoon thinly sliced basil

1 tablespoon extra-virgin olive oil

½ teaspoon red wine vinegar

½ teaspoon crushed red pepper flakes

Salt

Freshly ground black pepper

Put the tomato, cucumber, red and yellow bell peppers, onion, garlic, basil, oil, vinegar, and red pepper flakes in a small bowl. Season generously with salt, then with black pepper, toss, and let marinate for at least 1 hour, or up to 6, before serving. (It gets better the longer it marinates.)

CRISPY FRIED CLAMS
with Lemon-Coriander Aïoli

SERVES 4

Fried clams are *the* food of New England, a benchmark of whether or not a given cook is worth his salt, the way a roast chicken or French fries are in most other places. New England cooks need to be able to turn out great fried clams, because they show up in everything from hors d'oeuvres to sandwiches to salads to part of the quintessential fried-seafood platter. The secret to great New England–style flavor is the liberal use of celery salt and celery seed. These clams are pretty addictive, thanks to the simple, light breading and the cheese, lemon, and spices in the dipping sauce; you won't find them in a traditional fish-house sauce, but they get along great with the ingredients in the breading.

1 cup flour

½ cup cornmeal

⅓ cup cornstarch

1 teaspoon curry powder

¾ teaspoon salt, plus more for seasoning

¾ teaspoon celery salt

½ teaspoon celery seed

½ teaspoon cayenne

Canola oil, for frying

About 1 pound Atlantic surf clams or soft-shell clams, shucked and sliced (¾ cup)

About 1 cup buttermilk

Lemon-Coriander Aïoli (recipe follows)

Put the flour, cornmeal, cornstarch, curry, salt, celery salt, celery seed, and cayenne in a bowl and stir together.

Pour the oil into a heavy-bottomed pot to a depth of 4 inches and set over medium-high heat. Heat to a temperature of 350°F. Line a plate with paper towels.

Dip the clams in the buttermilk, letting any excess milk run off. Then dredge them in the flour mixture. Add them to the oil in small batches and fry until golden and crisp, approximately 2 minutes. As they are done, remove from the oil using a slotted spoon and transfer to the paper-towel-lined plate. Season immediately with salt. Let the oil return to a temperature of 350°F and repeat until all of the clams have been breaded and fried.

Serve from a bowl with the lemon-coriander aïoli alongside.

NOTE TO THE COOK I use a mix of cornmeal and cornstarch instead of pure cornmeal because the starch becomes fluffier when fried.

Lemon-Coriander Aïoli

This isn't your typical tartar or rémoulade sauce; the inclusion of cheese and anchovies makes it turn a corner toward Caesar salad dressing. All I can tell you is that it's delicious with these clams, and with all the same foods recommended for the two previous fish-house sauces. You can also emulsify it into some hot chicken stock to make a fast sauce that's outstanding with roasted chicken.

½ teaspoon coriander seed
1 egg yolk
1 anchovy fillet
½ teaspoon chopped garlic
Juice of 1 medium lemon
Leaves from ½ bunch cilantro

1 tablespoon red wine vinegar
½ tablespoon Dijon mustard
2 tablespoons grated Pecorino Romano
1 cup canola oil
Salt
Freshly ground black pepper

Put the coriander seed in a pan and toast over high heat until lightly toasted and fragrant, approximately 2 minutes. Transfer to a cutting board and coarsely chop it. Let cool.

Put the yolk, anchovy, garlic, lemon juice, cilantro, vinegar, mustard, and Pecorino in the bowl of a food processor fitted with the steel blade. Process for 3 minutes, then gradually add the oil in a thin stream to make a thick, creamy, white emulsion. After all of the oil has been added, add the coriander seed, and season with salt and pepper, being mindful that the anchovy and cheese are salty.

The aïoli can be covered and refrigerated for 2 to 3 days. Try to make it at least a day in advance, because it's always better the next day.

NOTE TO THE COOK If you don't have a food processor, chop the anchovy and cilantro leaves by hand and put them in a bowl. Add the remaining ingredients, stir well to combine, and season with salt and pepper.

BAKED FONTINA
with Garlic, Olive Oil, and Thyme

SERVES 4

This is a streamlined, simplified version of fondue without the fondue pot; without the cans of Sterno; and without the wine, cornstarch, or other supporting ingredients. You just take some cubed Fontina cheese, top it with slivered garlic, thyme leaves, and olive oil, and broil until it's melted and bubbly enough to scoop up with hunks of bread. It's a great appetizer, and paired with a green salad and a glass of wine, a pretty nifty lunch or dinner as well. (In fact, my writing partner, Andrew Friedman, and his wife, Caitlin, have just that for dinner at least once a week at The Red Cat's bar.) Be sure to use an Italian Fontina; the Danish varieties don't melt right for this recipe.

1½ pounds Italian Fontina, soft, brown rind trimmed and discarded, cut into 1-inch dice

¼ cup olive oil

6 cloves garlic, thinly sliced

1 tablespoon thyme

1 teaspoon chopped rosemary

Salt

Freshly ground black pepper

Sliced country bread or rolls

Preheat the broiler.

For individual servings, divide the Fontina among four 6-inch cast-iron pans. Drizzle with olive oil and scatter the garlic, thyme, and rosemary over the cheese. Season with salt and pepper. For one large pan, use a 12-inch cast-iron skillet and follow the same directions.

Broil until the cheese is melted and bubbly, 6 to 7 minutes.

Serve each person an individual pan, setting it on a trivet or napkin, or serve the 12-inch pan from the center of the table. Pass the bread alongside for dunking.

CHOPPED AIRPORT SALAD

SERVES 4

Why is this called an airport salad? To be honest, it's a bit of an in-joke in my family: My uncle used to ask my grandmother to make this for him all the time when he was a kid. It never had a name, until my uncle was about to leave home for the army. Just before heading for the airport, he requested this for his "last" meal, and the name was born. It's a virtual hit parade of Italian-American staples including salami, Provolone cheese, romaine lettuce, pepperoncini, oregano, and of course, oil and vinegar—but the presentation is different enough to make it interesting.

¼ cup extra-virgin olive oil

2 tablespoons red wine vinegar

¼ teaspoon Dijon mustard

Salt

Freshly ground black pepper

4 ounces Genoa salami, thinly sliced, cut into julienne strips (about 1 cup)

4 ounces Provolone cheese, thinly sliced, cut into julienne strips (about 1 cup)

1 heart romaine lettuce, thinly sliced crosswise

½ medium red onion, thinly sliced

2 stalks celery, thinly sliced diagonally

1 large carrot, peeled and cut into thin strips

6 large pepperoncini, thinly sliced on the bias, juice and seeds from cutting board reserved if possible

2 teaspoons chopped oregano

2 plum tomatoes, sliced crosswise into ½-inch slices

Make the vinaigrette: Put the oil, vinegar, and Dijon in a bowl and whisk together. Season to taste with salt and pepper. Set aside.

Put the salami, ¾ cup of the cheese, the lettuce, onion, celery, carrot, and pepperoncini and their juice and seeds in a large bowl. Add the vinaigrette and oregano and toss. Season to taste with salt.

Arrange a few tomato slices around the perimeter of each of 4 salad plates and season them each with a pinch of salt. Pile some salad on top of the tomatoes, top each serving with some of the remaining cheese, and serve.

CUCUMBER, WATERMELON,
AND FENNEL SALAD
with Ricotta Salata

SERVES 4

This crazy-sounding salad grew naturally out of my affection for two traditions: one old and one new. The former is *crudités*, or raw vegetables nibbled on as an hors d'oeuvre; the latter is a popular modern salad of watermelon paired with some kind of cheese, usually goat. This hybrid of those influences skews Italian, with the inclusion of fennel and ricotta salata, which is simply ricotta cheese that's been salted, pressed, and aged until crumbly and pleasantly salty. This salad is clean, fresh, and crisp and offers a great, uncomplicated way to enjoy summer vegetables, whether from your garden, a farm stand, or the supermarket.

5 medium cucumbers or 2 large, seedless hothouse cucumbers (about 10 ounces), very thinly sliced lengthwise, ideally on a mandoline

½ small bulb fennel, trimmed, very thinly sliced crosswise, ideally on a mandoline

2 teaspoons lemon juice

1 tablespoon plus 1 teaspoon extra-virgin olive oil

Salt

Freshly ground black pepper

3 ounces ricotta salata, crumbled

1 tablespoon sliced parsley

1 pound watermelon, rind removed (about 12 ounces), cut into eight wedges

Put the cucumber and fennel slices in a bowl. Add the lemon juice and oil, season with salt and pepper, and toss the salad well.

Pile some salad in the center of each of 4 salad plates. Top each one with some crumbled cheese, and scatter some parsley over the top. Set a watermelon wedge on both sides of each salad and serve.

NOTE TO THE COOK Use your best, fruitiest extra-virgin olive oil on this salad; it really brings out the other flavors.

SUNFLOWER SALAD

SERVES 4

Ah, the element of surprise: Most people only know sunflower seeds as a health snack, or part of a trail mix, so when they see them in a salad, you've already won them over. I've been eating sunflower seeds in salads my whole life, because I grew up in a half-crunchy household: My (divorced) dad's girlfriend was an out-and-out health-food nut who belonged to a food co-op, shopped at the farmer's market, and tried every new tofu product in town. (Favorite memory: grinding our own organic peanut butter at the market, years before Whole Foods made it trendy to do so.) We were known to eat scrambled tofu, rather than eggs, for breakfast and bake carob-, rather than chocolate-, chip cookies. We even germinated our own sprouts. When microgreens became all the rage in the 1990s, I thought, "It's about time." I'd been eating delicate greens for decades, so I whipped up this salad featuring those dependable ol' sprouts and the ever-popular seeds. It's a light, simple salad punched up with the vibrant flavor of beets, salty Parmesan cheese, and the vinaigrette, which calls on three types of vinegar.

Salt

2 large beets (about 12 ounces)

6 baby golden beets (about 6 ounces)

1/4 cup shelled sunflower seeds

1 tablespoon extra-virgin olive oil

Freshly ground black pepper

2 heads Bibb lettuce, about 5 ounces each, separated into leaves

1 1/2 cups packed sunflower sprouts, trimmed to 1 1/2 to 2 inches

2 1/2 ounces Parmigiano-Reggiano cheese, 1 ounce grated (1/4 cup), remaining cut into shards with a vegetable peeler

Sunflower Vinaigrette (recipe follows)

Bring a medium or large pot of salted water to a boil. Add the beets and boil until tender to a knife-tip, approximately 12 minutes for the baby beets and 40 minutes for the large beets.

While the beets are boiling, heat a skillet over medium-high heat. Add the sunflower seeds and toast until lightly browned, 3 to 5 minutes. Transfer to a small bowl and set aside.

When the beets are done, drain them, and when cool enough to handle, peel and quarter the baby beets. Transfer to a bowl and dress with the extra-virgin olive oil. Season with salt and pepper and set aside.

Peel the large beets and slice them very thin crosswise, ideally on a mandoline. Arrange the beets in an overlapping pattern over the surface of 4 salad plates.

Tear the lettuce into bite-size pieces, gathering them in a large bowl. Add the sprouts and grated cheese, and season with salt and pepper. Drizzle the vinaigrette over the salad and gently toss. Divide among the beet-covered salad plates. Top with the seeds and a cheese shard. Arrange some baby beet wedges around each salad and serve.

recipe continues

NOTE TO THE COOK Be sure to use sunflower sprouts for this salad. They stay crisp and waxy and make the salad pleasantly fluffy. Other sprouts tend to collapse when tossed into a salad and to wilt when dressed with vinaigrette.

Sunflower Vinaigrette

MAKES ABOUT ½ CUP

This is an all-purpose vinaigrette that you can use as an everyday house dressing. This recipe makes enough for roughly four portions; just multiply accordingly to make as much as you need.

1 shallot, finely diced

1 tablespoon rice vinegar

1 tablespoon sherry vinegar

1 tablespoon champagne vinegar

2 tablespoons extra-virgin olive oil

1 tablespoon sunflower oil

1 teaspoon sugar

Salt

Freshly ground black pepper

Whisk the shallot; rice, sherry, and champagne vinegars; sunflower oil; and sugar together in a small bowl. Season to taste with salt and pepper.

This dressing can be covered and refrigerated for 2 to 3 days.

SLICED HEIRLOOM TOMATOES
with Blue Cheese Puffs

SERVES 4

For my money, tomatoes and blue cheese are a classic combination: The clean, sweet, and acidic fruit goes perfectly with the intensity of the cheese, and this is especially true of soft, juicy heirloom varieties. Putting the blue cheese in a warm *gougère*, or cheese puff, adds another texture and temperature to the plate. The puffs are delicious on their own; think about making three times as many as you need and snacking on the extra, or serving them as an hors d'oeuvre.

½ cup hot water

½ cup milk

8 tablespoons (1 stick) butter, plus more for greasing the baking sheet

Salt

1 cup flour

3 eggs

2 ounces blue cheese, crumbled (½ cup)

1 teaspoon dry mustard, or 1 tablespoon Dijon mustard

Pinch of cayenne

2 large heirloom tomatoes or ripe beefsteak tomatoes, thinly sliced

1 medium red onion, minced

¼ cup sliced parsley

¼ cup basil, torn into small pieces

Extra-virgin olive oil, for serving

Freshly ground black pepper

Preheat the oven to 400°F.

Put the water, milk, butter, and a pinch of salt in a heavy-bottomed pot and heat until the butter melts. Add the flour and stir vigorously with a wooden spoon until the dough forms a firm ball and pulls away from the edges of the pot, approximately 5 minutes.

Transfer the dough to a bowl and beat in the eggs, one by one, stirring each one in until well incorporated and the dough is firm, smooth, and waxy, a few minutes. Stir in the cheese, mustard, and cayenne.

Grease a baking sheet and drop the dough by rounded tablespoonfuls onto it, or use a pastry bag fitted with a medium round tip.

Bake the cheese puffs until puffy and golden, approximately 20 minutes. Turn off the oven and let the puffs sit in the oven for 5 minutes.

Divide the tomato slices among 4 salad plates. Scatter the onion, parsley, and basil over the tomatoes. Drizzle with oil and season with salt and pepper. Top with warm cheese puffs and serve.

QUICK SAUTÉ OF ZUCCHINI
with Toasted Almonds and Pecorino

SERVES 4

We've served this dish at The Red Cat since our first dinner back in 1999. It sums up a lot of what I think makes a dish comfortable to both cook and diner: a mere handful of ingredients, each contributing its own important flavor and texture; the whole thing held together with a fine extra-virgin olive oil. It's that simple, but the flavor is very complex and complete.

Technically speaking, "quick sauté" is almost redundant; to sauté something means to make it "jump in the pan." But I include *quick* in the title to emphasize the importance of just barely cooking the zucchini: As soon as it begins to give off a little moisture, get the pan off the burner. The zucchini should be warm, but not too hot. You just want to unlock its flavor and help it meld with those of the almonds and oil.

¼ cup extra-virgin olive oil, plus more for serving
¼ cup sliced almonds
3 to 4 small zucchini, sliced lengthwise into ⅛-inch-thick slices, then crosswise into matchsticks (about 5 cups)

Salt
Freshly ground black pepper
4 ounces Pecorino Romano, thinly sliced into 12 triangular sheets with an old-fashioned cheese slicer or very sharp knife, or shaved into shards with a vegetable peeler

Divide the oil among 2 large, heavy-bottomed skillets and heat it over high heat. When the oil is hot but not smoking, add half of the almonds to each pan. Cook, tossing or stirring, until the almonds are golden brown, approximately 30 seconds. Add half of the zucchini to each pan and toss or stir to coat the zucchini with the hot oil, just a few seconds. Remove the pans from the heat, season with salt and pepper, and return to the heat for 30 seconds, tossing to distribute the seasoning.

Divide the zucchini and almonds among 4 warm salad plates, drizzle with extra-virgin olive oil, arrange the Pecorino sheets in a pyramid over each serving, and get it to the table while it's still nice and hot.

SHAVED MUSHROOM AND FENNEL SALAD
with Dry Jack Cheese

SERVES 4

This is a tribute to the cold vegetable salads of Italy, where everything from peas to artichokes to fennel to porcini mushrooms are often served raw. (I use cremini mushrooms—popular among Manhattan chefs—to honor my New York sensibility.) Visually, it's a quiet stunner, composed of various shades of white, with a surprisingly complex flavor.

1 large, or 2 medium, fennel bulbs, sliced
    paper-thin, ideally on a mandoline

12 ounces cremini mushrooms, sliced
    paper-thin, ideally on a mandoline

1 small head frisée, ends trimmed, white and
    yellow parts only, separated into leaves

2 tablespoons canola oil

1½ tablespoons extra-virgin olive oil

2 tablespoons plus 1 teaspoon lemon juice

2 large shallots, finely diced

Salt

Freshly ground black pepper

1½ ounces Dry Jack cheese (see Note),
    rind removed, shaved into shards with a
    vegetable peeler

Put the fennel, mushrooms, and frisée in a bowl. Drizzle with the canola oil, extra-virgin olive oil, and lemon juice, and scatter the shallots over the top. Season with salt and pepper and toss well.

Divide the salad among 4 plates, top each with a few shards of cheese, and serve.

NOTE TO THE COOK True story: Dry Jack cheese was created in Sonoma County, California, to replace Parmigiano-Reggiano for Americans who couldn't put their hands on the real thing during World War II. It's creamier and a bit less robust than Parmigiano. This is the only salad I use it in but, man, does it belong here.

ASPARAGUS AND EGGS
with Bacon Tempura

SERVES 4

So, late one night, I was in the dining room of The Red Cat with our chef, Bill McDaniel. Bill loves bacon. He loves to cook with bacon. He *needs* to cook with bacon. A customer remarked that there was bacon all over our menu. "Did you ever make tempura bacon?" he asked. We hadn't, but Bill and I liked the guy's moxie. So he went into the kitchen and fried up a batch of bacon tempura. I couldn't think of anything I'd rather pair it with than bacon's best friend, eggs. Here's my version: The asparagus lightens up the whole dish, and if you want to lighten it up even further, toss a teaspoon or two of lemon juice into the asparagus salad.

10 ounces large asparagus (about 16 spears)

2 tablespoons extra-virgin olive oil

2 tablespoons grated Parmigiano-Reggiano

Salt

Freshly ground black pepper

Canola oil, for frying

4 egg whites plus 4 whole eggs

3 cups flour

2¾ cups plus 2 tablespoons club soda or seltzer

8 thick slices double-smoked bacon, preferably applewood smoked (see Sources, page 249)

2 tablespoons butter

4 slices country bread, grilled or toasted

Using a vegetable peeler, slice the asparagus into long, paper-thin strips, gathering them in a bowl. Drizzle with the extra-virgin olive oil, and scatter the cheese over the asparagus. Toss, season with salt and pepper, and toss again. Set aside.

Line a large plate with paper towels. Pour canola oil into a large heavy-bottomed pot to a depth of 3 inches, and heat to a temperature of 350°F.

Meanwhile, in a large bowl, whisk the egg whites until soft peaks form. Whisk in the flour and club soda. Dip a few bacon slices into the batter, letting any excess batter run off, and carefully lower the bacon into the oil in small batches so they do not stick together. (Do not overcrowd, or the oil can overflow, and the bacon will not cook evenly.) Cook the bacon, stirring periodically to keep the slices from sticking together, until lightly golden brown, approximately 6 minutes. Remove the slices from the oil using a slotted spoon and transfer to the paper-towel-lined plate. Season immediately with salt.

Let the oil return to a temperature of 350°F and repeat with another batch of bacon. Continue to repeat until all of the bacon has been battered and fried.

Heat the butter in a heavy-bottomed sauté pan over medium-high heat. Break the eggs into the pan and cook sunny-side up, approximately 3 minutes.

Put 1 egg on each of 4 salad plates. Pile some asparagus to one side and set 2 slices of bacon tempura on the other. Serve with the bread alongside.

FIG TART

with Caramelized Onions and Blue Cheese

SERVES 4

A simple, savory way to make figs into a course all their own: Individual tartlets are filled with cara-melized onions, dotted with blue cheese, and topped with sliced figs. You taste each primary ingredient loud and clear, and the three of them establish a perfect harmony.

You will need four 4-inch tart molds.

1¼ cups flour, plus more for rolling

¼ teaspoon salt, plus more for seasoning

8 tablespoons (1 stick) butter

About 4 tablespoons ice water

2 large Spanish onions, thinly sliced

Freshly ground black pepper

4 ounces blue cheese, crumbled (1 cup)

6 ounces Mission figs, quartered lengthwise

Mix the flour and salt in a large bowl. Using a pastry blender or your fingertips, cut in 6 tablespoons of the butter, working the mixture until pea-size crumbs form. Add the ice water in 1-tablespoon increments, mixing it in until the dough holds together. Form the dough into a disk, wrap in plastic wrap, and refrigerate for 30 minutes.

Melt the remaining 2 tablespoons butter in a wide, deep, heavy-bottomed sauté pan set over medium heat. Add the onions and cook, stirring occasionally, until deeply caramelized, approxi-mately 30 minutes, adding a few drops of water when necessary to keep them from scorching. Season with salt and pepper and remove the pan from the heat.

Preheat the oven to 350°F. Line a cookie sheet with parchment paper and top with four 4-inch tart rings or molds.

On a floured surface, roll the dough out to a thickness of ⅛ inch. Cut four 4¾-inch circles out of the dough and fit them into the tart rings. Weight the dough with beans or pie weights, bake for 10 minutes, then remove the beans and bake until lightly golden, another 10 minutes. Trim the excess dough from the molds and let cool for 20 minutes. Do not turn off the oven.

Fill each tart with a layer of caramelized onions, then dot with blue cheese. Top with figs, stand-ing the quarters up in the onions. Bake for 2 to 3 minutes, just to warm the onions, cheese, and figs. Serve.

GRILLED HEN-OF-THE-WOODS MUSHROOMS
on Soppressata

SERVES 4

Most people like their salami raw, but every once in a while I like mine cooked, as in this starter based on the stark contrast between sweet soppressata and grilled hen-of-the-woods mushrooms. The mushrooms have a funky, earthy quality that gets along great with the meat. The red wine vinaigrette perks things up and helps hold the flavors together.

2 pounds hen-of-the-woods mushrooms,
    separated into 12 equal-size pieces
    attached at the root
About ¼ cup olive oil
Salt

Freshly ground black pepper
Red Wine Vinaigrette (recipe follows)
6 ounces sweet soppressata, cut into eight
    ⅛-inch-thick slices
1 cup arugula, coarsely chopped

Preheat a gas grill to high, or prepare a charcoal grill for grilling, letting the coals burn until covered with white ash.

Lightly brush the mushrooms with olive oil, and season with salt and pepper. Grill until lightly charred on all sides, approximately 4 minutes per side. Transfer to a bowl, toss with about half of the vinaigrette, and set aside.

Grill the soppressata until nice grill marks form on each side, approximately 60 seconds for the first side and 30 seconds for the other side.

Transfer 2 soppressata slices to each of 4 plates. Top with some arugula and 3 mushroom pieces, and drizzle some of the remaining vinaigrette over the mushrooms. Serve hot.

Red Wine Vinaigrette

MAKES ABOUT ¾ CUP

This is a good, all-purpose red wine vinaigrette.

2 tablespoons extra-virgin olive oil
3 tablespoons canola oil
3 tablespoons red wine vinegar
2½ tablespoons finely diced shallot

2½ tablespoons sliced basil
1 tablespoon minced garlic
Salt
Freshly ground black pepper

Put the extra-virgin olive oil, canola oil, vinegar, shallot, basil, and garlic in a small bowl and whisk together. Season with salt and pepper.

PEACH, RED ONION, AND PECAN SALAD
with Goat Cheese

SERVES 4

This is a fun and efficient dish to make: You crank up the oven, roast a few ingredients—pecans sweetened with honey and spiced with cayenne, onion slices, and goat cheese—then toss 'em all together in a salad, along with spinach, peaches, and a couldn't-be-simpler vinaigrette. It breaks the unspoken salad rule of delicacy and refinement in favor of bigger, bolder flavors and textures.

¾ cup pecans

2 teaspoons honey

⅛ teaspoon cayenne

Salt

2 small red onions, cut into eight ¼-inch-thick
    rings each

2 tablespoons olive oil

Freshly ground black pepper

¼ cup canola oil

1½ teaspoons sherry vinegar

1½ tablespoons red wine vinegar

⅛ teaspoon chopped garlic, mashed to a paste
    with a pinch of salt

4 ounces fresh goat cheese, in 4 equal pieces

6 ounces baby spinach (about 6 cups tightly
    packed)

2 medium peaches, pitted and thinly sliced

Preheat the oven to 350°F.

Put the pecans in a bowl. Add 1 teaspoon of the honey and toss to coat. Add the cayenne and season with salt. Toss well. Spread out on a cookie sheet and bake for 8 minutes. Remove from the oven and toss with the remaining teaspoon honey. Return to the oven and roast until golden and crisp, 8 more minutes. Remove the sheet from the oven, set aside, and let the pecans cool.

While the pecans are cooling, put the onions in a baking dish. Drizzle with 1 tablespoon of the olive oil, season with salt and pepper, and toss to coat the onions with the oil and seasoning. Spread the slices out in a single layer and roast until softened, approximately 10 minutes. When cool enough to handle, separate the slices into rings.

Make the vinaigrette: Put the canola oil, the remaining tablespoon olive oil, the sherry vinegar, red wine vinegar, and garlic paste in a small mixing bowl and whisk them together. Season with salt and pepper, and set aside.

Put the goat cheese on a baking dish and bake in the oven until softened, 4 to 6 minutes.

Put the spinach in a salad bowl. Add the pecans, peaches, onions, and vinaigrette. Toss and divide among 4 salad plates. Top each salad with a piece of warm cheese, and serve.

BITTER GREENS SALAD

with Gruyère Fondue

SERVES 4

That old saying that opposites attract applies to food as much as it does to people. One of my favorite matchmaking techniques is to put hot and cold food on the same plate. In this combination salad and fondue, many of the ingredients can be dipped in the melted cheese. It's sort of based on a raclette, a classic Swiss dish of melted cheese served right on a plate, along with various vegetables for scooping it up. It's a stick-to-your-ribs salad, if there is such a thing.

4 medium Yukon Gold potatoes, quartered

Salt

Freshly ground black pepper

10 ounces sliced bacon (about 10 strips)

1/2 tablespoon butter

1/2 tablespoon flour

1 cup dry white wine

2 medium shallots, chopped

1 cup heavy cream

About 2 cups grated Gruyère cheese (about 8 ounces)

1/2 tablespoon sherry vinegar

1/2 tablespoon extra-virgin olive oil

1 1/2 tablespoons canola oil

1/2 teaspoon Dijon mustard

4 Belgian endive spears, cut crosswise into 3 pieces

8 ounces mixed bitter greens, such as arugula, dandelion greens, or watercress

1/2 medium head radicchio, torn into bite-size pieces

Preheat the oven to 400°F.

Put the potatoes on a cookie sheet. Season with salt and pepper and bake until tender to a knife-tip, 35 to 40 minutes. Meanwhile, put the bacon strips on a cookie sheet and cook in the oven until crisp, approximately 7 minutes. Drain on paper towels, cut into 1-inch pieces, and set aside.

Make a roux by melting the butter in a heavy-bottomed saucepan over medium heat. Whisk in the flour and continue to cook, whisking, until the mixture is golden, but not browned, approximately 10 minutes. Remove from the heat and set aside.

Put the wine and shallots in a medium saucepan set over medium-high heat. Bring the wine to a simmer and let simmer until reduced by two thirds. Whisk in the heavy cream and the roux. Cook for about 1 minute, then whisk in the cheese, a few tablespoons at a time. If the mixture seems hopelessly thick, whisk in a tablespoon or so of hot water. If it seems too thin, add some more cheese. Season with salt and pepper. Keep warm over a low flame.

In a large bowl, whisk together the sherry vinegar, extra-virgin olive oil, canola oil, and Dijon mustard. Season with salt and pepper. Add the warm potatoes, bacon, endive, greens, and radicchio to the bowl. Season with salt and pepper, and toss.

Ladle some fondue onto each of 4 salad plates and top with some salad.

[51]

PAN-FRIED ARTICHOKES
with Lemon and Parmesan

SERVES 4

Artichokes are one of my favorite vegetables. Not only are they versatile—just as good baked as they are fried, boiled, or pureed—but they also put me in mind of springtime. Raw baby artichokes, shaved and tossed with lemon juice and Parmesan cheese, make up one of my favorite Italian starters—but you don't need a cookbook to throw that little bit of perfection together. This recipe takes a fresh look at the same combination, adding crunch by pan-frying the artichokes.

2 lemons

2 pounds baby artichokes, about 16 artichokes

Salt

2 tablespoons canola oil

2 tablespoons chopped rosemary

Freshly ground black pepper

2 cups arugula (loosely packed)

3 tablespoons extra-virgin olive oil

2 tablespoons sliced parsley

1½ ounces Parmigiano-Reggiano, shaved into
    shards with a vegetable peeler

Cut one of the lemons into wedges and reserve. Cut the remaining lemon in half and squeeze the juice from it. Measure 1 tablespoon plus 1 teaspoon juice and reserve. Pour the remaining lemon juice into a large bowl and fill the bowl halfway with cold water.

Prepare the artichokes: Cut off the top third of the artichokes with a heavy kitchen knife, then trim the stems to 1 inch, and peel them to remove the bitter green exterior. As the artichokes are trimmed, place them in the lemon water to keep them from turning brown.

Bring a large pot of salted water to a boil. Add the artichokes, cover with a lid slightly smaller than the pot to weight the artichokes down and keep them submerged, and simmer until tender to a knife-tip, approximately 8 minutes. Drain the artichokes and spread them out on a large plate or two to cool slightly. Pull off and discard the tough outer leaves and cut each artichoke in half. Pat dry with paper towels.

Heat half of the canola oil in a large skillet until lightly smoking. Add half the artichokes and half the rosemary, and cook over high heat, stirring occasionally, until the artichokes are golden and crisp, 4 to 5 minutes. Season with salt and pepper and transfer to a plate or platter. Repeat with the remaining canola oil, artichokes, and rosemary.

Meanwhile, put the arugula in a medium bowl. Drizzle with 1 tablespoon of the extra-virgin olive oil and 1 teaspoon of the reserved lemon juice, and season with salt and pepper.

Pile some arugula in the center of each of 4 wide, shallow bowls. Top with the artichokes, sprinkle with the remaining tablespoon lemon juice and 2 tablespoons extra-virgin olive oil, and scatter the parsley and Parmigiano-Reggiano shards over the artichokes. Serve with the reserved lemon wedges alongside for squeezing over the artichokes.

WARM JERSEY CORN SALAD

SERVES 4

This is one of those come-home-from-work, make-dinner-fast dishes. My longtime publicist and pal, Phil Baltz, and I made this up to see if we could pull off a little challenge we set for ourselves: to make a salad with no added acid. Sure, there's a touch in the tomatoes, but no vinegar at all. As a result, the dish lets you focus on each and every ingredient with no distraction.

Salt

6 small Yukon Gold potatoes, diced (4 cups)

1 pound thin asparagus, trimmed and cut crosswise into 1½-inch pieces

6 ears fresh corn, shucked, kernels removed from the cob (about 5 cups)

5 ripe plum tomatoes, seeded and diced

1 tablespoon chopped thyme

¼ cup plus 2 tablespoons extra-virgin olive oil

Freshly ground black pepper

Fill a large pot halfway with cold water. Season with salt and bring to a boil. Add the potatoes and boil until tender to a knife-tip, approximately 5 minutes. Drain through a fine-mesh strainer set over another pot. Transfer the potatoes to a large mixing bowl and return the water to a boil over high heat. Add the asparagus and boil until al dente, approximately 2 minutes. Drain and add to the bowl with the potatoes.

Heat a wide, deep-sided, heavy-bottomed sauté pan over medium-high heat. Add the corn in batches, to avoid crowding, and toast until lightly browned, approximately 3 minutes. As each batch is done, add it to the bowl with the potatoes and asparagus. Add the tomatoes, thyme, and oil, and season with salt and pepper. Toss, divide among individual plates, and serve warm.

NOTE TO THE COOK You can use other potatoes such as Red Bliss or fingerling in place of the Yukon Gold.

BAKED SEAFOOD IMPERIAL

SERVES 4

Baked crab imperial is one of those classics of Americana, the kind of thing you might have seen at a 1960s cocktail party: a dish of crabmeat tossed with cream, stuffed into a clean shellfish shell, then breaded and gratinéed. In those days, you didn't come anywhere near the mid-Atlantic in America and not know what an imperial was. The same was true in my family: In the twenty-plus times I dined out with my grandmother, Grandmom Bradley, I never saw her order anything other than crab imperial. My version features a mix of shellfish—crab, shrimp, scallops, and calamari. We serve it at The Mermaid Inn, where I developed it with the restaurant's chef, Mike Price, who, being from Maryland, took to this like a fish to water. You can make it any size you like, using scrubbed tiny littleneck clam shells or larger scallop or crab shells or even ramekins, and serve it accordingly, as an hors d'oeuvre or appetizer.

3 tablespoons butter

3 teaspoons minced garlic

1¼ cups dry bread crumbs (preferably Japanese panko)

2 tablespoons finely sliced chives

2 tablespoons sliced parsley

½ small onion, finely diced

¼ cup finely diced fennel

¼ cup finely diced celery

3 ounces large shrimp, peeled, deveined, and cut into bite-size pieces

3 ounces sea scallops, cut into bite-size pieces (see Note)

3 ounces squid, cleaned and cut into bite-size pieces

3 ounces jumbo lump crabmeat

1 teaspoon chopped tarragon

¼ teaspoon Old Bay seasoning

1 teaspoon Dijon mustard

Salt

Freshly ground black pepper

1 lemon, cut into wedges

1 cup cream

¼ cup grated white Cheddar cheese

¼ cup grated Parmigiano-Reggiano

Preheat the oven to 350°F.

Melt 1 tablespoon of the butter in a heavy-bottomed, ovenproof sauté pan set over medium-high heat. Add 1 teaspoon of the garlic and cook for 1 minute. Add the bread crumbs, 1 tablespoon chives, and 1 tablespoon parsley. Stir and transfer the pan to the oven. Toast until the bread crumbs are crispy, 3 to 5 minutes, stirring once to ensure even cooking. Remove the pan from the oven and set aside. Do not turn off the oven.

Melt 1 tablespoon of the butter in a wide, deep, heavy-bottomed sauté pan. Add the onion, fennel, celery, and remaining 2 teaspoons garlic, and cook until softened but not browned, approximately 4 minutes. Transfer to a large bowl.

recipe continues

In the same pan, melt the remaining tablespoon of butter. Add the shrimp, scallops, and squid, and sauté for 30 seconds. Add to the bowl with the vegetables. Add the crab, tarragon, Old Bay, mustard, and remaining 1 tablespoon chives and parsley. Season with 2 teaspoons of salt and black pepper to taste. Squeeze the juice from half of the lemon wedges over the mixture, catching the seeds in your hand.

Put the cream in a saucepan and cook at a simmer until reduced by half, approximately 8 minutes. Stir in the Cheddar and Parmesan until melted. Remove the pan from the heat and stir the cream mixture into the shellfish mixture.

Pack the mixture into clam or scallop shells, or individual ramekins; top with the seasoned bread crumbs; and bake until warm throughout, approximately 8 minutes. Serve immediately, with the remaining lemon wedges alongside for squeezing.

NOTE TO THE COOK There are three categories of sea scallops. By far, the superior ones are diver-harvested, or diver, sea scallops. Just like the name says, these are foraged by divers who hand-harvest them, guaranteeing freshness, a consistent size and weight, and a minimum of mud in the shell. Easier to find are dry-packed scallops, which aren't as fresh, but are still very good (they're shucked as soon as they're harvested, then shipped on ice). The ones to steer clear of are scallops packed in a milky white solution, a chemical preservative that mars their flavor and makes them irreversibly watery. If that's all you can find, make something else for dinner. (I also have to put in a word for delicate little bay scallops, which I don't use in the book. The best come from New England, especially around Nantucket, or the company Taylor Bay. Bay scallops are sweeter and more tender than sea scallops. They are best in the fall and are often sold in their own milk, which is perfectly acceptable; just pat them dry before searing them.)

VITELLO TONNATO
with Anchovy-Caper Mayonnaise
SERVES 4

If there's one case in which I've taken a classic and gone to town, this is it—my deconstructed take on the Italian dish of veal layered with a tuna sauce. Classically, it's served like a cold lasagna; this version uses fresh tuna instead of canned tuna, and room-temperature veal scallopini instead of cold veal. It's also a perfect example of a salad that can also be served as a lunch dish.

10 ounces filet mignon of veal or veal
    scallopini, in 8 equal pieces
Salt
Freshly ground black pepper
About 4 tablespoons canola oil
¼ cup black peppercorns, crushed
10 ounces tuna loin
¼ cup Citronette Dressing (recipe follows)

2 tablespoons finely diced red onion
2 tablespoons sliced parsley
1 tablespoon finely sliced chives
2 tablespoons chopped capers
4 teaspoons Anchovy-Caper Mayonnaise
    (recipe follows)
4 ounces baby lettuces
½ lemon

One by one, put the veal pieces between 2 sheets of plastic wrap and pound with a meat tenderizer or the bottom of a heavy pan to a thickness of ⅛ inch. Season the slices with salt and ground pepper. Heat a sauté pan over high heat and add 2 tablespoons of the oil. Sear the veal in batches until lightly browned on both sides, approximately 1 minute per side, adding more oil between batches if necessary. Set aside.

Put the peppercorns on a plate. Season the tuna loin with salt, and roll it in the peppercorns, pressing down so they adhere. Heat the remaining 2 tablespoons oil in a heavy-bottomed sauté pan over high heat and sear the tuna for approximately 1 minute on each side, keeping the center bright red and uncooked. Slice the tuna into ¼-inch cubes and transfer to a large bowl.

Add the citronette dressing, red onion, parsley, chives, and capers. Season with salt and ground pepper and toss to coat.

To serve, spoon 1 teaspoon of the anchovy-caper mayonnaise in the center of each of 4 salad plates. Lay two slices of the veal over the mayonnaise, coating the bottom of each veal slice with some of the mayonnaise. Place equal portions of the dressed tuna over each of the veal slices, garnish with baby greens, finish with a squeeze of lemon juice, and serve.

recipe continues

Citronette Dressing

MAKES ABOUT 1 CUP

Since the vinegar is replaced by lemon juice in this dressing, it seems odd to me to call this a vinaigrette, hence "citronette." Semantics aside, this is an all-purpose dressing that's one of my go-to choices at home. I put it on just about any salad I can think of.

½ cup canola oil

¼ cup extra-virgin olive oil

¼ cup lemon juice

2 tablespoons finely diced shallots

Salt

Freshly ground black pepper

Put the canola oil, extra-virgin olive oil, lemon juice, and shallots in a small bowl. Whisk together, then season with salt and pepper.

This vinaigrette can be covered and refrigerated for up to 1 day.

Anchovy-Caper Mayonnaise

MAKES ABOUT ½ CUP

Use this mayonnaise on sandwiches, especially those featuring roasted vegetables, chicken, or turkey.

½ cup mayonnaise

½ tablespoon minced anchovies

½ tablespoon minced capers

½ teaspoon hot sauce

1 teaspoon champagne vinegar

Put the mayonnaise, anchovies, capers, hot sauce, and champagne vinegar in a bowl and whisk them together. Whisk in about 2 tablespoons of room-temperature water, a few drops at a time, until the mayonnaise is speadable but still well emulsified.

This mayonnaise can be covered and refrigerated for up to 2 days.

SQUASH SALAD
with Soft Lettuce and Parmesan

SERVES 4

Let's say it's the fall, and you're craving some squash at lunchtime or dinner, or maybe you have a bumper crop of squash on hand and you're looking for a way to enjoy it. I say, do something different and use it in a salad, where you can see how well the roasted slices play against a brown-butter vinaigrette and soft lettuces. You can use just about any kind of winter squash, such as butternut, but if you use acorn squash, don't try to peel it; the deep ridges make it impossible. Just remember to trim away the peel when you eat it.

1 pound squash

1 tablespoon extra-virgin olive oil

2 teaspoons light brown sugar

1 teaspoon chopped thyme

Salt

Freshly ground black pepper

¼ teaspoon canola oil

Cayenne

2 tablespoons lemon juice

3 tablespoons butter

1½ tablespoons pumpkin seed oil (or sunflower oil, hazelnut oil, or walnut oil)

1 small head Bibb lettuce, separated into leaves, washed well, and spun dry

1½ ounces Parmigiano-Reggiano, shaved into shards with a vegetable peeler

Preheat the oven to 350°F.

Peel the squash. Halve it, scoop out the seeds, and set ¼ cup of them aside. Cut the squash into ¼-inch-thick slices and put it in a bowl. Add the extra-virgin olive oil, brown sugar, thyme, 1 teaspoon salt, and a few grinds of black pepper. Toss, then arrange the slices in a single layer on a cookie sheet and roast until light golden brown and soft to a knife-tip, approximately 15 minutes.

Meanwhile, pat the squash seeds dry with a paper towel and put them in an ovenproof sauté pan. Drizzle with the canola oil and season with ¼ teaspoon salt and a scant pinch of cayenne. Toss and then toast in the oven until the seeds are fragrant and lightly toasted, approximately 6 minutes. Remove from the oven and toss with ½ tablespoon of the lemon juice.

While the squash and seeds are in the oven, make the dressing: Melt the butter in a sauté pan set over medium-high heat, letting it turn brown. Whisk in the pumpkin seed oil and then the remaining 1½ tablespoons lemon juice. Season with salt and pepper and remove the vinaigrette from the heat.

To serve, arrange the squash slices on 4 salad plates. Put the lettuce in a bowl, toss with the vinaigrette, and season with salt and pepper. Top the squash with some lettuce, garnish with cheese shards, and serve.

GRILLED BELGIAN ENDIVE
with Gorgonzola Gratinée and Balsamic Vinegar

SERVES 4

This proudly unsubtle dish sets soft, grilled endive against two assertive accompaniments: Gorgonzola and balsamic vinegar. You'll use the grill and the broiler, but I promise this recipe is pretty simple and straightforward: Once the endive's grilled (which can be done a day ahead), it takes five minutes or less to finish. It's packed with flavor, the char of the grill matched by sweet balsamic vinegar. Bonus feature: It will make your home smell like a fine cheese cave.

4 Belgian endives, halved lengthwise

2 tablespoons canola oil

Salt

Freshly ground black pepper

6 ounces Gorgonzola dolce latte, or other soft, creamy blue cheese, crumbled

2 tablespoons extra-virgin olive oil

2½ tablespoons balsamic vinegar

2 tablespoons sliced parsley

Preheat the broiler. Preheat a gas grill to high, or prepare a charcoal grill for grilling, letting the coals burn until covered with white ash.

Meanwhile, slice each endive half lengthwise into 5 equal slices, attached at the root; brush with canola oil and season with salt and pepper. Grill the endive in batches, fanning the pieces of each half out on the grill, and turning, until tender and browned, approximately 5 minutes. Lift the fan-shaped clusters with a spatula and transfer them to a baking dish. Top the endive with the Gorgonzola and broil for 3 to 5 minutes, or until the cheese has melted and is bubbly.

Transfer 2 gratinéed endive halves to each of 4 salad plates. Drizzle with the extra-virgin olive oil and vinegar and garnish with the parsley. Serve warm.

NOTES TO THE COOK When you want to melt blue cheese in your cooking, choose a soft, wet one such as Gorgonzola or Roquefort. If crumbling raw cheese, select a relatively dry one such as Maytag Blue.

You can use the grilled endive, without its blue-cheese topping, as a vegetable accompaniment to fish or meat. It's especially good with grilled salmon.

SEARED TUNA CROSTINI

SERVES 4

One of the most popular contemporary appetizers, tuna tartare, gets the Italian treatment here: Cubed tuna is tossed with some of my favorite ingredients—red onion, capers, parsley, lemon juice, and extra-virgin olive oil—then set atop a slice of grilled bread, making it a *crostini* (Italian for "crouton"). Searing the tuna before chilling it adds a nice char flavor to the mix.

I love serving this tartare on toast, but you can experiment with other vehicles, such as potato chips, endive spears, fried wonton skins, and lettuce leaves. You can also make this a do-it-yourself affair for your guests by arranging one or more of those choices on a platter, and setting the tuna out in a bowl set in a larger bowl of ice to keep it chilled, with a spoon for serving.

8 ounces sushi-grade tuna steak

Salt

Freshly ground black pepper

2 tablespoons canola oil

4 slices country bread, halved

2 teaspoons finely diced red onion

1 teaspoon chopped capers

1 teaspoon sliced parsley

Pinch of finely sliced chives

1 tablespoon extra-virgin olive oil

2 teaspoons lemon juice

Season the tuna generously with salt and pepper.

Heat the canola oil in a heavy-bottomed skillet over high heat. Add the tuna and sear, flipping it once, just until golden brown on the outside (the inside should still be rare), approximately 2 minutes. Quickly transfer the tuna to a plate, let cool to room temperature, then cover with plastic wrap and chill in the refrigerator until cold at the center, approximately 1 hour, or up to 3 hours.

When ready to serve, toast or grill the bread.

Slice the tuna into ¼-inch cubes. Transfer to a bowl and add the onion, capers, parsley, chives, extra-virgin olive oil, and lemon juice. Toss, taste, and adjust the seasoning with salt and pepper, if necessary.

To serve, arrange the toast slices on a plate or platter, top each slice with some of the tuna mixture, and serve.

CLAMS OREGANATA

SERVES 4

In the summer in New England, we have some sort of shellfish before every meal. If it's clams, and they're not raw, then this is how we cook them. Some New Englanders make these with crushed Ritz crackers; I go with dried bread crumbs because their crunch survives the cooking process. The saltiness of the clams gets along perfectly with the garlicky, buttery sauce. Any great Mediterranean chef will tell you he only needs five ingredients to make dinner: olive oil, oregano, lemon, salt, and a fish. This dish is fashioned after that spirit of simplicity.

2 pounds littleneck clams (approximately 20 clams)

8 tablespoons (1 stick) butter

1 medium onion, finely diced

2 teaspoons finely chopped garlic

1¼ cups dried bread crumbs (preferably Japanese panko)

2 teaspoons chopped oregano

¼ cup Shellfish Stock (page 247) or bottled clam juice

Juice of 1 lemon

¼ cup dry white wine

2 tablespoons sliced parsley

Preheat the oven to 400°F.

Shuck the clams, reserving 1 half-shell from each clam.

Melt 4 tablespoons of the butter in a heavy-bottomed, ovenproof sauté pan over medium-high heat. Add the onion and garlic and sauté until lightly browned, approximately 6 minutes. Add the bread crumbs and oregano, toss, and transfer to the oven. Bake until the crumbs are crispy and lightly golden, approximately 4 minutes. Keep the oven at 400°F.

Arrange the reserved half-shells on one or two rimmed cookie sheets and place 1 clam on each half-shell. Pack 1 tablespoon of breading atop each clam. Put the stock, lemon juice, and wine in a small bowl, stir together, and drizzle the mixture over the clams. Cut the remaining 4 tablespoons butter into bits and dot the clams with the butter. Bake in the oven until the clams are golden and crisp, approximately 8 minutes.

Use tongs to transfer the clams to a serving plate. Swirl the parsley into the pan juices in the cookie sheet(s), then pour the sauce over the clams and serve.

SEARED LAMB CARPACCIO
with Chopped Egg and Scallions

SERVES 4

There's a rich tradition of raw-meat appetizers in Western cuisine, and this dish borrows from two of them. First off, there's carpaccio, a Venetian legend comprising thin slices of chilled raw beef topped with a mayonnaise. I took its name for this recipe because the lamb, while not truly raw (it's seared, then refrigerated), is served cold. The accompaniments—hard-boiled eggs and red onion—are on loan from another raw-meat institution, steak tartare. Topping the lamb with frisée adheres to my philosophy of finding a place for a salad on an appetizer's plate, and adds texture to boot. You won't find this on any menu in Venice, but this is a carpaccio for everyone.

8 ounces lamb loin

2 tablespoons chopped thyme

Salt

Freshly ground black pepper

1 tablespoon plus 1/3 cup canola oil

1 egg yolk

1/4 teaspoon Dijon mustard

2 teaspoons balsamic vinegar

1 teaspoon cold water

1 teaspoon lemon juice

2 small heads frisée, ends trimmed, white and yellow parts only, separated into leaves

1 large scallion, very thinly sliced

2 hard-boiled eggs, halved lengthwise and sliced

1/2 cup parsley

Pickled Red Onions (recipe follows)

1 1/2 ounces Parmigiano-Reggiano, shaved into shards with a vegetable peeler

Season the lamb all over with the thyme, then season generously with salt and pepper, pressing them into the meat to make sure they adhere. Heat 1 tablespoon of the oil in a heavy-bottomed skillet over high heat. Add the lamb loin and sear, turning the lamb as needed to brown well on all sides, approximately 6 minutes. Transfer the lamb to a plate and let cool, then cover with plastic wrap and refrigerate until chilled, at least 1 hour, or up to 6 hours.

Make the vinaigrette: Put the egg yolk in a medium bowl. Add the Dijon mustard, balsamic vinegar, cold water, and lemon juice. Slowly add the remaining 1/3 cup canola oil in a thin stream, whisking to form an emulsion. Taste and adjust the seasoning with salt and pepper.

Add the frisée, scallion, hard-boiled eggs, and parsley to the bowl and toss together. Taste and adjust the seasoning with salt and pepper, if necessary. Thinly slice the lamb and fan out one fourth of it on each of 4 plates. Top the lamb with salad, then top the salad with pickled onion and Parmesan shards. Serve.

Pickled Red Onions

These onions are delicious in salads and alongside fish. They're also perfect in a roast beef sandwich or chopped up as a garnish to salmon tartare or smoked salmon.

1 small red onion, halved and thinly sliced

¼ cup plus 2 tablespoons red wine vinegar

1 tablespoon balsamic vinegar

1 teaspoon sugar

½ teaspoon salt

½ teaspoon freshly ground black pepper

2 tablespoons cold water

Put the onions in a heat-proof container. Put the vinegars, sugar, salt, pepper, and cold water in a small saucepan, stir together, and bring to a simmer over medium-high heat. Pour the hot mixture over the onions. Let cool to room temperature, then cover and refrigerate for at least 6 hours, or up to 2 weeks.

SOUPS

COLD CORN SOUP

with Chili Oil

TOMATO-BREAD SOUP

with Parmesan

PUREE OF CELERY ROOT SOUP

SPICY SWISS POTATO SOUP

MULLIGATAWNY

NEW ENGLAND FISH CHOWDER

CURRIED LOBSTER AND EGGPLANT SOUP

GOULASH SOUP

WHITE BEAN, ESCAROLE, AND SWEET SAUSAGE SOUP

BEET AND CABBAGE BORSCHT

SPRING GARLIC AND BREAD SOUP

SPLIT PEA SOUP

with Rum

I happen to love a great soup, but I'll let you in on a little secret: For me, soups are about convenience as much as they are about flavor. In fact, to tell the truth, I rarely *plan* to make soups. They're a spontaneous phenomenon in my life. I find myself cooking them when I have the right stuff on hand and don't feel like working too hard. In the spring and summer I lean toward elemental stuff that really goes to town on one ingredient and doesn't take too long: garlic, corn, tomatoes—the usual seasonal suspects. In the winter, I turn to soups that take their time cooking, usually populating them with stuff like beans, split peas, pork shoulder, celery root, and so on—ingredients that really fill the house with aroma and warm you up before you even take your first spoonful.

For me, soups are one of those things that put you in touch with the long history of food: There's something inevitable about those combinations that have stood the test of time, such as split pea and ham, or sausage, white beans, and escarole—ingredients that seem positively made for one another. A lot of the soups I gravitate toward are considered peasant food in their countries of origin—tomato-bread soup (Italy), goulash (Hungary), borscht (Poland and Russia, primarily)—because they are easy to make and don't call for a lot of expensive ingredients, and yet taste great. In fact, you have to wonder if it isn't time we stopped using the phrase "peasant food," because a lot of what falls into that category is some of the best food you'll ever eat.

Many of the soups in this chapter, like the majority of dishes in the book, serve four, but for those soups that can survive, or even improve with, a day or two in the refrigerator, the recipes serve eight to ten. Serve these to a large group, or refrigerate or freeze leftovers for another day.

A few notes about soup making:
- First of all, a safety tip: If a recipe calls for blending a hot liquid, do so with *extreme caution* because the heat released while blending can blow the lid right off the blender. Only fill the blender about one third of the way with hot liquid, and put a damp towel, rather than the blender lid, over the top to allow the steam and heat to escape.
- An immersion blender, aka a hand blender, can be a fine tool for blending soup, especially since it eliminates the hot-liquid-in-a-blender issue, but it's not always ideal. Use it to puree a portion of a soup to thicken it, but do not use it when you want to puree a soup thoroughly; it doesn't do as good a job as a regular blender.
- Do not cook your soups to death. Just as in all other recipes, the cooking times are there for a reason. Let a stage of the process go too long and beans will disintegrate, sturdy greens will lose their tooth, and seafood will become rubbery. By the same token, when a recipe says to "simmer," don't boil, thinking you can move things along. Patience, my dear reader, patience.

COLD CORN SOUP
with Chili Oil

SERVES 4

There's a small window of opportunity to make this soup each year: late summer, when you should use corn purchased from a farm or roadside stand and cook it as soon as possible after you get home. All that's in the bowl is corn and milk, with a garnish of shallot, chives, and smoked trout, which hits the summer note a little harder with a smokiness that suggests the grill. The heat of the chili oil perks the whole thing up a bit.

¼ cup crushed red pepper flakes

½ cup extra-virgin olive oil

Salt

6 ears fresh corn

2 cups milk

Sugar, if needed

1 small shallot, finely diced

1 tablespoon finely sliced chives

6 ounces smoked trout, flaked into small pieces

Make the chili oil: Put the red pepper flakes and oil in a jar and cover. Let marinate for 2 to 3 days, ideally in a sunny part of the kitchen. Strain. (Alternatively, you can use store-bought chili oil.) The chili oil can be kept, in an airtight container, in the refrigerator for up to 1 month.

Fill a soup pot three-quarters full with salted water and bring to a boil over high heat. Add the corn and boil until the kernels are tender, approximately 5 minutes. Use tongs to transfer the cobs to a colander set in the sink and refresh under cold running water to cool the corn.

Stand the corn cobs on end and cut the kernels from them. Scrape the cobs with the back of the knife after you've cut off the kernels, and reserve any juices. You should have about 6 cups kernels. Transfer to a blender, along with any juice, in 4 batches, adding ½ cup of the milk to each batch, and blending each batch for about 2 minutes to liquefy. Pass each batch through a fine-mesh strainer set over a bowl, pressing down on the solids with a rubber spatula to extract as much liquid as possible. Season with salt. Taste and, if the soup doesn't seem sweet, add a pinch of sugar.

Chill the soup, then divide among bowls and serve, garnished with the shallot, chives, trout, and a drizzle of chili oil.

NOTE TO THE COOK For a more substantial soup, use more smoked trout, making a little island of it in the center of each bowl before carefully ladling the soup around it.

TOMATO-BREAD SOUP
with Parmesan

SERVES 4

In the classic tomato-bread soup, day-old bread is softened into a tomato soup, thickening it. My version deconstructs the original, floating toasted, garlicky bread cubes on a cheese-infused tomato soup. If you love dunking bread in your spaghetti sauce, you'll love this soup, which creates the same effect in every bite.

¼ cup olive oil

1 medium onion, finely diced

2 cloves garlic, thinly sliced

1 28-ounce can whole peeled tomatoes, with their juices, crushed by hand

2 cups White Chicken Stock (page 245) or low-sodium, store-bought chicken broth

Parmigiano-Reggiano rind (see Note) plus ½ cup grated Parmigiano-Reggiano cheese

Salt

Freshly ground black pepper

¼ cup plus 2 tablespoons extra-virgin olive oil

2 tablespoons sliced basil

2 tablespoons sliced parsley

2 tablespoons chopped thyme

Garlic Croutons (page 84), made with 2 tablespoons chopped thyme (added with the bread)

Heat the olive oil in a heavy-bottomed soup pot. Add the onion and garlic and sauté until softened but not browned, approximately 4 minutes. Add the tomatoes, stock, and Parmesan rind and simmer until the cheese flavor permeates the soup, 15 to 20 minutes. Use tongs or a slotted spoon to remove and discard the cheese rind. Season the soup with salt and pepper, and stir in the extra-virgin olive oil, basil, parsley, and thyme.

Serve the soup in bowls, garnished with the croutons and grated cheese.

NOTE TO THE COOK Unlike most cheese rinds, which go right into the garbage can, Parmigiano-Reggiano rinds should be saved, in a plastic bag, in the refrigerator. That's because Parmesan rinds add a subtle essence of the cheese to soups, stews, and other dishes by infusing them with Parmesan flavor. Generally, the rinds are added after the recipe is pretty well under way, allowed to simmer for a while, and removed with tongs or a slotted spoon before blending and/or serving.

PUREE OF CELERY ROOT SOUP

SERVES 4

The understated flavor of celery root is captured in this smooth and creamy, but creamless, soup. When you make it, be careful to not overwhelm the delicate root: Don't let the onion, celery, or garlic brown at all, and go especially easy on the salt and pepper.

3 tablespoons butter

1 small leek, white part only, coarsely chopped

1/2 medium onion, coarsely chopped

1 stalk celery, coarsely chopped

2 cloves garlic, thinly sliced

1/2 large celery root, peeled and coarsely chopped (about 2 1/2 cups)

3 cups White Chicken Stock (page 245) or low-sodium, store-bought chicken broth

1/4 cup milk

Salt

Freshly ground black pepper

2 tablespoons sliced chervil or tarragon

Melt 2 tablespoons of the butter in a soup pot set over medium heat. Add the leek, onion, celery, and garlic, and sauté until the vegetables have softened but not browned, approximately 4 minutes. Add the celery root and stock, bring to a boil, then lower the heat and simmer until the celery root is tender to a knife-tip, approximately 20 minutes.

Transfer the soup to a blender in batches and puree until smooth. Add the remaining tablespoon butter and the milk to enrich the soup. Taste and season with salt and pepper.

Divide among individual bowls, garnish with the chervil, and serve.

SPICY SWISS POTATO SOUP

SERVES 4

A potato soup is spiced up with cayenne, ladled over grated Gruyère, and topped with sliced scallions, giving a full complement of flavors and textures that is fun to eat and delicious. If you have leftover mashed potatoes, this is a great way to use them; you'll need about 2 cups. Start the recipe after the food-mill step, leaving out half of the cream and milk and substituting White Chicken Stock for the cooking liquid.

3 tablespoons butter

1 small shallot, finely chopped

1½ pounds Idaho potatoes (about 2 medium potatoes), peeled and quartered

3 cups White Chicken Stock (page 245) or low-sodium, store-bought chicken broth

1½ cups milk

1½ cups heavy cream

Salt

Freshly ground black pepper

Cayenne

¾ cup grated Gruyère cheese (about 6 ounces)

2 teaspoons hot paprika

2 scallions, white and green parts, finely sliced

Melt 2 tablespoons of the butter in a heavy-bottomed soup pot over medium-high heat. Add the shallot and sauté until softened but not browned, approximately 3 minutes. Add the potatoes, chicken stock, and 3 cups water. Bring to a boil and then lower the heat so the liquid simmers. Cook until the potatoes are soft to a knife-tip, approximately 15 minutes. Pour the contents of the pot into a fine-mesh strainer set over a bowl. Set the cooking liquid aside.

Pass the potatoes through a food mill or ricer. Return the potatoes to the pot over medium heat and add the milk, cream, and 1½ cups of the cooking liquid. Whisk gently to incorporate, but do not overwork the potatoes. Season with salt, pepper, and cayenne to taste. Finish by whisking in the remaining tablespoon butter.

To serve, put some shredded Gruyère in the bottom of each of 4 bowls, and ladle in the hot soup. Garnish with a dusting of paprika and the scallions.

MULLIGATAWNY

SERVES 4

Mulligatawny was borrowed from India by British citizens stationed there in the late eighteenth century. These Brits carried the Indian soup known as "pepper water" back home with them, freely adapting it to their own taste, and other passersby, including Australians, did the same. So, in the Western world, there's no one way of making Mulligatawny because each returning adventurer did his own thing with it. But there are a few constants, the essential one being that the soup is a curried cream of chicken.

Here's my New York answer to Mulligatawny, with an exotic mix of spices and some cilantro added at the last second.

2 tablespoons butter

1 medium carrot, cut into ¼-inch dice

½ medium onion, cut into ¼-inch dice

1 stalk celery, cut into ¼-inch dice

1 tablespoon curry powder

½ teaspoon ground cumin

¼ teaspoon ground turmeric

Pinch of cayenne

¼ cup flour

6 cups White Chicken Stock (page 245) or
   low-sodium, store-bought chicken broth

½ cup canned, unsweetened coconut milk

1 boneless, skinless chicken breast,
   cut into ½-inch dice

2 tablespoons lemon juice

Salt

Freshly ground black pepper

2 tablespoons sliced cilantro

Melt the butter in a heavy-bottomed pot set over medium heat. Add the carrot, onion, and celery and cook until softened but not browned, approximately 4 minutes.

Add the curry, cumin, turmeric, cayenne, and flour. Cook, stirring, for 3 to 5 minutes. Gradually add the stock, stirring to keep lumps from forming, then add the coconut milk in the same manner.

Add the chicken and cook at a simmer until cooked through, approximately 5 minutes. Stir in the lemon juice and season with salt and pepper.

To serve, ladle the soup into individual bowls and garnish with the cilantro.

NEW ENGLAND FISH CHOWDER

SERVES 4

Okay, let's get something straight: I live in Manhattan, but my heart will always, *always*, belong to New England fish chowder, which is thicker and creamier than the Rhode Island–style chowder, which is thin and milky.

This is the fish chowder of my memories, the one I grew up on. It starts with a smoky bacon base; features celery, thyme, and potatoes; is thickened with milk; and is cooked until the fish falls apart, but not long enough that it's overcooked. Finally, it's served with oyster crackers or saltines, which are just as important as the fish itself.

Salt

2 medium Yukon Gold potatoes, peeled and cut into 1/2-inch dice (1 1/2 cups)

4 strips bacon, cut into 1/2-inch dice

1 large white onion, cut into 1/4-inch dice

4 stalks celery, cut into 1/4-inch dice

1/2 teaspoon chopped thyme

4 tablespoons (1/2 stick) butter

1/4 cup flour

4 cups Shellfish Stock (page 247) or bottled clam juice

1 1/2 to 2 cups milk

Freshly ground black pepper

1/2 pound white fish trimmings or fillets, such as cod, scrod, or haddock, cut into 1/2-inch pieces

Oyster crackers or saltines

Bring a medium pot of salted water to a boil and add the potatoes. Cook until tender to a knife-tip, approximately 7 minutes. Drain in a colander set in the sink, refresh under cold running water, and set aside.

Heat a heavy-bottomed soup pot over medium heat. Add the bacon and sauté until crisp and golden and the bacon has rendered enough fat to coat the bottom of the pot, approximately 7 minutes. Add the onion and celery and sauté until translucent and slightly browned, approximately 5 minutes. Add the thyme and butter and cook until the butter is melted. Sprinkle the flour over the contents of the pot and cook, stirring for a minute or two to work the butter and flour together, making a roux. Add the shellfish stock, whisking to incorporate it smoothly.

Add the potatoes and bring the mixture to a simmer. Stir in 1 1/2 cups of the milk, return to a simmer, and simmer until slightly thickened, approximately 8 minutes. Taste and add more milk, if necessary, and season with salt and pepper. Add the fish, let the soup return to a simmer, and cook, stirring gently to heat the fish and break the pieces apart, approximately 4 minutes.

Divide the soup among individual bowls and serve with oyster crackers or saltines alongside.

CURRIED LOBSTER AND EGGPLANT SOUP

SERVES 8 TO 10

I've always loved the combinations of crab and curry and eggplant and curry, so I decided to put the two pairings together and see what happened. I was so happy with the result that I decided to give the soup—a creamy, complex, and deeply satisfying concoction—an upgrade by substituting lobster for crab. This is packed full of tangy, exotic flavor, and the luxurious lobster makes it appropriate for any occasion, from the most casual to the most formal.

2 live lobsters, 1½ pounds each

2 tablespoons canola oil

1 large onion, coarsely chopped

2 stalks celery, coarsely chopped

1 bulb fennel, coarsely chopped

¼ cup brandy

1¾ cups whole canned tomatoes, chopped,
 drained of juice (from about 15 tomatoes)

6 tablespoons (¾ stick) butter

8 small shallots, finely diced

8 cloves garlic, thinly sliced

8 cups ¼-inch-diced peeled eggplant (from
 about 1 pound)

3 tablespoons curry powder

1 teaspoon cayenne

Hot sauce

Salt

Freshly ground black pepper

Preheat the oven to 350°F.

Kill the lobsters by driving a heavy chef's knife between their eyes and pulling it down like a lever. Separate the tails from the bodies and tear off the claws. (Alternatively, you can cook the lobsters in boiling water for 1 minute to kill them.)

Bring a large pot of water to a simmer over medium-low heat. Add the lobster claws and poach for 5 to 6 minutes, then remove with tongs or a slotted spoon and set aside. Add the tails and poach for 3 minutes, then remove with tongs or a slotted spoon and set aside. When the lobster parts are cool enough to handle, remove the meat from the shells (be sure to remove and discard the dark intestine from the tail portion) and cut it into ½-inch pieces. Wrap in plastic wrap and refrigerate until ready to make the soup.

Rinse and chop up the lobster bodies (the upper part that includes the head) and spread the pieces out on a cookie sheet or in a roasting pan. Roast until they turn bright red, approximately 15 minutes.

Meanwhile, heat the canola oil in a heavy-bottomed soup pot set over medium-high heat. Add the onion, celery, and fennel and cook until softened but not browned, approximately 4 minutes. Add the roasted lobster pieces and cook, stirring, to incorporate the flavors for a minute or two. Add the brandy and cook, stirring to loosen up any bits cooked onto the bottom of the pot. Add one quarter of the tomatoes and enough cold water to cover by 1 inch. Bring to a simmer, lower the heat, cover,

recipe continues

[79]

and simmer gently for 3 hours. Pour the liquid through a fine-mesh strainer set over a bowl. Discard the solids and reserve the stock; you will need 2 quarts to make the soup.

Melt 4 tablespoons of the butter in a heavy-bottomed soup pot set over medium-high heat. Add the shallots and garlic and cook until softened but not browned, approximately 4 minutes. Add the eggplant and sauté until tender, 3 to 4 minutes. Add the curry powder and stir to coat the other ingredients. Add the remaining tomatoes and the lobster stock, bring to a simmer, and simmer until the flavors are nicely integrated, 20 to 30 minutes.

Ladle about one third of the soup into a blender, puree, and return to the pot to thicken the soup. (Alternatively, you can give the pot of soup a few quick zaps with an immersion blender.) Whisk in the remaining 2 tablespoons butter. Season with the cayenne and the hot sauce, salt, and pepper to taste. Stir in the lobster meat and let cook for 1 minute to warm the meat through, but do not boil or the meat will toughen.

The soup can be cooled and refrigerated for up to 2 days in an airtight container, or frozen for up to 2 months. Reheat gently before serving.

Ladle the soup among individual bowls and serve.

GOULASH SOUP

SERVES 8 TO 10

The best-known Hungarian export, at least in culinary terms, goulash is one of the oldest meat-and-potato dishes on Earth. I make it with veal, thicken it with tomatoes, and season it generously with Hungarian paprika. This might be my favorite soup of all time because, like the original goulash, it's essentially a soupy stew, hearty and satisfying enough to be served as a meal.

Salt

3 medium Idaho or russet potatoes, peeled and cut into ½-inch dice

1½ pounds veal shoulder, cut into ½-inch cubes

Freshly ground black pepper

2 tablespoons sweet Hungarian paprika

¼ cup olive oil

1½ medium onions, cut into ¼-inch dice

5 cloves garlic, thinly sliced

¼ cup flour

½ teaspoon cayenne

8 whole peeled canned tomatoes, crushed by hand and drained

3 tablespoons tomato paste

About 4 cups Veal Stock (page 246) or low-sodium, store-bought beef broth

About 4 cups White Chicken Stock (page 245), or low-sodium, store-bought chicken broth

Bring a medium pot of salted water to a boil and add the potatoes. Cook until tender to a knife-tip, approximately 7 minutes. Drain in a colander set in the sink, refresh under cold running water, and set aside.

Put the veal in a bowl and season with salt, pepper, and the paprika.

Heat the olive oil in a heavy-bottomed soup pot over medium-high heat. Add the veal and sauté until browned all over, approximately 4 minutes, then add the onions and garlic and sauté until softened but not browned, approximately 4 minutes. Add the flour and stir to coat the meat, cooking for 2 minutes.

Add the cayenne, tomatoes, tomato paste, and stocks, and stir to loosen any flavorful bits stuck to the bottom of the pot. Simmer, covered, until the veal is tender, 60 to 90 minutes. Stir in the potatoes. The soup should be thick but distinctly soupy (versus stew-like). If it's too thick, stir in some more stock. Taste and season with salt and pepper.

The soup can be cooled and refrigerated for up to 2 days in an airtight container, or frozen for up to 2 months. Reheat before serving.

To serve, ladle the soup into individual bowls.

NOTES TO THE COOK There are many kinds of Hungarian paprika, the primary factors distinguishing them being degrees of sweetness and spiciness. If you get just one, get the sweet one; it's more all-purpose. If you're a dabbler, though, keep both on hand and play around with them in your cooking. They're a quick way to add complexity to a variety of dishes.

Stir ¼ to ½ cup sour cream into this soup for a richer result.

WHITE BEAN, ESCAROLE, AND SWEET SAUSAGE SOUP

SERVES 8 TO 10

This soup demonstrates why Italian cooking is so popular: a coming-together of great, inexpensive ingredients without a lot of fuss. It's hearty and comforting, and it gets better after a day or two in the fridge.

8 ounces dried Great Northern beans (1 cup)

3 strips bacon, cut into very small dice

2 large carrots, peeled and cut into large pieces

2 stalks celery, cut into large pieces

1 tablespoon olive oil

1 pound sweet Italian sausage, removed from casings and crumbled into bite-size pieces

1 medium onion, finely diced

4 cloves garlic, coarsely chopped

¼ cup chopped thyme

¼ cup sliced basil

¼ cup chopped oregano

6 cups White Chicken Stock (page 245) or low-sodium, store-bought chicken broth

½ large head escarole, thinly sliced

¼ cup sliced parsley

Extra-virgin olive oil, for serving

Grated Parmigiano-Reggiano, for serving

Soak the white beans overnight in enough cold water to cover by 4 inches. Drain.

Cook the bacon in a heavy-bottomed pot set over medium heat until it renders enough fat to coat the bottom of the pot, approximately 7 minutes. Add the carrots and celery and cook until softened but not browned, approximately 6 minutes. Add the beans and stir gently to coat with fat. Add 3 cups water, bring to a simmer, cover, and simmer until the beans are al dente, 40 to 50 minutes. Remove from the heat and let the beans cool in their cooking liquid. Use tongs or a slotted spoon to fish out and discard the pieces of carrot and celery.

Heat the olive oil in a heavy-bottomed soup pot set over medium heat. Add the sausage and cook until browned and enough fat has rendered to coat the bottom of the pot, approximately 7 minutes. Add the onion and garlic and sauté until softened but not browned, approximately 4 minutes. Stir in the thyme, basil, and oregano. Add the stock and bring to a simmer. Drain the beans and add them to the pot. Ladle about one eighth of the soup into a blender and puree. (Alternatively, you can give the pot of soup a few quick zaps with an immersion blender.) Return to the soup to thicken it. Stir in the escarole and parsley.

The soup can be cooled and refrigerated for up to 2 days in an airtight container, or frozen for up to 2 months. Reheat gently before serving.

Divide the soup among bowls and finish each serving with a drizzle of extra-virgin olive oil and a scattering of grated cheese.

NOTE TO THE COOK You can quick-soak beans in 2 hours: Put them in a pot, cover by 3 inches with cold water, bring to a boil, cover, and remove the pot from the heat. Let soak for 2 hours and drain.

BEET AND CABBAGE BORSCHT

SERVES 8 TO 10

If you love beets, then you have to love borscht, which is a dolled-up beet soup. My version of this Eastern European classic adds beans and diced pork shoulder for an unexpected flavor and texture.

1 cup dried Gigante beans

Salt

3 large beets, about 6 ounces each, trimmed

¼ cup canola oil

1 pound pork shoulder, cut into 1-inch dice

Freshly ground black pepper

2 cups very thinly shredded cabbage

1 medium onion, diced

Pinch of light brown sugar

5 cups White Chicken Stock (page 245) or low-sodium, store-bought chicken broth

3 cups Veal Stock (page 246), or low-sodium, store-bought beef broth

2 canned whole tomatoes, crushed by hand, with their juice

Soak the beans overnight in enough cold water to cover by 4 inches. Drain.

Put the beans in a medium, heavy-bottomed pot set over medium heat. Add 3 cups water, bring to a simmer, lower the heat, cover, and simmer until the beans are al dente, 40 to 50 minutes. Remove from the heat and let the beans cool in their cooking liquid. Drain and set aside.

Meanwhile, bring a large pot of salted water to a boil. Add the beets and boil until tender to a knife-tip, approximately 40 minutes. Drain, and, when the beets are cool enough to handle, peel and cut them into a ½-inch dice.

Heat the canola oil in a heavy-bottomed soup pot set over medium-high heat. Add the pork, season with salt and pepper, and sear it all over until browned, about 5 minutes. Use tongs or a slotted spoon to transfer the pieces to a plate. Add the cabbage, onion, and brown sugar, and cook until the cabbage and onion are softened but not browned, approximately 5 minutes. Add the pork, chicken stock, and veal stock, bring to a simmer, and continue to simmer for 20 minutes. Add the beets and tomatoes, and simmer for another 20 minutes. Add the beans and cook just enough to warm them through.

The soup can be cooled and refrigerated for up to 2 days in an airtight container, or frozen for up to 2 months. Reheat gently before serving.

Ladle the borscht into individual bowls and serve.

SPRING GARLIC AND BREAD SOUP

Garlic turns up in my cooking, and that of most cooks whose homes I never decline an invitation to eat at, as much as any other ingredient. I love it so much that I also enjoy making it the center of attention, as in this soup, which is built on a base of garlic, with minced garlic added at the last second, and garlic croutons on top. Each garlic incarnation contributes its own effect: the cooked is mellow and sweet; the raw adds a spike of pure, fresh garlic; and the croutons are nutty, toasted, and lingering. Punched up with hot sauce, it's a real treat; just make sure your girlfriend or boyfriend eats this when you do or you might not get any lovin' after the meal.

¼ cup extra-virgin olive oil

10 cloves garlic, mashed to a paste with a
    sprinkle of salt, plus 1 clove, minced

4 ounces day-old bread, crusts removed,
    cut into 1-inch pieces (2 cups)

5 cups White Chicken Stock (page 245), or
    low-sodium, store-bought chicken broth

4 thyme sprigs

2 eggs, beaten

Salt

Freshly ground black pepper

A few shakes of hot sauce

Garlic Croutons (recipe follows)

2 tablespoons sliced parsley

¼ cup grated Parmigiano-Reggiano

Heat the oil in a large, heavy-bottomed soup pot set over medium-high heat. Add the garlic paste and cook, stirring, until lightly browned, approximately 5 minutes. Add the bread, stock, and thyme. Bring to a simmer, and let simmer, stirring occasionally, for 20 minutes. Use tongs to fish out and discard the thyme sprigs. Stir in the eggs and cook, stirring, for 3 minutes. Stir in the minced garlic. Taste and season with salt, pepper, and hot sauce.

    Divide the soup among 4 bowls, garnish with the croutons, parsley, and grated cheese, and serve.

Garlic Croutons

¼ cup olive oil

1 clove garlic, minced

4 ounces day-old bread, crusts removed,
    cut into 1-inch pieces (2 cups)

Salt

Freshly ground black pepper

Heat the oil in a heavy-bottomed sauté pan over medium-high heat. Add the garlic and sauté until it begins to brown, approximately 2 minutes. Add the bread cubes and toss, letting the bread soak up the oil, until the cubes are crispy, approximately 3 minutes. Season the cubes with salt and pepper.

SPLIT PEA SOUP
with Rum

SERVES 8

Split pea soup gets a makeover here, thanks to two touches: Carrots cooked in pancetta fat are stirred into the finished soup just before serving (so they don't break down during the long cooking time), and the soup is topped off with rum, which adds a bracing, cool undercurrent and cuts the richness of the soup. If you're wondering where this cockamamie idea comes from, I conceived of this dish as a sailor's porridge. Split pea soup is one of the most famous ship meals in nautical history, and seamen always have a bottle of rum around.

3 tablespoons butter

1 medium onion, finely diced

1 large shallot, finely diced

3 cups (1½ pounds) dried split peas

3 to 4 pounds ham hock

2 quarts plus 2 cups White Chicken Stock
   (page 245), or low-sodium, store-bought
   chicken broth

¼ cup finely diced pancetta (from about
   4 ounces)

4 large carrots, peeled and finely diced

About 1 tablespoon dark rum, for serving

Melt the butter in a heavy-bottomed soup pot set over medium heat. Add the onion and shallot and cook until softened but not browned, approximately 4 minutes. Add the peas and stir to coat with the butter, then add the ham hock and stock. Bring to a simmer, lower the heat, and let simmer until the peas are soft, approximately 1 hour.

Use tongs or a slotted spoon to remove the ham hock from the soup and set it aside to cool.

Ladle about one quarter of the soup into a blender, puree it, and stir it back into the soup to thicken it. (Alternatively, you can give the pot of soup a few quick zaps with an immersion blender.)

Shred the meat from the ham hock by hand, discard the skin and bones, and return the meat to the soup.

Put the pancetta in a heavy-bottomed sauté pan and sauté until crispy and enough fat has been rendered to coat the bottom of the pan, approximately 5 minutes. Add the carrots and sauté until tender, approximately 5 minutes. Stir the carrots into the soup.

The soup can be cooled and refrigerated for up to 2 days in an airtight container, or frozen for up to 2 months. Reheat gently before serving.

Ladle the soup into individual bowls and float a thin layer of rum on top.

Pasta & Risotto

BUCATINI

with Anchovy, Sweet and Hot Peppers,
Lemon, and Toasted Bread Crumbs

LINGUINE

with Clams, Pancetta, Butternut Squash,
and Wilted Greens

PASTINA

with Vegetables in Broth

ORECCHIETTE

with Chicken, Greens, Thyme, and Goat Cheese

SPAGHETTI

with a Salad on Top

CAPELLINI SALSA FRESCA

PEACH AND PANCETTA RISOTTO

SWEET AND SOUR MUSHROOM RISOTTO

POTATO RAVIOLI

with Mushrooms, Shallots, and Chives

FALL SQUASH AGNOLOTTI

with Brown Butter and Brussels Sprouts

CAVATELLI

with Braised Veal Cheeks

There aren't many foods that you could safely say *everyone* loves, but my nominees for that short list would include pasta and risotto for sure. Who doesn't crave the firm, toothsome bite of a perfectly cooked al dente pasta, sauce clinging to its ridges or dripping from its strands, or a creamy risotto, loaded up with big-flavored ingredients?

As you cook your way through this chapter, you might notice that I prefer dried pasta when it comes to strands and tubular shapes, and homemade or high-quality fresh pasta (such as pappardelle or fettuccine) or wonton skins for ravioli and shapes such as cavatelli. The simple reason is that I like the firm bite you get from dried pasta, whereas fresh pasta, even if you cook it al dente, will always end up limp (though if you make your own you can achieve some tooth). With filled pastas, like ravioli, I'm not looking for that bite; in fact, I like wonton skins because the real thin ones let the colors of the ingredients within show through, as they would with properly made fresh pasta.

Most pasta dishes need to be very well tossed. If you don't have the proficiency to do this, my advice is to put all the ingredients in a big, heat-proof bowl and toss them with wooden spoons or salad tongs.

Just like pasta, risotto is a great playground for flavor combinations, both classic and new. It's also a very user-friendly dish to prepare because most risottos are essentially made the same way: You cook the rice and then fold in ingredients that have been prepared and/or cooked separately. When cooking risotto, the effect you're looking for is something that appears creamy to the eye, even though there's no cream in the preparation—the result of the suspension of the starch released from the rice by cooking.

As for the risotto rice, many contemporary cookbooks call interchangeably for Arborio, Vialone Nano, or Carnaroli. But these varieties do have distinctions: Arborio is best suited for dense risottos, bound up with lots of cheese and butter; Vialone Nano, favored in the Veneto, is a better choice for seafood, producing a wavy (*all'onda*, as the Italians say) result. And Carnaroli, which didn't come along until 1945, is—get this—a hybrid of Italian and Japanese rice strains that's the closest of the three to being all-purpose. All of that said, don't stress out over the choice of rice. Most markets only offer one variety and generally speaking any of them will do fine for any of the risottos in this chapter.

Every so often a dish, such as the Spaghetti with a Salad on Top on page 95, says "no cheese necessary," but for the most part I add Parmigiano-Reggiano or Pecorino Romano cheese. Some people find adding cheese to fish dishes sacrilege, but I usually find leaving cheese *out* of a pasta or risotto, even those featuring shellfish, unforgivable. The cheese is often stirred into the dish, essentially acting as a seasoning, and helping to pull the flavors together. It makes the ingredients cling to one another and helps sauce thicken and stick to the noodles. Basically, the cheese is a clean-up batter, not unlike butter in so many classic French recipes.

BUCATINI

with Anchovy, Sweet and Hot Peppers, Lemon, and Toasted Bread Crumbs

SERVES 6 AS AN APPETIZER, OR 4 AS A MAIN COURSE

This dish was inspired by one of the quintessential dishes of Sicily, *pasta con le sarde*, or pasta with sardines. There are no actual sardines visible in *pasta con le sarde*; they're "melted" into hot olive oil, tossed with hot pasta (sometimes with tomato), and the dish is often topped with bread crumbs and/or chopped nuts. My version uses anchovies rather than sardines for a lighter, cleaner flavor, tosses in the bread crumbs, and rounds out the dish with garlic, hot peppers, lemon juice, Parmesan, and parsley. You can make this with spaghetti, but the thicker bucatini—a long, tubular pasta—stands up better to all those assertive flavors. There's a high ratio of other ingredients to pasta so when the bucatini's gone, you're left with a little warm bread salad of sorts on the plate.

Get all your ingredients together and you can cook the anchovies and peppers while the pasta's boiling.

Salt

1 pound dried bucatini

½ cup olive oil

6 large cloves garlic, thinly sliced

12 canned anchovy fillets, minced

6 ounces Italian frying peppers, or hot cherry peppers (about 6 peppers), seeded and thinly sliced crosswise

½ cup thinly sliced pepperoncini

¾ cup dried bread crumbs (preferably Japanese panko)

¼ cup plus 2 tablespoons grated Parmigiano-Reggiano (from about 1½ ounces cheese)

Pinch of crushed red pepper flakes, or more to taste

¼ cup plus 2 tablespoons sliced parsley

1 lemon, halved

Bring a large pot of salted water to a boil. Add the bucatini and cook until al dente, approximately 7 minutes.

Meanwhile, heat the oil in a wide, deep, heavy-bottomed sauté pan over medium-high heat. Add the garlic and anchovies, and cook, mashing the anchovies with a wooden spoon, until they dissolve, approximately 3 minutes. Add the Italian frying peppers and cook, stirring to integrate the flavors, until the peppers wilt just a bit, approximately 3 minutes. Add the pepperoncini.

When the bucatini is done, drain it and add it to the pan with the anchovy and pepper mixture. Add the bread crumbs, Parmigiano, pepper flakes, and parsley. Squeeze half a lemon over the pan, catching any seeds in your hand, and toss to combine well. Taste and adjust with more pepper flakes and/or lemon juice if necessary.

Divide the pasta among dinner plates or wide, shallow bowls, and serve.

LINGUINE

with Clams, Pancetta, Butternut Squash, and Wilted Greens

SERVES 6 AS AN APPETIZER, OR 4 AS A MAIN COURSE

As a cook, I'm very devoted to the seasons, but I'm not above straying a bit when seduced by a compelling idea. This dish came about one fall night when I was in the mood for linguine and clams, a dish that for me evokes summer. I began playing around, expanding the dish with earthy pancetta and bitter, crunchy greens. The most incongruous, autumnal ingredient in this dish—the squash—is the one that holds it all together. Its sweetness unites the briny clams and the other elements.

Salt

½ cup dry white wine

1 pound Manila clams (about 24 clams)

1 tablespoon olive oil

¾ cup diced pancetta, from about 3 ounces pancetta

¼ cup thinly sliced garlic

1 pound dried linguine

2 cups 1-inch-cubed butternut squash, from about 8 ounces squash

3 cups torn escarole

½ cup grated Parmigiano-Reggiano, plus more for serving

½ cup sliced parsley

½ cup sliced basil

½ cup chopped oregano

2 teaspoons crushed red pepper flakes

1 tablespoon butter

Bring a large pot of salted water to a boil.

Meanwhile, pour the wine into a large, heavy-bottomed pot and heat it over medium-high heat. Add the clams, cover, and steam until the clams open, 3 to 5 minutes. Discard any clams that have not opened. Strain the clams' cooking liquid through a fine-mesh strainer set over a bowl and set the strained liquid aside.

Pour the oil into a wide, deep, heavy-bottomed sauté pan and heat it over medium-high heat. Add the pancetta and cook until it gives off enough fat to coat the bottom of the pan, approximately 5 minutes. Add the garlic and cook until lightly browned, approximately 3 minutes.

Add the pasta to the boiling water and cook until al dente, approximately 7 minutes.

Meanwhile, add the squash to the pan with the pancetta and garlic, and cook until lightly browned on all sides, approximately 6 minutes.

Drain the pasta in a colander and add it to the pan with the other ingredients. Add ½ cup of the reserved clam cooking liquid. Add the escarole and toss just to warm and wilt it slightly. Add the clams to the pan, along with the Parmigiano, parsley, basil, oregano, red pepper flakes, and butter, and toss very gently.

Divide the pasta among 4 to 6 bowls, getting an even number of clams in each portion; top with some grated cheese; and serve.

PASTINA
with Vegetables in Broth

SERVES 6 AS AN APPETIZER, OR 4 AS A MAIN COURSE

I hate to use the phrase "comfort food" but that's what this is—chicken noodle soup, Italian style. Pastina is just what it sounds like: little pasta. It comes in a number of shapes and sizes, including stars and letters of the alphabet for kids. If this dish sounds very simple, that's because it is—a quick, quietly delicious hybrid of pasta and soup that's homey and easy to adapt to whatever you have in the fridge or pantry. You can refrigerate any leftovers for several days, and they will taste better each day.

3 tablespoons olive oil

½ medium onion, finely diced

1 clove garlic, thinly sliced

3½ cups White Chicken Stock (page 245) or low-sodium, store-bought chicken broth

5 whole peeled canned tomatoes, crushed by hand and drained

Parmigiano-Reggiano rind (see Note, page 72) plus ¼ cup grated Parmigiano-Reggiano cheese

Salt

½ cup dried pastina

2 tablespoons sliced parsley

1 tablespoon sliced basil

Freshly ground black pepper

2 cups baby spinach leaves

4 teaspoons extra-virgin olive oil

In a soup pot, heat 2 tablespoons of the olive oil over medium heat. Add the onion and garlic and cook until softened but not browned, approximately 2 minutes. Add the stock, tomatoes, and Parmigiano rind. Bring to a gentle simmer and continue to simmer for 20 minutes.

Meanwhile, bring a large pot of salted water to a boil. Add the pastina and cook until al dente, approximately 2 minutes. Drain in a fine-mesh strainer and refresh under cold running water. Toss with the remaining tablespoon olive oil and set aside.

After the stock has simmered for 20 minutes, add the pastina, parsley, and basil, and season to taste with salt and pepper. Add the spinach and simmer for 5 minutes. Use tongs or a slotted spoon to remove and discard the cheese rind.

Ladle the soup into bowls and top each serving with some grated cheese and 1 teaspoon extra-virgin olive oil.

NOTES TO THE COOK You can also make this dish with the short, tubular pasta called tubettini.
To make this more of a meal, fold in diced, cooked chicken or shrimp.

ORECCHIETTE
with Chicken, Greens, Thyme, and Goat Cheese
SERVES 6 AS AN APPETIZER, OR 4 AS A MAIN COURSE

This is a perfect example of using pasta as a vehicle for some planned leftovers, in this case the remains of a roasted chicken and some salad greens. I like this with chicken thighs and legs, but you could also make it with any part of the bird. For extra flavor, replace the pasta cooking liquid with White Chicken Stock (page 245) in making the quick sauce.

Salt

1 pound dried orecchiette

¼ cup olive oil

2 cloves garlic, thinly sliced

4 cups torn escarole leaves

4 leftover roasted chicken thighs, meat separated from the bone and shredded, at room temperature (2 large chicken breasts or 4 legs can be substituted)

¼ cup chopped thyme

¼ cup sliced parsley

½ cup grated Parmigiano-Reggiano

Freshly ground black pepper

2 tablespoons butter, at room temperature

1 beefsteak tomato, cut into ¼-inch dice

4 ounces aged goat cheese, crumbled (1 cup), at room temperature

Bring a large pot of salted water to a boil. Add the orecchiette and cook until al dente, approximately 8 minutes.

Meanwhile, heat the oil in a wide, deep, heavy-bottomed sauté pan over medium-high heat. Add the garlic and sauté until lightly browned, approximately 1 minute. Add the escarole and cook for 1 minute to wilt it. Add the chicken and sauté until warmed through, approximately 2 minutes. Stir in the thyme and parsley.

Reserve 1 cup of the pasta water and drain the pasta. Add the pasta to the pan with the chicken and vegetables. Add the Parmigiano and a few tablespoons reserved pasta water, and toss to melt the cheese into a creamy emulsion. Season with salt and pepper, add the butter, and toss to melt the butter.

Divide the pasta among 4 or 6 wide, shallow bowls and top each serving with some tomatoes and goat cheese.

NOTE TO THE COOK If desired, spice up this dish with a pinch or two of crushed red pepper flakes.

SPAGHETTI
with a Salad on Top

SERVES 6 AS AN APPETIZER, OR 4 AS A MAIN COURSE

Diners at The Mermaid Inn find this funny-sounding all-in-one dish irresistible, and I dare say you'll love it just as much at home. (There's a photograph of it on page 6.) The spaghetti is dressed in a spicy red seafood sauce that gets its salty punch from a secret ingredient (soy sauce) and the peppery raw arugula offers a stark and pleasing contrast. The seafood in this dish cooks very quickly, so have all of your ingredients organized and nearby before starting.

2 cups arugula

2 scallions, white and green parts, thinly sliced

Salt

Freshly ground black pepper

6 large sea scallops, 1 to 2 ounces each, halved horizontally (see Note, page 56)

12 jumbo shrimp, peeled and deveined

1 pound spaghetti

2 tablespoons olive oil

¼ cup chopped garlic

½ teaspoon crushed red pepper flakes, plus more to taste

1 28-ounce can whole peeled plum tomatoes, with their juices, crushed by hand

1 cup soy sauce (do not use reduced sodium)

6 ounces squid, cleaned, tubes sliced into ¼-inch rings, and tentacles left whole if small

6 tablespoons (¾ stick) butter, at room temperature

2 teaspoons extra-virgin olive oil

Put the arugula and scallions in a bowl. Season with salt and pepper and set aside.

Bring a large pot of salted water to a boil over high heat. Add the scallops and shrimp and cook for 1 minute. Use tongs or a slotted spoon to transfer them to a bowl and set aside.

Let the water return to a boil, add the spaghetti to the water, and cook until al dente, approximately 8 minutes.

Meanwhile, heat a wide, deep, heavy-bottomed skillet over high heat until very hot. Add the olive oil to the skillet, warm for 1 minute, then add the garlic and cook until well browned, approximately 1 minute. Add the red pepper flakes and cook, stirring, for 30 seconds. Add the tomatoes and pan-fry them for 2 to 3 minutes. Add the soy sauce and cook until slightly reduced and the sauce begins to turn almost black, approximately 3 minutes. Add the scallops, shrimp, squid, and butter and cook, stirring, until the butter melts and the shellfish is cooked through, approximately 3 minutes.

Drain the spaghetti well in a colander, add it to the skillet with the sauce, and toss well.

Add the extra-virgin olive oil to the bowl with the arugula and quickly toss. Transfer the pasta to a serving platter and top with the arugula and scallions. Serve family style at the table.

CAPELLINI SALSA FRESCA

SERVES 6 AS AN APPETIZER, OR 4 AS A MAIN COURSE

To me, this pasta is the perfect expression of summer: garden tomatoes mingling with basil, olive oil, and garlic. It's as simple and as good as it sounds, provided you use high-quality ingredients (fresh tomatoes and basil, real Parmigiano-Reggiano) and are careful not to overcook the pasta or sauce. You just want to warm the ingredients, but each should maintain its own identity so you taste each of them distinctly.

Salt

1 pound dried capellini (angel hair) pasta

¼ cup extra-virgin olive oil

1 large red beefsteak tomato, finely diced

1 yellow beefsteak tomato, or another red tomato, diced

3 cloves garlic, minced

¼ cup sliced basil

½ cup finely grated Parmigiano-Reggiano

2 tablespoons butter, at room temperature

Freshly ground black pepper

Bring a large pot of salted water to a boil. Add the pasta and boil until al dente, approximately 3 minutes.

Meanwhile, heat the olive oil in a wide, deep, heavy-bottomed sauté pan over medium-high heat. Add the red and yellow tomatoes, garlic, and basil, and cook for 1 minute.

Drain the pasta and add it to the pan with the tomatoes, basil, and garlic. Add the cheese and butter, season with salt and pepper, and toss well to melt the butter and incorporate the ingredients.

Divide among wide, shallow bowls and serve hot.

PEACH AND PANCETTA RISOTTO

SERVES 6 AS AN APPETIZER, OR 4 AS A MAIN COURSE

I love fruit with my bacon, and not always in the morning. Here, sweet peaches and salty pancetta, two contrasting but complementary flavors, offer a pairing so powerful that you don't need many more ingredients to make it complete and satisfying. Risotto brings out the lunatic in me—I also make one with lobster and strawberry—but I promise you that as crazy as this sounds, it is delicious.

Normally, I'd say to use the same pot you used for browning the pancetta to cook the risotto, but you need to use a second pot here in order to preserve the pure flavor of the rice, keep the individual ingredients distinct, and make the dish a beautiful white with flecks of pink and orange. The fat gets stirred in at the end with the pancetta, but if you were to start the risotto in the same pot, it would be a much less pretty affair.

8 ounces pancetta, cut into ½-inch dice
6 cups White Chicken Stock (page 245) or
    low-sodium, store-bought chicken broth
4 tablespoons (½ stick) butter
2 tablespoons canola oil
½ medium onion, finely diced
1 pound risotto rice (see page 89)

½ cup dry white wine
½ cup grated Parmigiano-Reggiano
8 medium peaches, cut into 1-inch dice
½ cup sliced basil
Salt
2 tablespoons crushed pink peppercorns or
    1 teaspoon freshly ground white pepper

Put the pancetta in a cold pan and set over medium heat. Cook, stirring, until the pancetta is browned all over, approximately 5 minutes. Set aside, reserving the pancetta in any rendered fat.

Pour the stock into a pot and bring to a simmer over medium-high heat.

Meanwhile, heat 2 tablespoons of the butter and the oil in a large, heavy-bottomed pot over medium heat. Add the onion and sauté until softened but not browned, approximately 4 minutes. Add the rice and cook, stirring to coat it with the oil, for 2 minutes. Pour in the wine and cook, stirring and scraping the bottom of the pot, until the wine reduces by two thirds, approximately 3 minutes. Begin ladling simmering broth into the pot, ½ cup at a time, and stir constantly until the broth is absorbed by the rice. Continue adding broth in ½-cup increments, stirring constantly and only adding the next ladleful when the previous one has been absorbed. After about 20 minutes, and after you've used up almost all or all of the stock, the rice should appear to have softened slightly and turned creamy, but the individual grains should still be firm in the center. Bite into one to test it if you're not sure.

Stir in the Parmigiano and remaining 2 tablespoons butter, then fold in the pancetta and its fat, the peaches, and basil. Season with salt and pepper. Divide among dinner plates or large, shallow bowls. Garnish each serving with some of the pink peppercorns, and serve immediately.

SWEET AND SOUR MUSHROOM RISOTTO

SERVES 6 AS AN APPETIZER, OR 4 AS A MAIN COURSE

Sausage, mushrooms, radicchio, raisins, and Parmigiano hit all the flavor buttons: spicy, earthy, bitter, sweet, and salty. That's not to say you can't adapt this dish to meet your personal taste preferences. You can, for example, use hot sausage instead of sweet (andouille is especially good), or a combination of the two; you can use button mushrooms instead of cremini, and you can leave out the radicchio, or replace it with spinach or arugula leaves, if you find it too bitter.

$4\frac{1}{2}$ cups White Chicken Stock (page 245) or
    low-sodium, store-bought chicken broth

12 ounces sweet Italian sausage, casings
    removed

3 cloves garlic, minced

10 ounces cremini or button mushrooms
    (about 16 mushrooms), quartered

Salt

Freshly ground black pepper

2 tablespoons butter

2 tablespoons olive oil

$\frac{1}{2}$ medium onion, finely diced

$\frac{1}{4}$ cup minced celery

1 pound risotto rice (see page 89)

$\frac{1}{2}$ cup dry white wine

1 small head radicchio, shredded

$\frac{1}{2}$ cup golden raisins

$\frac{1}{2}$ cup grated Parmigiano-Reggiano

1 tablespoon chopped thyme

1 tablespoon sliced basil

1 tablespoon sliced parsley

Pour the broth into a small pot and bring it to a simmer over medium-low heat.

Meanwhile, put the sausage meat and garlic in a skillet and set the skillet over medium heat. Using the back of a fork, break up the meat and cook, stirring, until the meat loses its pink color and begins to brown, approximately 8 minutes. Turn the heat down a bit, add the mushrooms, and continue to cook until the mushrooms begin to give off their liquid, approximately 10 minutes. Season with salt and pepper. Remove the skillet from the heat, cover to keep warm, and set aside.

Heat the butter and oil in a large, heavy-bottomed pot over medium heat. Add the onion and celery and sauté until softened but not browned, approximately 4 minutes. Add the rice and cook, stirring to coat it with the oil, for 2 minutes. Pour in the wine and cook, stirring and scraping the bottom of the pot, until the wine reduces by two thirds, approximately 3 minutes. Begin ladling simmering broth into the pot, $\frac{1}{2}$ cup at a time, and stir constantly until the broth is absorbed by the rice. Continue adding broth in $\frac{1}{2}$-cup increments, stirring constantly, and only adding the next ladleful when the previous one has been absorbed. After about 20 minutes, and after you've used up all or almost all of the stock, the rice should appear to have softened slightly and turned creamy, but the individual grains should still be firm in the center. Bite into one to test it if you're not sure.

Fold in the reserved sausage mixture, the radicchio, raisins, Parmigiano, thyme, basil, and parsley, and stir gently but thoroughly. Season with salt and pepper. Divide among dinner plates or large, shallow bowls and serve immediately.

POTATO RAVIOLI

with Mushrooms, Shallots, and Chives

SERVES 6 AS AN APPETIZER, OR 4 AS A MAIN COURSE

Sometimes putting background ingredients in the foreground can create unexpected results, as when mashed potatoes, usually a side dish, take center stage. Here, they're made into a ravioli filling, and the ravioli are served with sautéed mushrooms in a quick sauce of mushroom stock and grated Parmigiano-Reggiano. The combination of simple, earthy ingredients adds up to something surprisingly elegant.

2 teaspoons canola oil

10 ounces mushrooms, preferably honshimeji, oyster, or shiitake, stems removed and set aside

1 medium Yukon Gold potato

¾ cup milk

4 tablespoons (½ stick) butter, finely diced and frozen, plus 2 tablespoons at room temperature

Salt

Freshly ground black pepper

1 tablespoon plus 1 teaspoon mascarpone cheese

1 tablespoon white truffle oil (optional)

3 teaspoons finely sliced chives

48 wonton skins

1 egg, beaten

1 medium shallot, minced

1 tablespoon grated Parmigiano-Reggiano, plus more for serving

Make a quick mushroom stock: Heat 1 teaspoon of the canola oil in a medium pot set over medium heat. Add the mushroom stems and sauté until they just begin to soften, approximately 5 minutes. Add 1 quart water, bring the water to a simmer, and let simmer for 45 minutes. Strain through a fine-mesh strainer set over a bowl. Discard the solids. Reserve 2 cups of the stock; refrigerate or freeze any extra for another use.

Make the mashed potatoes: Put the potato in a pot, cover by several inches with cold water, set over high heat, and bring to a boil. Continue to boil until a sharp, thin-bladed knife pierces easily to the center of the potato, approximately 12 minutes. Drain, and when cool enough to handle, peel and quarter the potato. Return the potato to the pot and cook over medium-high heat for a few minutes, stirring, to evaporate any excess moisture, but do not brown the skin. Transfer to a bowl and mash with a potato masher. Gradually add the milk and frozen, cubed butter, mashing to incorporate them. Season with salt and pepper. You should have ¾ cup mashed potatoes. Fold in the mascarpone, truffle oil (if using), and 1 teaspoon of the chives.

Keeping a damp cloth over the package to keep the wonton skins moist, lay 6 wonton skins on a clean, dry cutting board or work surface. Put 1 generous teaspoon of mashed potatoes in the center of each skin. Brush the edges of each square with the beaten egg and top with another wonton skin. Seal the ravioli, leaving one corner open. Gently squeeze out any air, then seal the open corner. Repeat with the remaining skins, filling, and beaten egg to make 24 ravioli.

Bring a pot of salted water to a boil.

Meanwhile, heat the remaining teaspoon canola oil in a large, heavy-bottomed sauté pan over medium heat. Add the mushrooms, shallot, and 1 tablespoon of the butter. Cook until the mushrooms are lightly browned, approximately 5 minutes. Season with salt and pepper, transfer the mushrooms to a bowl, and set aside.

Melt the remaining tablespoon butter in a medium saucepan set over medium-high heat. Cook until the butter browns, approximately 5 minutes. Add the mushrooms and 2 cups mushroom stock, bring to a simmer, and continue to simmer until the stock is reduced by half, approximately 12 minutes.

Meanwhile, add the ravioli to the boiling water and cook just until they float to the surface, 2 to 3 minutes. Drain the ravioli and add them to the pot with the mushrooms and sauce. Add the Parmigiano and remaining 2 teaspoons chives and toss well.

To serve, divide the ravioli among 4 to 6 bowls and ladle some sauce over them. Top with some grated cheese.

NOTES TO THE COOK You can skip the mushroom stock step and reconstitute $1/2$ cup dried porcini in 2 cups hot water for 20 minutes. Strain and use the liquid in place of the stock, and use the porcini as the mushrooms in the dish.

While excellent on their own, these ravioli and their sauce are a perfect accompaniment to roast chicken.

FALL SQUASH AGNOLOTTI
with Brown Butter and Brussels Sprouts

SERVES 6 AS AN APPETIZER, OR 4 AS A MAIN COURSE

Seasonal cooking at its best, these agnolotti (folded-over ravioli) bring together some of fall's most popular flavors: butternut squash, Brussels sprouts, and sage. I have a special fondness for Brussels sprouts because of their musky, almost turnip quality, a great match for the sweet squash and brown butter. The toasted squash seeds add another layer of squash-like nuance, as well as essential crunch.

1½ pounds butternut squash

4 tablespoons (½ stick) plus 1 teaspoon butter

Salt

Freshly ground black pepper

8 ounces Brussels sprouts, quartered

1 tablespoon olive oil

2 tablespoons grated Parmigiano-Reggiano, plus more for serving

2 teaspoons sliced parsley

24 ravioli or wonton skins

1 egg, beaten

15 sage leaves

½ cup White Chicken Stock (page 245) or low-sodium, store-bought chicken broth

Preheat the oven to 350°F.

Halve the squash, scoop out the seeds, and set ¼ cup of them aside.

Put ½ tablespoon butter in the seed cavity of each squash half and set the two halves on a cookie sheet or in a roasting pan. Season with salt and pepper and roast, cut side up, without browning, until soft to a knife-tip, approximately 35 minutes.

Meanwhile, in a bowl, toss the Brussels sprouts with the olive oil and season with salt and pepper. Spread out on a cookie sheet and roast until lightly browned, approximately 12 minutes. Remove from the oven and set aside.

Pat the squash seeds dry with a paper towel. Put the seeds in an ovenproof skillet or baking dish and toast in the oven until fragrant, approximately 12 minutes. Toss with 1 teaspoon of the butter and season with salt and pepper. Set aside.

Remove the squash from the oven and let cool. Transfer the flesh to the bowl of a food processor fitted with a steel blade. Puree, then transfer to a bowl and stir in half of the Parmigiano and the parsley, and season with salt and pepper. You should have about ¾ cup.

Keeping a damp cloth over the package to keep the wonton skins moist, lay 6 wonton skins on a clean, dry cutting board or work surface. Put 1½ teaspoons of squash puree in the center of each skin. Brush the edges of each square with the beaten egg and fold the skin over diagonally. Seal the agnolotti, leaving one corner open. Gently squeeze out any air, then seal the open corner. Repeat with the remaining wonton skins, filling, and beaten egg to make 24 agnolotti.

Bring a pot of salted water to a boil.

Melt 2 tablespoons of the butter in a wide, deep sauté pan, letting it turn brown. Add the sage leaves and let them frizzle in the butter.

Meanwhile, boil the agnolotti in the salted water until they rise to the surface, approximately 2 minutes. Use a slotted spoon to transfer them to the pan with the butter and sage. Add the Brussels sprouts and stock, bring to a simmer, and season with salt and pepper. Stir in the Parmigiano and remaining tablespoon butter and remove from the heat.

To serve, divide the agnolotti among plates or bowls. Top each serving with a scattering of squash seeds and some more grated cheese.

CAVATELLI
with Braised Veal Cheeks

SERVES 6 AS AN APPETIZER, OR 4 AS A MAIN COURSE

There are simple pastas that involve little more than herbs and cheese. This is not one of those pastas. It's a hearty, stick-to-your-ribs dish that Joey Campanaro, who was the opening chef of The Harrison, and I developed together. The real beauty of it is Joey's grandmother's recipe for cavatelli made with ricotta cheese.

This pasta is best approached the same way as the recipe for the orecchiette with chicken (page 94): Prepare the veal cheeks the day before. Trust me, this dish is worth the effort of making your own cavatelli; when you combine them with the veal and add the Pecorino and escarole, it's truly over the top. Break out a good bottle of red wine and serve this to some people who are worth the trouble.

1 cup plus 2 tablespoons canola oil

1 pound veal cheeks

Salt

Freshly ground black pepper

1 carrot, peeled and coarsely chopped

1 onion, peeled and coarsely chopped

1 stalk celery, coarsely chopped

1 35-ounce can whole peeled tomatoes, crushed by hand, with their juice

2 cups Veal Stock (page 246) or low-sodium, store-bought beef broth

1 cup red wine, preferably Barolo or Cabernet Sauvignon

5 thyme sprigs

2 large cloves garlic, coarsely chopped

½ medium head escarole

Cavatelli (recipe follows) or 1 pound store-bought cavatelli or orecchiette

3 ripe plum tomatoes, seeded and diced

1 cup grated Pecorino cheese, preferably Locatelli, plus more for serving

2 tablespoons sliced basil

Extra-virgin olive oil, for serving

Preheat the oven to 325°F.

Pour 1 cup of the canola oil into a heavy-bottomed roasting pan and heat over high heat.

Meanwhile, season the veal cheeks with salt and pepper. Add them to the pan and brown well on both sides, approximately 5 minutes per side. Remove the cheeks from the pan and set them on a plate. Pour off all but 2 tablespoons of fat from the pan. Add the carrot, onion, and celery and brown them, approximately 5 minutes. Add the canned tomatoes, stock, wine, and thyme and bring to a simmer. Return the meat to the pan and transfer to the oven. Cover and braise until the meat is almost falling apart, approximately 2½ hours. As the cheeks braise, periodically check on them to be sure the liquid isn't boiling aggressively; it should be at the mildest of simmers. If it's bubbling violently, reduce the temperature by 25 degrees; if it isn't boiling at all, raise the oven temperature by 25 degrees.

Transfer the meat to a plate and set aside. Pass the braising liquid through a food mill to make a sauce. When cool enough to handle, shred the meat by hand and return it to the sauce.

Bring a large pot of salted water to a boil over high heat.

Heat the remaining 2 tablespoons canola oil in a wide, deep-sided, heavy-bottomed sauté pan set over medium-high heat. Add the garlic and cook until it's just beginning to brown, approximately 2 minutes. Add the escarole and sauté for a minute or two, then add the meat and sauce and cook for 2 to 3 minutes to warm the meat and integrate the flavors.

Add the cavatelli to the boiling water and cook until they float to the surface, 2 to 3 minutes; 8 to 9 minutes if using dried pasta. Strain them and add them to the sauce. Toss in the fresh tomatoes, Pecorino, and basil, and taste and adjust the seasoning with salt and pepper.

Divide the pasta and sauce among 4 to 6 bowls, drizzle with some extra-virgin olive oil, top with some grated cheese, and serve.

Cavatelli

MAKES ENOUGH FOR 6 APPETIZERS, OR 4 MAIN-COURSE DISHES

I believe that, even in an era when good-quality fresh pastas are available on the market, homemade pasta is a noble and rewarding undertaking. This is one of my favorites: slightly tangy nuggets with ricotta cheese right in the dough. To make this, you will need a cavatelli maker, which can be had for $25 to $35. If you don't have one, you can make orecchiette from this dough (see below).

2 cups fresh ricotta cheese

2 eggs

2 tablespoons salt

4 cups flour, plus extra for shaping

Extra-virgin olive oil (optional)

Put the cheese and eggs in the bowl of a standing mixer fitted with the paddle attachment, add the salt, and beat on medium speed until well incorporated and smooth, approximately 3 minutes. With the motor running, slowly add the flour and continue beating on medium speed until the dough pulls together in a ball, but remains a little sticky.

Remove the dough from the bowl, form into a ball, wrap in plastic wrap, and refrigerate for at least 25 minutes, or up to 2 days.

Lightly flour a work surface. Remove the dough from the plastic and set it out on the surface. Cut the dough into 6 equal pieces, and roll each piece into a log-shaped roll, 1 inch in diameter and about 30 inches long. Feed the logs, one at a time, through the cavatelli cutter. Or, if you don't have a cavatelli cutter, make orecchiette by cutting each log crosswise into ¼-inch pieces. Flour your palm and, one by one, place the pieces into the center of your palm. Press down with your thumb, twist, and flick the piece into a bowl. Repeat with the remaining pieces, re-flouring your hands as necessary.

If not cooking the cavatelli immediately, toss with olive oil, cover, and refrigerate for up to 2 days.

FISH & SHELLFISH

STEAMED AND ROASTED MANILA CLAMS
with Red Pepper Soffritto and Sherry

SCALLOPS
with Morel Risotto and Pea Sauce

GRILLED SOFT-SHELL CRABS
with Baby Spinach, Mango, and Bacon Salad

STEAMED MUSSELS
with Orzo and Herbs

GRILLED SARDINES
with Spicy Black Olive and Tomato Salsa Cruda

SAUTÉED SKATE
with White Gazpacho of Sweet Grapes

HALIBUT
with Grapefruit, Parsley, Red Onion, and Shiitake Mushrooms

GRILLED TUNA
*with Grilled Potato, Parsley, and Red Onion Salad
and Tapenade Vinaigrette*

LOBSTER THERMIDOR

BABY CUTTLEFISH STEW
on Bread

SAUTÉED CODFISH NEW ENGLAND STYLE

PAN-CRISPED WHOLE FISH
with Braised Greens and Reds

SALMON
with Corn, Sugar Snap Peas, and Shiitake Mushrooms

GRILLED SWORDFISH ON ROSEMARY BRANCHES
*with Grilled Vegetables
and Yellow Pepper Vinaigrette*

MUSTARD-CRUSTED TROUT
with Burst Cherry Tomato Sauce and Lemon Oil

taly and New England, certain parts of them anyway, are worlds apart in more ways than one. But they do have things in common, and one of them is love for fish and shellfish. Both of my ancestral bloodlines have fish swimming through them, so I suppose I was destined to love all things seafood myself. I'm so fond of it that I opened The Mermaid Inn, my own interpretation of a clam shack, right in New York City's East Village.

I grew up in the seaside town of Narragansett, Rhode Island, specifically in an area called Point Judith, at the southernmost tip of the state. There, fish was as immediate and available as a vegetable you'd yank out of your backyard garden or a piece of fruit you might pluck from a nearby tree; in fact, we had the largest fishing community in the state.

In Point Judith, you bought your fish down at the docks, when the commercial fishermen returned from their day on the sea, pulling in on their day boats. Those guys each fished for a specific catch. Codfish, squid, lobster, and bluefish were the most popular, and there were also people who specialized in working the scallop, clam, and oyster beds.

But every boat runs into fish they're not looking for. Some of it ends up in their nets or on the end of their lines by sheer happenstance, and some of it's worth making an extra effort for. The financial model of a fishing boat is like this: The captain keeps the lion's share of the profit from the boat's species of choice, with the rest going to the crew. But the captain will also let the crew pocket any money they can make from the other fish.

To load up with as much fish as possible, and as a security precaution, also, every boat has a shotgun in tow. When they see an especially prized specimen swimming along—perhaps a large tuna or swordfish—the crew put a slug in it, scoop it up with a net, and bring it back to the docks. When the boats pull in at the end of the day, the guys—many of whom have become my personal friends, though at the time they were my friends' older brothers—set up a table right next to their docking slot. And that table is called a *shack*.

But I digress, as I'm apt to do when talking about New England. The point is that I'm sure due to the fact that I grew up in one of the fishing capitals of the nation, my fish and shellfish dishes employ a bit of nostalgia and a little whimsy. They're also unmistakably seasonal, with a lot of emphasis on spring and summer, seasons when you think of eating light, simple food that can be prepared quickly and enjoyed outside. There's also some Mediterranean influence in here, such as sardines that you just flash on the grill and lay over a salsa cruda, and a dish of grilled tuna and vegetables that requires only a drizzle of vinaigrette before you can dig in.

For all of my praise of New England fishermen, I must point out that you can make any of these dishes no matter where you live, thanks to the legions of mail-order businesses (see page 249) that have mastered the art not just of fishing but of express delivering just about any fish to any destination, in pristine condition. Avail yourself of this option, and you can enjoy whatever fish—from these pages or elsewhere—you love.

STEAMED AND ROASTED MANILA CLAMS
with Red Pepper Soffritto and Sherry

SERVES 4

This Basque-inspired dish is fun eating that's broken up into three stages: First, you eat the clams, fat and garlicky from the broth. Then, you take to the broth itself with a spoon, eating it like a soup. Finally, you mop the bowl clean with the bread.

Soffritto is one of the fundamentals of a lot of Mediterranean cooking, the base from which sauces, soups, braising liquids, and other components are built. The word means "under fried," and it's generally a stewed mixture of minced carrot, onion, and celery cooked in olive oil. Here, the soffritto is powered by bacon, peppers, onion, and thyme; because you start the dish with those elements, they become part of its DNA, making their flavor felt throughout.

5 tablespoons extra-virgin olive oil

4 thick slices double-smoked bacon (about 2 ounces), diced

2 red bell peppers, seeded and cut into 1-inch dice

1 medium onion, cut into 1-inch dice

2 tablespoons chopped thyme

Salt

Freshly ground black pepper

3 cloves garlic, sliced, plus 8 cloves peeled and left whole

4 slices country bread, ½ inch thick, toasted or grilled

2 pounds Manila or mahogany clams, scrubbed

⅓ cup dry sherry

½ cup Shellfish Stock (page 247) or bottled clam juice

4 tablespoons (½ stick) butter, cut into 4 pieces, at room temperature

To make the soffritto, pour 1 tablespoon of the oil into a large, deep, heavy-bottomed sauté pan set over medium heat. Add the bacon and sauté until it is almost crisp and has released enough fat to coat the bottom of the pan, approximately 5 minutes. Add the peppers, onion, and 1 tablespoon of the thyme, and season with salt and pepper. Cook, stirring, until the peppers are tender, but have not browned, approximately 15 minutes. Turn the soffritto out of the pan and onto a cutting board and coarsely chop. Set aside.

To make the garlic puree, heat 3 tablespoons of the oil in a skillet set over low heat. Add the whole garlic cloves and cook, stirring, until golden brown and soft to a knife-tip, 12 to 15 minutes. Strain off the oil and mash the cloves with the back of a kitchen spoon. Spread it on the warm toast.

To cook the clams, heat a large, heavy-bottomed pot over medium-high heat. Pour in the remaining tablespoon oil and let it get nice and hot. Add the sliced garlic and sauté until it starts to brown, approximately 3 minutes. Add the clams and pan-roast them, stirring gently to let them all get a good dose of heat, but without cracking the shells, for 1 minute. Pour in the sherry and stir for a minute to scrape up any tasty bits stuck to the bottom of the pan, again being careful not to bust the shells. Add the stock, soffritto, and the remaining tablespoon thyme. Stir gently, cover, and steam until the clams have opened, approximately 5 minutes. (Discard any clams that have not opened.) Gently stir in the butter, 1 piece at a time, and season with salt and pepper to taste.

To serve, give everyone a small fork (if you have any seafood forks, this is a good time to break them out) and a soup spoon. Divide the clams and broth among 4 bowls and serve the toast alongside. Have a few extra bowls on the table for empty shells.

NOTES TO THE COOK If you can find it, I prefer Nueske's double-smoked bacon. (See Mail-Order Sources, page 249.)

The best way to scrub clams is with a scouring pad under cold running water. It's important to be gentle with them; if they sense too much movement, they seize up, making them tough to open.

SCALLOPS
with Morel Risotto and Pea Sauce
SERVES 4 AS A MAIN COURSE

Morels and peas belong in the spring cooking Hall of Fame, right alongside soft-shell crabs, rhubarb, and shad roe in my book. Serving them with scallops and risotto adds heft and protein to these light, seasonal ingredients, making them substantial and satisfying.

I'm not going to lie to you: This dish takes a bit of concentration and uses most of the burners on your stovetop. It's not really difficult, but you'll need to make a pea sauce and a risotto, then cook up some scallops. But I promise you, the combination of the three—the pot of gold at the end of the rainbow—is worth the effort. My advice is to make the pea sauce ahead of time (a full day ahead if you like), and then just get everything organized and ready to go. You'll need a sauté pan for the mushrooms, a pot for the risotto stock, and a pot for the risotto. You'll also need a pot for reheating the pea sauce just before serving, but I'll let you in on a little secret: You can use the same pot that held the risotto stock, which will be empty just in time for this quick task. (If there's a bit of stock left, just pour it into a storage container, or dump it—there won't be more than a few tablespoons.)

The cool thing about this dish is that it's packed with big flavors, but they're all clean and fresh so the result is anything but heavy. To get there, treat all of the ingredients gently: When making the pea sauce, cook the peas just enough, gently simmering rather than boiling the stock. Don't brown any of the vegetables here, and be especially careful not to scorch the risotto. Same goes for the mushrooms—as soon as they soften, get the pan off the heat.

Believe it or not, frozen peas can be a better choice than fresh for the sauce. Once peas are snipped from the vine, their natural sugars begin converting to starch, and they give up their sweetness. Once frozen, that process stops and peas that are frozen soon after they are picked are apt to be sweeter than fresh peas that have been sitting around for a day or two. So, unless you have access to a farmer's market, or your own backyard garden, make this with frozen peas, accentuating their sweetness with some sugar, if necessary.

Salt

½ cup shelled fresh peas or defrosted frozen peas

9 tablespoons (1 stick plus 1 tablespoon) butter

1 tablespoon minced shallot

½ small white onion, finely diced

2¼ cups plus 2 tablespoons White Chicken Stock (page 245) or low-sodium, store-bought chicken broth

Sugar (optional)

4 ounces morel mushrooms, wiped clean with a damp towel, larger ones halved

¼ cup plus 2 tablespoons olive oil

1 cup risotto rice (see page 89)

½ cup dry white wine

½ cup grated Parmigiano-Reggiano cheese

16 large sea scallops, approximately 1½ pounds total weight (see Note, page 56)

Freshly ground black pepper

1 tablespoon sliced tarragon

1 tablespoon sliced chervil

1 teaspoon sliced parsley

Make the pea sauce: Bring a small pot of salted water to a boil. Add the peas and cook for 1 minute if frozen, or 5 minutes if fresh. Drain in a strainer, then cool them off under cold running water. Drain again and set aside. Melt 1 tablespoon of the butter in a sauté pan set over medium heat. Add the shallot and 2 tablespoons or so of the diced onion and sauté until softened but not browned, approximately 4 minutes. Add ¼ cup of the stock and bring to a gentle simmer. Add the peas, return to a simmer, and let simmer for 1 minute, then transfer to a blender and blend until smooth. Strain through a fine-mesh strainer set over a bowl, pressing down with a rubber spatula to extract as much puree as possible. Season with salt and, if needed, sugar—you want to taste the peas loud and clear, with just a hint of sweetness and no salt flavor. Cover and chill for at least 1 hour, or up to 24 hours.

When ready to proceed, sauté the mushrooms: Melt 2 tablespoons of the butter in a sauté pan over medium-high heat. Add the morels, season with salt, and cook until they soften slightly and begin to give off some liquid, approximately 5 minutes. Add 2 tablespoons of the stock and 1 table-spoon of the butter, stir to blend the mushrooms, stock, and butter, then remove the pan from the heat and set aside.

Make the risotto: Put the remaining 2 cups stock in a small pot and bring to a simmer on a back burner. Heat 2 tablespoons of the butter and 2 tablespoons of the olive oil in a large, heavy-bottomed pot over medium heat. Add the remaining onion and sauté until softened but not browned, approximately 4 minutes. Add the rice and cook, stirring to coat it with the oil, for 2 minutes. Pour in the wine and cook, stirring and scraping the bottom of the pot, until the wine reduces by two thirds, approximately 3 minutes. Begin ladling simmering broth into the pot, ½ cup at a time, and stir con-stantly until the broth is absorbed by the rice. Continue adding broth in ½-cup increments, stirring constantly, and only adding the next ladleful when the previous one has been absorbed. After about 20 minutes, and after you've used up almost all or all of the stock, the rice should appear to have softened slightly and turned creamy, but the individual grains should still be firm in the center. Bite into one to test it if you're not sure. When the risotto is done, gently fold in the mushrooms and the cheese. Set aside and cover to keep warm.

Divide the remaining ¼ cup oil between 2 wide, heavy-bottomed sauté pans over high heat. Season the scallops with salt and pepper, put 8 in each pan, and sear for 3 to 4 minutes on each side. Divide the remaining 3 tablespoons butter between the pans in the final few minutes of cook-ing, and baste the scallops with the melted butter.

Meanwhile, remove the pea sauce from the refrigerator and give it a stir; if it seems excessively thick, stir in a few drops of cold water to loosen it up. Transfer the pea sauce to a pot and gently heat it over medium heat.

To serve, fold the tarragon, chervil, and parsley into the risotto. Spoon some pea sauce onto the bottom of each of 4 plates. Top with some risotto and 4 scallops, and serve.

GRILLED SOFT-SHELL CRABS
with Baby Spinach, Mango, and Bacon Salad

SERVES 4

Growing up in New England, we didn't eat a lot of soft-shell crabs. But there are few things more popular in certain Mid-Atlantic communities, including New York City, and therefore I've come to think of soft-shell crabs as one of my favorite springtime arrivals. A soft-shell crab is a blue crab that's hoisted up out of the water within hours of when it molts, or sheds its hard, outer shell, and before the new one hardens. The crabs are rushed to market, where you purchase them still alive. I love that you eat the crab whole, because the soft shell is edible.

Grilling soft-shell crabs is actually pretty easy: You don't need to dredge them in flour or bread crumbs or anything like that because their soft shells turn nice and crispy if you grill them patiently over indirect heat, letting the shell gradually crisp and lightly blacken.

This dish grew out of a predilection of mine: When I grill, I like to grill all the key ingredients in that particular dish because . . . well . . . why not? Grilling is a simple technique and adds great flavor. So in this recipe, the crabs and the bacon are both cooked on the grill.

1 teaspoon sesame seeds

1 cup baby spinach

½ cup frisée

1 very ripe mango, thinly sliced

½ medium red onion, thinly sliced

4 jumbo soft-shell crabs

Salt

Freshly ground black pepper

4 thick slices bacon

Lemon-Sambal Vinaigrette (recipe follows)

Preheat a gas grill to high, or prepare a charcoal grill for grilling, letting the coals burn until covered with white ash.

Meanwhile, put the sesame seeds in a sauté pan and toast over medium heat (or over the grill) until the seeds are very lightly browned and fragrant and they begin to pop, approximately 2 minutes. Transfer to a salad bowl and let cool, then add the spinach, frisée, mango, and onion. Set aside.

Prepare the crabs: Rinse them under cold running water. Lift the two sides of the shell and pull off and discard the feathery gills, then turn the crabs over and remove the apron, the flap that covers the underside of the crab. Snip off the front pincers and eyes using kitchen shears.

Season the crabs with salt and pepper and grill over low, indirect heat until the soft shells turn hard and crispy, approximately 4 minutes per side. Transfer to a plate and set aside.

Grill the bacon over indirect heat for 90 seconds per side until crispy. Break the slices into 1-inch pieces, and add them to the salad bowl. Dress with the lemon-sambal vinaigrette and toss well.

Divide the salad among 4 plates and top each portion with a crab. Serve.

recipe continues

Lemon-Sambal Vinaigrette

This vinaigrette gets it juice from sambal, a chili pepper condiment used pervasively in Indonesian and Malaysian cooking. Different brands feature different spices, and perhaps sugar, but the heat is the main thing, especially when used in as small a quantity as it is here.

½ teaspoon sambal

2 tablespoons lemon juice

¼ cup extra-virgin olive oil

1 teaspoon chopped oregano, or cilantro, or a combination

Put the sambal, lemon juice, extra-virgin olive oil, and chopped oregano in a bowl and whisk together. The vinaigrette can be covered and refrigerated for up to 4 days.

STEAMED MUSSELS
with Orzo and Herbs

SERVES 6 AS AN APPETIZER, OR 4 AS A MAIN COURSE

Toss mussels with tomatoes, corn, peas, and herbs and you've got . . . well, you've got a bit of a mess. But add some pasta—orzo is great here—and it fills out the flavors and textures, taking the weight of the dish off the mussels' shoulders. Basically this dish turns an appetizer of mussels into a quick main course, with the pasta filling in for the bread you'd normally serve alongside to dunk in the broth. Just as that bread does, the orzo soaks up all of the awesome flavor.

One note of caution: The mussels go in early, so be careful not to break apart their shells when you stir the dish.

1 cup defrosted frozen peas, or shelled fresh
    peas

Salt

1 cup orzo

4 tablespoons olive oil

4 cloves garlic, thinly sliced

1½ pounds Prince Edward Island mussels
    (approximately 30 mussels)

¼ cup dry white wine

1 medium zucchini, quartered lengthwise,
    seeds sliced off and discarded, quarters
    sliced crosswise into ¼-inch pieces

Kernels from 2 large ears of corn (about 2 cups)

3 plum tomatoes, diced

Pinch of crushed red pepper flakes

1 cup Shellfish Stock (page 247) or bottled
    clam juice

1 tablespoon sliced basil

2 tablespoons sliced parsley

1 tablespoon thyme

1 tablespoon butter

Freshly ground black pepper

2 medium scallions, white and light green
    parts, thinly sliced diagonally

If using fresh peas, bring a small pot of salted water to a boil. Add the peas and blanch for 1 minute. Drain, refresh under cold running water, drain again, and set aside. (If using frozen peas, they need only be defrosted, not cooked.)

Bring a large pot of salted water to a boil. Add the orzo and cook until al dente, approximately 8 minutes. Drain, refresh under cold running water, and drain again. Transfer to a bowl, toss with 2 tablespoons of the oil, and set aside.

Pour 2 tablespoons of the oil into a large, heavy-bottomed pot, and heat it over high heat. Add the garlic and sauté until lightly browned, approximately 1 minute. Add the mussels and cook for 1 minute. Add the wine and cook for 1 minute, stirring to scrape up any flavorful bits cooked onto the bottom of the pot. Add the orzo, peas, zucchini, corn, tomatoes, red pepper flakes, stock, basil, parsley, and thyme. Cover the pan and steam until the mussels open, approximately 5 minutes. Use tongs to fish out and discard any mussels that do not open. Stir in the butter and season with salt and pepper.

To serve, divide the pasta, mussels, and vegetables among bowls, making sure to get a good mix of ingredients in each serving. Top each portion with a generous amount of scallions.

GRILLED SARDINES
with Spicy Black Olive and Tomato Salsa Cruda

SERVES 4 AS A MAIN COURSE, OR 6 AS AN APPETIZER

When I think of summer cooking, this is one of the first dishes that comes to mind: quickly grilled sardines served with a slightly spicy, refreshing sauce made of chopped raw vegetables. I love how the oily fish stands up to an aromatic marinade, and the contrast of the crispy, grilled skin with the moist dark flesh within.

I've always been a big fan of sardines. To me, they epitomize the magnificence of an oily fish. I know some people think oil makes fish taste "fishy," but to me it's all a matter of balancing the fish with the right accompaniment, in this case a salsa loaded with heat, acidity, and salinity. I only cook with fresh sardines, and prefer them whole because the bones impart more flavor. When shopping for sardines, look for ones that are firm and as straight as torpedoes. They should be bluish-gray, not red, and they should smell like the ocean, not like fish.

12 fresh whole sardines, about 5 ounces each, cleaned and gutted by your fishmonger
½ cup olive oil
Juice of ½ lemon
Grated zest of 1 lemon
1 teaspoon crushed red pepper flakes

3 cloves garlic, thinly sliced
1 teaspoon chopped oregano
Salt
Freshly ground black pepper
Salsa Cruda (recipe follows)
Lemon wedges, for serving

Put the sardines in a baking dish or other shallow vessel. Drizzle with the olive oil and lemon juice and scatter the zest, red pepper flakes, garlic, and oregano over them. Turn them to coat with the marinade and let marinate for 1 hour.

Preheat a gas grill to high, or prepare a charcoal grill for grilling, letting the coals burn until covered with white ash.

Remove the sardines from the marinade and brush off any solids. Season with salt and pepper and grill until cooked through, approximately 3 minutes per side.

Divide the salsa cruda evenly among serving plates. Top with sardines, crossing them over the salsa. Serve right away, with lemon wedges alongside.

Salsa Cruda

MAKES ABOUT 4½ CUPS

Salsa cruda literally means "raw sauce" and this is a highly adaptable condiment to have in your repertoire. It's delicious with just about any grilled fish or poultry, and you can vary it to include, say, diced, grilled vegetables such as fennel or peppers, or diced avocado for creaminess.

2 medium ripe tomatoes, cut into ¼-inch dice (2 cups)
1 15½-ounce can chickpeas, rinsed and drained
½ cup pitted, chopped black olives
½ small cucumber, peeled, seeded, and cut into ¼-inch dice (¼ cup)
¼ red bell pepper, seeded and cut into ¼-inch dice (¼ cup)
¼ yellow bell pepper, or an additional ¼ red bell pepper, seeded and cut into ¼-inch dice (¼ cup)

½ small red onion, cut into ¼-inch dice (¼ cup)
1 tablespoon sliced basil
1 teaspoon minced garlic
½ jalapeño pepper, seeded and minced
1 tablespoon plus 1 teaspoon red wine vinegar
3 tablespoons extra-virgin olive oil
1 teaspoon salt
½ teaspoon freshly ground black pepper

Put all of the ingredients in a bowl, gently toss, cover, and let rest at room temperature for at least 1 hour, or refrigerate for up to 2 days. Bring to room temperature before serving.

SAUTÉED SKATE
with White Gazpacho of Sweet Grapes
SERVES 4

Like the New England–style cod on page 129, this is a case of turning a soup into a sauce. In this case, the soup itself is pretty cool, a white gazpacho of green grapes, cucumber, and almonds. It's sweeter and less acidic than the tomato-based gazpacho most people know, and it's not at all spicy. In addition to being soothing and cold, it's also the perfect, understated match for the delicate flesh of a skate wing. The salad uses many of the same ingredients as the sauce—a neat trick for keeping the ingredient list short and the recipe concise and guaranteeing that one component complements the other.

1½ cups sliced blanched almonds

3 slices white bread, crusts removed, cut into ½-inch cubes

2 cups milk

1 large cucumber (if using an American cucumber, peel it; if using a European, or hothouse, cucumber, don't)

2½ cups halved seedless green grapes

1 small red onion, thinly sliced

¼ cup plus 2 tablespoons extra-virgin olive oil

3 tablespoons lemon juice

Salt

Freshly ground black pepper

1 small head frisée lettuce, ends trimmed, white and yellow parts only, separated into leaves

4 pieces boneless, skinless skate wings, 4 to 5 ounces each

1 cup flour

½ cup canola oil

1 tablespoon butter

Heat a sauté pan over medium-high heat. Add the almonds and toast, shaking the pan constantly to keep them from browning or scorching, until well toasted and very fragrant, approximately 5 minutes. Transfer the almonds to a plate and let cool.

To make the gazpacho sauce, put the bread in a small bowl and pour the milk over it. Let soak for 15 minutes.

Meanwhile, dice about half of the cucumber (1 cup); then halve lengthwise, seed, and thinly slice the remaining cucumber and set aside.

Remove the bread from the bowl, squeezing out the excess milk by hand. Put the bread in the bowl of a food processor fitted with the steel blade. Add the diced cucumber, 1¼ cups of the grapes, ½ cup of the almonds, and half of the onion. Process until smooth, then pour through a fine-mesh strainer set over a bowl, pressing down on the solids with a rubber spatula or wooden spoon to extract as much liquid as possible. Whisk in 2 tablespoons of the extra-virgin olive oil and 1 tablespoon of the lemon juice. Season with salt and pepper, cover, and refrigerate for at least 2 hours, or up to 24 hours to develop the flavor. Let come to room temperature before proceeding.

To make the salad, put the remaining 1¼ cups grapes, 1 cup almonds, and onion, the sliced cucumber, and the frisée in a medium bowl. Add the remaining ¼ cup extra-virgin olive oil and 1 tablespoon of the lemon juice, season to taste with salt and pepper, and toss well.

To cook the fish, season the skate wings with salt and pepper, then dredge them in flour, gently shaking off the excess flour. Heat the canola oil in a large, deep sauté pan set over medium-high heat. Add the wings without crowding and cook until nicely browned on one side, approximately 4 to 5 minutes, then turn, add the butter to the pan, and cook for 30 seconds to 1 minute on the other side. (To check for doneness, you can use a sharp, thin-bladed knife to peek between two of the fish's ridges and confirm that the flesh is opaque; just be sure to serve the fish with that side facing down.) Drizzle the remaining tablespoon lemon juice over the fish.

Spoon some sauce onto the center of each of 4 dinner plates. Top with some salad, then a skate wing, so the heat of the wing causes the salad to wilt just a little. Serve at once.

NOTE TO THE COOK Skate is a member of the same family of fish as the ray. Fish in this family have triangular fins that help them glide through the water. The fins, the edible portion of the fish, are called wings because their function resembles that of a bird's wings more than fins. They are moist, sweet, and delicate, with a flavor not unlike that of a scallop. Buy them boneless and skinless.

HALIBUT
with Grapefruit, Parsley, Red Onion, and Shiitake Mushrooms

SERVES 4

Grapefruit on the dinner table? That's right. The sweet and tangy ruby red brings together earth (mushrooms) and sea (halibut) in this dish, with the flavors rounded out by the cream in the sauce, the sharpness of the red onion, and the herbaceous parsley, which gives the dish a nice lift.

1½ large pink grapefruits

¾ cup torn parsley

¼ medium red onion, very thinly sliced

1 tablespoon extra-virgin olive oil

Salt

Freshly ground black pepper

1 tablespoon cream

8 tablespoons (1 stick) butter, cut into 8 pieces

Dash of hot sauce

½ cup canola oil

10 ounces shiitake mushrooms, caps only,
    thinly sliced (2 cups)

4 skinless halibut fillets, 6 ounces each

Section the grapefruit: Peel it by hand, then run a sharp, flexible knife blade over the surface of the fruit to remove as much pith as possible without cutting into the flesh. Separate the grapefruit into sections, then carefully remove the skin from 12 sections with the aid of a paring knife. Finally, remove and discard the seeds. Set the peeled sections aside. Squeeze ½ cup juice from the remaining sections, catching any seeds in your hands and discarding them.

To make the salad, put the grapefruit sections, parsley, onion, and extra-virgin olive oil in a bowl, season with salt and pepper, and very gently toss. Set aside.

To make the sauce, pour the grapefruit juice into a nonreactive saucepan and bring to a boil over high heat. Let boil until reduced to a glaze, approximately 5 minutes. Whisk in the cream and let reduce for 1 minute. Remove the pan from the heat and whisk in the butter, 1 piece at a time. Whisk in a dash of hot sauce and season to taste with salt and pepper. Cover and set aside.

Heat ¼ cup of the canola oil in a sauté pan over medium heat. Add the mushrooms and sauté until they begin to crisp, approximately 4 minutes. Season with salt and pepper and set aside, covered, to keep warm.

Heat the remaining ¼ cup canola oil in a sauté pan set over medium-high heat. Season the fillets with salt and pepper and add them, skinned side up, to the pan. Sear for 3 to 4 minutes. Turn the fish over and cook for another 3 minutes. (To check for doneness, you can use a sharp, thin-bladed knife and apply slight pressure to peek between the fish's flakes and confirm that the flesh is opaque.)

Spoon some mushrooms onto the center of each of 4 dinner plates. Top with some salad, then a halibut fillet. Spoon the sauce around the mushrooms, and serve.

GRILLED TUNA

with Grilled Potato, Parsley, and Red Onion Salad and Tapenade Vinaigrette

SERVES 4

Someone once summed up the red-meat-like qualities of tuna by calling this fish "a steak that swims." That principle is put to the test here as grilled tuna is paired with some traditional steak accompaniments—red onions, tomatoes, and potatoes. A grill can take just about anything to a new level; here, it heightens the sweetness of the red onion and tomato. The parsley really pops against that char flavor, which helps pull all the flavors together.

Salt

2 Idaho potatoes, sliced crosswise into ½-inch-thick slices

Olive oil, for grilling vegetables and fish

Freshly ground black pepper

2 large red onions, sliced crosswise into ½-inch-thick rings

2 large beefsteak tomatoes, sliced crosswise into ½-inch-thick slices; or 4 plum tomatoes, cut in half lengthwise

4 tuna steaks, 6 ounces each

¼ cup Red Wine Vinaigrette (page 48), leave out the basil

½ cup parsley

⅓ cup pitted black olives, such as kalamata or Gaeta (from about 15 olives)

Tapenade Vinaigrette (recipe follows)

Preheat a gas grill to high, or prepare a charcoal grill for grilling, letting the coals burn until covered with white ash.

Bring a large pot of salted water to a boil. Add the potato slices and parboil for 5 minutes. Remove with tongs or a slotted spoon and carefully pat dry with paper towels.

Drizzle the potato slices with oil and season with salt and pepper. Lay them on the grill and grill until nice char marks form on the bottom, then turn over and grill until marks form on the other side, approximately 5 minutes per side.

While the potatoes are cooking, drizzle the onions, tomato slices, and tuna with oil and season with salt and pepper.

Grill the onion slices until blackened at the edges, then turn over and grill on the other side, approximately 3 minutes per side.

Add the tomato slices to the grill and grill for about 1 minute per side.

When the potato slices are done, remove them to a plate and drizzle with the red wine vinaigrette. Transfer the grilled onion and tomato slices to another plate.

Add the tuna to the grill, and grill for approximately 3 minutes per side for rare, or a bit longer for more well-done.

On each of 4 dinner plates, arrange some potato, onion, and tomato slices, then top with a tuna steak. Scatter the parsley and olives over the other ingredients. Drizzle the tapenade vinaigrette over each plate and serve.

Tapenade Vinaigrette

MAKES ABOUT ½ CUP

Use this olive dressing on fish or poultry, chicken livers, avocado salads, as a crostini topping, and in sandwiches.

2 tablespoons pureed black olives, or store-
　　bought olive paste
1 anchovy fillet, minced
1 clove garlic, minced
1½ teaspoons coarsely chopped capers
1 teaspoon chopped parsley

¼ cup extra-virgin olive oil
2 teaspoons sherry vinegar
Juice of ½ lemon
Salt
Freshly ground black pepper

Put the olives, anchovy, garlic, capers, parsley, and oil in a bowl and stir together. Stir in the sherry vinegar and lemon juice and season to taste with salt and pepper.

The vinaigrette can be covered and refrigerated for up to 4 days.

LOBSTER THERMIDOR

SERVES 4

The attention-grabbing presentation of this American classic—lobster meat is cooked in an aromatic cream sauce which is then baked right in the split lobster shell—might make you forget how traditional this rendition is. I add a variety of herbs and diced mushrooms to round out the flavors and textures. To keep the tail absolutely straight (it's easier to stuff, bake, and eat that way), you will need eight 8-inch metal skewers.

4 2-pound live lobsters
2¾ cups cream
¼ cup olive oil
1 small shallot, chopped
2 tablespoons chopped fennel or celery
20 ounces button mushroom, caps only, diced (6 cups)
½ cup dry white wine, such as Chablis
¼ cup Cognac

½ teaspoon chopped thyme
1 teaspoon sliced tarragon
2 teaspoons sliced parsley
½ teaspoon cayenne
Salt
Freshly ground black pepper
2 tablespoons butter, melted
¼ cup finely grated Parmigiano-Reggiano
Juice of ½ lemon

Preheat the oven to 400°F. Bring a large pot of water to a boil.

Kill the lobsters by driving a heavy chef's knife between their eyes and pulling it down like a lever. (Alternatively, you can cook the lobsters in boiling water for 1 minute to kill them. Just keep in mind that the tails will curl.) Split the lobsters with the knife, cutting all the way through the meat but not through the bottom shell, and spread the lobsters open. Remove and discard the dark intestine that runs along the tail. Twist off the claws.

Boil the claws for 5 minutes, then remove them with tongs or a slotted spoon and set aside.

Put the lobsters, cut side up, on one or two baking sheets. Pour 2 tablespoons of the cream onto each lobster, and bake for 5 minutes. Remove the sheets from the oven and set aside.

Shell the lobster claws and cut the meat into a 1-inch dice.

Heat the oil in a sauté pan over medium heat. Add the shallot, fennel, and mushrooms, and sauté until softened but not browned, approximately 5 minutes. Deglaze with the wine and Cognac and cook until the liquid is reduced to 2 tablespoons. Add 2 cups of the cream and reduce until you have about ½ cup liquid in the pan. Add the thyme, tarragon, parsley, and cayenne. Add the diced lobster and the lemon juice, and season with salt and pepper.

Spoon the mixture into the lobster shells. Skewer the lobsters from head to tail, using one skewer for each side of each lobster. (This will keep the tail from curling when roasted; if you boiled your lobsters, skip this step.) You can also weight down the head and tail ends of the lobster with pie weights. Top with the melted butter, the remaining ¼ cup cream, and the Parmigiano. Bake for 10 minutes, then remove from the oven. Place 1 lobster on each of 4 dinner plates, and serve.

BABY CUTTLEFISH STEW
on Bread

SERVES 4

When it comes to seafood soups and stews, I gotta have a hunk of bread to dunk into the broth. I'm not alone: There are entire *nations* that share my disposition. For example, you just don't serve French dishes like bouillabaisse or *soupe de poisson* (fish soup) without baguette croutons spread with *rouille*.

For me, the ultimate combination of bread and broth is the family of Italian *zuppe di pane*, or bread soups. To serve these soups, you put a piece of grilled bread right in the bottom of the bowl, then ladle the soup over it. By the time you get to the bread, it is completely soggy with soup and needs to be eaten with a spoon. That tradition gave rise to this stew.

You can also make this with squid, but I prefer cuttlefish because of its toothsome quality. When you buy cuttlefish, you need to remove the skin under cold running water, yanking it off like a cellophane wrapper, then pull out the exoskeleton.

2 tablespoons olive oil

3 cloves garlic, thinly sliced, plus 1 clove peeled and left whole

2 shallots, thinly sliced

1 pound fresh or frozen cuttlefish, cleaned and cut into rings

1 cup halved cherry tomatoes

½ cup thinly sliced black olives, such as kalamata or Gaeta (from about 20 olives)

½ teaspoon crushed red pepper flakes

½ cup dry white wine

½ cup Shellfish Stock (page 247) or bottled clam juice

2 tablespoons butter

Salt

Freshly ground black pepper

1 tablespoon sliced basil

1 tablespoon finely sliced chives

4 slices country bread, ½ inch thick

2 lemons, halved

Heat 1 tablespoon of the olive oil in a wide, deep, heavy-bottomed pot over high heat. Add the sliced garlic and the shallots and cook, stirring, until softened but not browned, approximately 4 minutes. Add the cuttlefish and stir to coat them with oil, cooking them for about 2 minutes. Add the tomatoes, olives, and red pepper flakes and cook until the tomatoes begin to break down and give off their liquid, approximately 2 minutes.

Add the wine and cook, stirring to loosen any flavorful bits stuck to the bottom of the pot, for 2 minutes. Add the stock, bring to a simmer, lower the heat, and let simmer until reduced by about one third, 3 to 5 minutes. Add the butter and stir until it melts into the stew. Taste and season with salt and pepper. Stir in the basil and chives.

Grill or toast the bread. Brush the slices with the remaining tablespoon oil, rub with the whole garlic clove (you can impale the clove on a fork for greater control), and season with salt and pepper.

To serve, place a piece of warm bread in the bottom of each of 4 wide, shallow bowls, and spoon some stew over the bread. Serve each bowl with a lemon half for squeezing over the stew.

SAUTÉED CODFISH
New England Style

SERVES 4

Using New England clam chowder as the inspiration for a sauce is a perfectly logical leap, especially when you use it on the quintessential New England catch: codfish. I'm usually pretty loose when it comes to ingredients: If you don't have red wine vinegar, use a little sherry vinegar, and so on. But when it comes to anything even *inspired* by New England chowder, I'm as strict as a prison warden: It must have bacon, the Holy Trinity of celery (celery stalks, celery salt, and celery seed), and thyme.

Salt

½ small Idaho potato, peeled and cut into ¼-inch dice (½ cup)

4 tablespoons (½ stick) butter

1 strip double-smoked bacon, diced

¼ small onion, finely diced

¼ stalk celery, finely diced

¼ cup plus 2 tablespoons flour

¾ cup cream

1 cup Shellfish Stock (page 247) or bottled clam juice

1 teaspoon celery seed

1 tablespoon finely chopped thyme

Celery salt

Freshly ground black pepper

2 tablespoons olive oil

4 codfish fillets, 6 ounces each, skin on if desired

Bring a small pot of salted water to a boil over high heat. Add the potato and cook until tender to a knife-tip, approximately 5 minutes. Drain and refresh under cold running water. Drain again and set aside.

Melt 2 tablespoons of the butter in a heavy-bottomed pot set over medium-high heat. Add the bacon and cook until it renders its fat, approximately 5 minutes. Add the onion and celery and cook until softened but not browned, approximately 4 minutes. Add the remaining 2 tablespoons butter and cook, stirring, until it melts. Add the flour, a little at a time, stirring to combine the flour and butter and not letting the butter brown. Then, add the cream, a little at a time, stirring to incorporate it into the butter-flour mixture. Gradually add the stock, stirring to make a thick sauce, and simmer for 10 minutes. Gently stir in the potatoes, celery seed, and thyme. Taste and adjust the seasoning with celery salt and pepper. Cover and set aside.

Heat the oil in a wide, deep, heavy-bottomed sauté pan. Season the codfish with salt and pepper, and sear in the pan until nicely browned, approximately 4 minutes per side. (To check for doneness, you can use a sharp, thin-bladed knife and apply slight pressure to peek between the fish's flakes and confirm that the flesh is opaque.)

To serve, put 1 fillet on each of 4 dinner plates and spoon some sauce over the top.

PAN-CRISPED WHOLE FISH
with Braised Greens and Reds

SERVES 4

This dish is pure and simple: You cook whole fish, and while they're in the oven, quickly stove-braise leafy greens and reds such as escarole, Swiss chard, and kale. Then you make a quick sauce by swirling butter, red wine and balsamic vinegars, and lemon juice into the pan.

You want a white-fleshed fish such as snapper, sea bass, dourade, or sea bream, something that will soak up the flavors of the greens and their juice.

4 whole fish such as snapper, sea bass, dourade, or sea bream, 1½ to 2 pounds each, cleaned and gutted (ask your fishmonger to do this)

Salt

Freshly ground black pepper

1 cup olive oil

1½ tablespoons red wine vinegar

1 teaspoon balsamic vinegar

2 teaspoons lemon juice

1 large shallot, minced

5 cups bite-size pieces escarole, chard, and/or kale leaves (from about ½ large head)

1 cup chopped broccoli rabe (from about 2 stalks)

3 cups shredded red cabbage (from about ½ medium head)

2 tablespoons butter

Preheat the oven to 400°F.

Season the fish with salt and pepper. Heat ½ cup of the oil in a wide, deep, heavy-bottomed sauté pan. Add one of the fish, and sear until crisp, approximately 4 minutes. Turn over and sear for 1 minute, then transfer to a roasting pan. Repeat with the remaining fish. After all four fish have been seared, transfer the pan to the oven and roast for 7 to 10 minutes, depending on their size. (To check for doneness, you can use a sharp, thin-bladed knife and apply slight pressure to peek between the head and the fillet of the fish and check that the flesh is opaque.)

Put 6 tablespoons of the oil in a small bowl. Add the red wine vinegar, balsamic vinegar, and lemon juice. Whisk together, season with salt and pepper, and set the vinaigrette aside.

Meanwhile, heat the remaining 2 tablespoons oil in the same pan you used to sear the fish over medium-high heat. Add the shallot and cook until softened but not browned, approximately 2 minutes. Add the greens, broccoli rabe, and cabbage, and cook until wilted, approximately 5 minutes. Add the vinaigrette and cook for 2 minutes, scraping up any flavorful bits stuck to the bottom of the pan. Add the butter and swirl to melt it and make a sauce.

To serve, spoon some greens onto each of 4 dinner plates, and top with a fish. Spoon some sauce over and around the fish.

SALMON

with Corn, Sugar Snap Peas, and Shiitake Mushrooms

SERVES 4

Corn, snap peas, and a piece of simply cooked fish is perfect summer eating. This recipe pulls out the stops with a pureed corn sauce that has kernels of corn added at the last second. The mushrooms aren't necessarily a summer ingredient, but they offer a contrast in texture and flavor to the corn and peas and take some of the richness out of the dish.

This dish would also be delicious made with halibut, cod, or any large-flaked white fish.

4 tablespoons (½ stick) butter

3 medium shallots, minced, plus 2 medium shallots, sliced and separated into rings

2½ cups corn kernels, preferably fresh (from 2 to 3 ears corn)

¼ cup sherry

2 cups White Chicken Stock (page 245) or low-sodium, store-bought chicken broth

Salt

Freshly ground black pepper

1½ cups sugar snap peas (about 6 ounces)

4 tablespoons canola oil

10 ounces shiitake mushrooms, caps only, thickly sliced

Pinch of thyme

4 salmon fillets, 6 ounces each, with the skin on

½ cup pea shoots (optional)

Melt 1 tablespoon of the butter in a saucepan over medium heat. Add the minced shallots and cook, stirring, until softened but not browned, approximately 3 minutes. Add 2 cups of the corn kernels and the sherry and cook, scraping up any tasty bits cooked onto the bottom of the pan, until the sherry has reduced by about three quarters, approximately 30 seconds. Add the stock, bring to a boil over high heat, then lower the heat and simmer until slightly thickened, approximately 5 minutes. Season to taste with salt and pepper.

Carefully transfer the contents of the pan to a blender, add 1 tablespoon butter, and puree until smooth.

Bring a medium saucepan of salted water to a boil over high heat. Fill a medium bowl halfway with ice water. Add the snap peas to the boiling water and blanch for 1 minute. Drain and transfer to the ice water to stop the cooking and set the color. Drain again and set aside.

Heat 2 tablespoons of the oil in a sauté pan over medium-high heat. Add the shallot rings and sauté until they are golden, approximately 3 minutes. Add the mushrooms and sauté until they begin to soften and crisp up, approximately 2 minutes. Add the peas and thyme, cook for approximately 1 minute to warm the peas, then season to taste with salt and pepper. Remove the pan from the heat, cover, and set aside.

Carefully wipe out the pan and melt 1 tablespoon of the butter over medium heat. Add the remaining ½ cup corn kernels and sauté until al dente, approximately 4 minutes. Pour the corn puree into the pan to reheat it. Stir in the remaining tablespoon butter and season to taste with salt and pepper. Remove from the heat, cover, and keep warm.

Heat the remaining 2 tablespoons canola oil in a wide, deep sauté pan over high heat. Season the salmon with salt and pepper and add the fillets to the pan, skin side down, without crowding, and sear for 4 minutes. Turn the fillets over and cook for another 3 to 4 minutes for medium rare, or a bit longer for more well-done. (To check for doneness, you can use a sharp, thin-bladed knife and apply slight pressure to peek between the fish's flakes and confirm that the flesh is opaque.)

Spoon some sauce into the center of each of 4 dinner plates or wide, shallow bowls. Top with some vegetables, then a salmon fillet. Garnish with pea shoots, if desired.

GRILLED SWORDFISH ON ROSEMARY BRANCHES

with Grilled Vegetables and Yellow Pepper Vinaigrette

SERVES 4

This is pure, vibrant summer cooking at its best: grilled fish, a bright yellow pepper vinaigrette, and lots of herbs. Using the rosemary branches as skewers for the fish adds tons of flavor but also a sense of playfulness. Let the fish marinate for the full 24 hours if you can to infuse it with the most flavor.

1½ cups extra-virgin olive oil

1½ tablespoons grated lemon zest (from 2 medium lemons)

1½ tablespoons grated orange zest

1 tablespoon chopped thyme

4 rosemary branches, each 12 inches long, leaves removed and chopped, branches reserved

2 pounds swordfish, cut into approximately 16 cubes

2 yellow bell peppers, roasted and seeded (page 244), and still warm

Pinch of saffron threads

¼ cup rice vinegar

1 clove garlic, coarsely chopped

1 tablespoon honey

½ tablespoon Dijon mustard

Salt

Freshly ground black pepper

1 tablespoon sliced basil

½ tablespoon chopped oregano

1 medium zucchini, cut lengthwise into ¼-inch-thick strips

1 medium yellow squash, cut lengthwise into ¼-inch-thick strips

1 medium red onion, cut crosswise into ¼-inch-thick rings

½ large bulb fennel or 1 medium bulb, cut lengthwise into ⅛-inch-thick slices

4 ripe plum tomatoes, halved lengthwise

Make a marinade for the swordfish by pouring ¼ cup of the oil into a wide, shallow, nonreactive dish. Stir in the lemon and orange zests, ½ tablespoon of the thyme, and all but 1 tablespoon of the chopped rosemary. Add the swordfish, turn to coat, then cover, and refrigerate for at least 2 hours or up to 24 hours.

Preheat a gas grill to high, or prepare a charcoal grill for grilling, letting the coals burn until covered with white ash.

Put the yellow peppers and saffron in the bowl of a food processor fitted with the steel blade, or in a blender. Puree, then add the rice vinegar, garlic, honey, and mustard and blend until smooth. Slowly blend in 1 cup of the oil. (Note: The mixture will emulsify briefly, then loosen into a thick dressing.) Season with salt and pepper and set aside.

Make a marinade for the vegetables by pouring the remaining ¼ cup of the oil into a bowl and stirring in the basil, oregano, remaining ½ tablespoon thyme, and remaining tablespoon chopped rosemary, and seasoning with salt and pepper. Dip the zucchini, squash, red onion, fennel, and toma-toes into the marinade, letting any excess marinade run off. Season the vegetables with salt and pep-per and grill them in groups of one or two vegetable types until cooked through and nice grill marks have formed on each side—approximately 4 minutes per side for the zucchini and squash, 3 minutes per side for the onion and fennel, and 1 minute per side for the tomatoes. As they are done, gather them on a platter and keep covered with foil to keep warm.

Remove the swordfish from the marinade, brushing off any solids. Skewer the pieces on the rose-mary branches (about 4 per branch), and season with salt and pepper. Place on the grill and grill, turning as needed, until cooked through, approximately 4 minutes.

Arrange the fish and vegetables decoratively on a large platter. Drizzle with the yellow pepper vinaigrette and serve.

NOTE TO THE COOK If you can't find long or sturdy rosemary branches, use bamboo skewers. Soak them in warm water for 15 minutes before using them to keep them from catching fire on the grill.

MUSTARD-CRUSTED TROUT
with Burst Cherry Tomato Sauce and Lemon Oil

SERVES 4

Trout fillets are dredged in a mixture of Dijon and whole-grain mustards, breaded and fried, then topped with a fresh sauce of stewed tomatoes and a drizzle of lemon oil. This is fresh, simple, elemental cooking: three complementary components that add up to more than the sum of their parts. It all works because the firmness and texture of the trout can stand up to this kind of breading, and to such a juicy sauce, without turning soggy.

1 cup Dijon mustard

1 cup whole-grain mustard

2 tablespoons hot sauce

4 cups dried bread crumbs (preferably
  Japanese panko)

4 tablespoons chopped thyme

Salt

Freshly ground black pepper

4 brook trout, approximately 10 ounces each,
  filleted

2¼ cups canola oil

2 large cloves garlic, sliced

½ small white onion, diced

2 pints red cherry tomatoes, halved (about
  4 cups)

1½ pints yellow cherry tomatoes, halved (about
  3 cups)

¼ cup dry white wine

2 tablespoons sliced parsley

1 tablespoon butter

Lemon Oil (recipe follows)

Put the Dijon mustard, whole-grain mustard, hot sauce, and ⅓ cup cold water in a bowl and whisk together well. Set aside.

Mix the bread crumbs, 3 tablespoons of the thyme, and 1 teaspoon salt in a bowl and season with pepper. Dredge the fillets through the mustard mixture, letting any excess liquid run off, then dredge in the bread-crumb mixture. If you have time, lay the fillets on a nonstick cookie sheet and refrigerate for 1 to 2 hours to help the coating stick to the fish.

Preheat the oven to 350°F.

Pour ¼ cup of the canola oil into a large saucepan and set over high heat. Add the garlic and onion and cook until the onion is translucent, approximately 2 minutes. Add the red and yellow tomatoes, then pour in the wine, lower the heat, and cook until the wine is reduced and the tomatoes break down and start to reduce, 10 to 15 minutes. Add the remaining tablespoon of thyme and the parsley, stir in the butter, and season with salt and pepper. Set aside.

In a large skillet over medium-high heat, heat ½ cup of the canola oil. Add 2 of the fillets and pan-fry until golden and crisp, approximately 2 minutes on each side. Transfer the fillets to a roasting pan. Repeat with the remaining oil and fillets, discarding the oil between batches, adding a fresh ½ cup, and letting it heat up before adding another batch of fillets. Once all of the fillets are in the roasting pan, put the pan in the oven and cook until warmed through, approximately 3 minutes. (To check for doneness, you can use a sharp, thin-bladed knife and apply slight pressure to peek between the fish's flakes and confirm that the flesh is opaque.)

Spoon some sauce onto the center of each of 4 dinner plates. Top each serving with 2 fillets. Drizzle with lemon oil to finish, and serve.

NOTE TO THE COOK This is delicious with mashed potatoes, and the breading is also delicious with bluefish.

Lemon Oil

MAKES 1 CUP

This is delicious drizzled over just about any fish, used in chicken salads, as a base for light vinaigrettes, and for finishing sautéed green vegetables, especially spinach.

Zest of 2 lemons, removed with a vegetable
   peeler, with no pith

1 cup canola oil
Salt

Put the lemon zest in a bowl and add the oil and a pinch of salt. Set in a sunny spot for 5 hours, strain, and refrigerate for up to 2 weeks.

POULTRY

CHICKEN, THE RED CAT WAY

SIMPLE SKILLET ROAST OF CHICKEN

. . . with Lemon Sauce and Summer Vegetable Salad

. . . with Red Onion, Sugar Plum, and Rosemary Sauce

. . . with Fried Tomato Sauce and Polenta

GRILLED POUSSINS
with Escarole, Sicilian Style

ROASTED QUAIL
on a Stew of Sausage, Tomato, Creminis, and Golden Raisins

CHICKEN LIVER TARTINE
with Port Wine Sauce, Warm Onion Salad, and Grilled Bread

DUCK BREASTS
with Roasted Fall Root Salad and Truffle Vinaigrette

DUCK BREASTS
with Radishes, Anchovy, and Orange

TURKEY SCHNITZEL
with Orzo Mac and Cheese and Black Mushroom Puree

If there's one thing I'd love for you to get out of this chapter—if you don't have it already—it's a love of dark meat. Because, when it comes to poultry and game birds, I'm all about the dark meat. Not just all-dark-meat birds like duck and quail; I also prefer a chicken's thigh and drumstick to, say, the breast. Just like some people always drink red wine, I always go dark.

There are many reasons for this predilection, and they all have to do with fat. Because dark meat has more fat woven into it, it has a richer, lustier flavor than white meat, and because the fat melts as it cooks, you can roast dark meats for a relatively long time, and they will stay juicy. That said, I also understand why a lot of people love white meat, especially in a good, organic, free-range chicken, with which you can pair just about anything. By using half-birds, the chicken dishes in this chapter present the best of both worlds, light and dark meat together.

If there's another thing I'd like to do in this chapter, it's to relieve you of the notion that dark-meat birds like duck and quail are meant only for the autumn and winter. That might be the most logical time to enjoy their charms, but my love of dark meat has led me to devise ways to enjoy duck all year long. Case in point: There's a summery duck dish in this chapter that features radishes and onion, while another pairs the bird with roasted fall root vegetables and truffle vinaigrette.

Of course all of this is just the tip of the iceberg. The world of poultry and game birds also includes squab, pheasant, or a nice hen. I love all those birds, but in the name of giving people what they want, and what they can usually find, I've confined myself in this book to the most popular birds. I would, however, encourage you to discover those others; they're all well worth knowing.

CHICKEN, THE RED CAT WAY

The most requested secret in The Red Cat kitchen is our method for roasting chicken. There are very few "food people" (cooks, chefs, journalists, even one of our book editors) who have the chicken at the restaurant who don't wave me over, or call or e-mail the next day, to ask for the recipe. And more than a few customers have worked up the gumption to ask for it as well.

This cracks me up, because—other than procuring boneless halved chickens—the recipe couldn't be simpler. Basically, we break all the chicken rules when we roast our chicken. Most recipes for roast chicken take one of two tacks: One is to roast a whole bird, trussing it before-hand to ensure even cooking and maintain an attractive shape. We don't do that. The other technique is to use a portion of a bird, maybe a half, weighting it down to ensure that as much surface area as possible is exposed to the heat, guaranteeing a crisp, crackling skin. This technique has different names all over the world, from the American "chicken under a brick" to the Cuban *pollo a la plancha* to the Italian *pollo al matone.* We don't do that either.

So what do we do? Well, at some point in my career, it occurred to me that an oven cranked up to over 450 degrees is way hot, and that the heat will find its way into the little nooks and crannies of a chicken all by itself; strings and weights only get in the way, caus-ing uneven heating and ruining the natural texture of the bird itself.

At The Red Cat, we simply sear a boned half chicken in a hot pan, then transfer the pan to the oven and let the heat do its thing. The result is a perfectly crisped skin and moist, suc-culent flesh. Just another case where less sometimes turns out to be more in the kitchen.

Now, about the boneless half chickens. The reason they need to be boneless is so that the chickens lay flat, with all the skin coming into contact with the oil to ensure a uniformity of crispiness, so to speak.

There are three ways to obtain boneless half chickens. The first is to do what we do at The Red Cat: Buy whole chickens, then split and debone them yourself. But I'll be honest; this requires more than a little experience and if you don't know how to do it, you sure ain't gonna learn from reading about it in a book. The second option—and my recommended course for most home cooks—is to support your local butcher, who should be more than happy to halve and bone out the chicken for you. If you watch him do it a few times—I'd even ask if you can come around to his side of the counter—you might find that—hey!—you *can* pull it off at home before too long, after all.

The final option, while not ideal, would be to purchase boneless chicken breasts and thighs with the skin on. Then you just cook the pieces instead of halves. It's not as impres-sive as serving half-chickens, but it'll taste the same, and get the job done.

Roasted Half Chickens

SERVES 4

2 chickens, 3 pounds each, halved and boned,
    skin on, or 2 to 2½ pounds boneless
    chicken parts, skin on

Salt
Freshly ground black pepper
4 tablespoons canola oil

Preheat the oven to 450°F.

Heat 2 wide, deep, heavy-bottomed ovenproof skillets over high heat. Season the chickens generously with salt and pepper. Add 2 tablespoons of the canola oil to each pan, let it get nice and hot, then put the chicken halves in the pans, skin side down, making sure they lie flat and all skin is in contact with the oil, and cook until the skin is golden, 3 to 5 minutes. Transfer the pans to the oven and roast until the juices from the thickest part of the white meat and the thickest part of the dark meat run clear when the meat is pierced with a sharp, thin-bladed knife, approximately 20 minutes.

Serve with one of the following recipes (I tell you where to start making the chicken in each recipe), or with your own favorite chicken accompaniments.

SIMPLE SKILLET ROAST OF CHICKEN
with Lemon Sauce and Summer Vegetable Salad

SERVES 4

Here, the roasted half chickens are paired with a salad of summer vegetables and a lemon-cream sauce. This very convenient dish is the next best thing to the simplicity of grilling in the summertime—you can make the salad in advance, and the sauce while the chicken roasts.

1 roasted red bell pepper (page 244), cut into thin strips

4 medium zucchini, quartered lengthwise, seeded, and thinly sliced crosswise

¾ cup corn kernels (from 1 ear of corn)

½ cup halved, pitted kalamata olives (from about 20 olives)

2 medium bulbs fennel, separated into layers and thinly sliced lengthwise

¼ cup extra-virgin olive oil

¼ cup plus 3 tablespoons lemon juice

½ cup sliced basil

¼ cup sliced tarragon

¼ cup plus 2 tablespoons chopped thyme

1 tablespoon sliced parsley

Roasted Half Chickens (page 143)

Salt

½ cup defrosted frozen peas, or shelled fresh peas

1 tablespoon cream

8 tablespoons (1 stick) butter, at room temperature, cut into 8 pieces

Pinch of cayenne

Freshly ground black pepper

Put the bell pepper, zucchini, corn, olives, and fennel in a large bowl. Toss and dress with the extra-virgin olive oil, ¼ cup of the lemon juice, the basil, tarragon, thyme, and parsley. Toss again and set aside. The salad can be refrigerated in an airtight container for up to 24 hours. Let come to room temperature before serving.

Start making the chicken now, preparing the rest of the dish as the chicken roasts.

Bring a small pot of salted water to a boil. Fill a large bowl halfway with ice water. Add the peas to the boiling water and blanch for 2 minutes for frozen, or 3 minutes for fresh. Drain, transfer to the ice water to stop the cooking and set the color, and drain again. Gently stir the peas into the vegetable salad.

Heat the remaining 3 tablespoons lemon juice in a small, nonreactive saucepan and simmer until it becomes syrupy, approximately 3 minutes. Add the cream. As soon as the cream simmers, remove the pan from the heat and whisk in the butter, 1 piece at a time. Season with cayenne, salt, and pepper.

To serve, spoon some sauce onto each of 4 dinner plates, set half a chicken next to it, and place some salad alongside.

SIMPLE SKILLET ROAST OF CHICKEN
with Red Onion, Sugar Plum, and Rosemary Sauce

SERVES 4

This dish starts with the key ingredients of a great French onion soup—namely caramelized onions and veal stock—then goes off in its own direction, adding prunes (aka dried sugar plums) and rosemary, which counteracts the intense sweetness of the onions and prunes. A lot of recipes featuring plums puree them into the sauce, but I wanted to maintain their plump, juicy character.

I recommend making this dish in the autumn, when the flavor and aroma of brown sugar and rosemary are most at home. Serve it with Red-Hot Rapini (page 193); the bitterness of the rapini is a perfect contrast to the sugar here. You can also serve the coarse, country-style sauce with roasted leg of lamb.

2 tablespoons canola oil

2½ small red onions, halved lengthwise and cut lengthwise into ¼-inch-thick strips

12 prunes, halved and pitted

1½ tablespoons light brown sugar

½ teaspoon chopped rosemary

1½ cups White Chicken Stock (page 245) or low-sodium, store-bought chicken broth

½ cup Veal Demi-Glace (page 246) or store-bought veal demi-glace

1 tablespoon butter

Juice of ½ lemon

Salt

Freshly ground black pepper

Roasted Half Chickens (page 143)

Preheat the oven to 450°F (for the chicken).

Make the sauce: Pour the canola oil into a heavy-bottomed sauté pan and heat it over medium heat. Add the onions and sauté until caramelized, approximately 10 minutes. Add the prunes and sauté for 5 minutes, then add the sugar and rosemary, and sauté for 30 seconds. Add the chicken stock and veal demi-glace, stir, bring to a boil over high heat, then lower the heat and simmer until the sauce thickens enough to coat the back of a wooden spoon, approximately 8 minutes. Whisk in the butter and lemon juice, and season with salt and pepper. Remove the pan from the heat and keep covered and warm.

Make the chicken now.

Spoon some sauce into the center of each of 4 dinner plates, making sure to include a nice amount of prunes in each serving. Top with a chicken half and serve.

SIMPLE SKILLET ROAST OF CHICKEN
with Fried Tomato Sauce and Polenta

SERVES 4

The crisp, crackling skin and succulent meat created by this chicken preparation are ideal matches for polenta and tomato sauce. You can adjust the sauce with herbs and spices to suit your own taste.

Roasted Half Chickens (page 143)

1½ cups White Chicken Stock (page 245) or low-sodium, store-bought chicken broth

½ cup milk

1 tablespoon butter

2 cups quick-cooking polenta

¼ cup finely grated Parmigiano-Reggiano

Salt

Freshly ground black pepper

¼ cup olive oil

½ small onion, finely diced

2 cloves garlic, thinly sliced

1 can (15 ounces) whole peeled tomatoes, crushed by hand, with their juice

1 tablespoon chopped oregano

Pinch of crushed red pepper flakes

½ cup parsley

½ cup celery leaves

Start making the chicken now, preparing the rest of the dish as the chicken cooks.

Make the polenta: Put the stock, milk, and butter in a nonreactive saucepan and bring to a simmer over medium heat. Gradually whisk in the polenta and keep whisking until the mixture comes together in a mashed-potato-like mass, approximately 8 minutes. Whisk in the cheese and season with salt and pepper. Turn off the heat and cover to keep it warm.

Heat the oil in a wide, deep, heavy-bottomed sauté pan over high heat. Add the onion and garlic and cook for 1 minute. Add the tomatoes and cook for 2 minutes, stirring to prevent scorching. Stir in the oregano and red pepper flakes and season with salt and pepper.

When the chickens are done, remove them from their pans. Set 1 pan over medium-high heat, add the parsley and celery leaves, and wilt them for 10 seconds.

To serve, spoon some sauce into the center of each of 4 dinner plates. Top with some polenta, then a half chicken, then some parsley and celery-leaf salad. Serve.

GRILLED POUSSINS
with Escarole, Sicilian Style

SERVES 4

The only grilled chicken recipe in this book (poussin is a baby chicken), this one offers a study in the difference between an oven-roasted chicken and a flame-licked grilled chicken. Chicken is one of those culinary litmus tests; you can tell a lot about a cook, a chef, or a restaurant by what they do with their chickens. The flavor here is jacked up by marinating the poussin for 24 hours, infusing the tender meat with garlic and lemon. The Sicilian-style escarole is an easy stovetop preparation, with raisins and red pepper flakes providing little bursts of flavor.

4 poussins, 1¼ pounds each, backbone and breastbone removed (ask your butcher to do this or do it yourself, see page 142), leg bones intact (see Mail-Order Sources, page 249)

3½ tablespoons olive oil

¼ cup plus ½ tablespoon lemon juice

1 tablespoon grated lemon zest

6 large cloves garlic, thinly sliced

½ teaspoon chopped thyme

1 cup golden raisins

1 medium white onion, thinly sliced

Salt

1 medium bulb fennel, thinly sliced

1 pound escarole, thinly sliced

2 tablespoons butter

Pinch of crushed red pepper flakes

Freshly ground black pepper

½ cup extra-virgin olive oil

½ teaspoon Dijon mustard

½ medium shallot, minced

½ teaspoon chopped oregano

Put the poussins in a large baking dish or other shallow nonreactive dish. Drizzle with 1½ table-spoons of the olive oil and ½ tablespoon of the lemon juice, and scatter the zest, one third of the sliced garlic, and the thyme over them. Turn the poussins over to coat with the marinade ingredients. Cover and refrigerate for at least 6 hours, or up to 24 hours.

When ready to proceed, preheat a gas grill to high, or prepare a charcoal grill for grilling, letting the coals burn until covered with white ash.

Bring a small pot of water to a boil over high heat. Meanwhile, put the raisins in a small bowl and the onion in another small bowl. When the water boils, pour enough into each bowl to cover the raisins and the onion with water. Let soak for 10 minutes, then drain.

Return the pot to the stove over high heat, salt the remaining water, and blanch the fennel for 1 minute. Drain, refresh under cold running water, and drain again. Set the fennel aside.

Heat the remaining 2 tablespoons olive oil in a sauté pan set over high heat. Add the remaining garlic and sauté until it just begins to brown, approximately 1 minute. Add the escarole, raisins, onion, fennel, and butter and cook, tossing, until the escarole wilts, approximately 1½ minutes. Stir in the red pepper flakes and season with salt and pepper. Cover the pan and set it aside while you grill the poussins.

Remove the poussins from the baking dish and brush off any thyme or garlic. Season on both sides with salt and pepper and grill until cooked through, nice grill marks form on each side, and the juices run clear when the meat is pierced at the thigh with a sharp, thin-bladed knife, 5 to 7 minutes per side. Transfer to a platter and let rest for 5 minutes.

Make a dressing by putting the remaining ¼ cup lemon juice and the extra-virgin olive oil, mustard, shallot, and oregano in a bowl and whisking them together. Pour any accumulated juices from the poussin plate into the bowl and whisk to incorporate. Season with salt and pepper.

To serve, make a small pile of escarole in the center of each of 4 plates. Top with a poussin and spoon some vinaigrette over and around the bird.

NOTE TO THE COOK The onion and raisins here are steeped in boiling water, and the fennel is blanched, to moderate their flavor. Softening the onion's bite, taking the raisins' sweetness down a bit, and toning down the fennel's anise quality enable these pronounced flavors to get along better.

ROASTED QUAIL
on a Stew of Sausage, Tomato, Creminis, and Golden Raisins

SERVES 4

I really hope you like this dish, because—dark meat aficionado that I am—I love quail, and it pained me to pick just one quail dish for the book. I limited myself because quail can be hard to find, and it's not the most popular game bird around, but it's well worth discovering and seeking out because its flavor is sublime. I selected this recipe not just because I think it's the best quail dish I've ever made, but because I think it's one of the best dishes I ever came up with, period. I devised it for The Red Cat, and it's become a long-running classic there, resistant to change. I went for the biggest contrast possible, with a sweet-and-sour stew that really offsets the gamey quality of the bird. And, of course, the sausage doesn't hurt either; its fat is used to cook and flavor the other ingredients.

If you want to substitute another bird, use chicken thighs or duck breasts.

8 semi-boneless quail, 2 to 3 ounces each (see
    Mail-Order Sources, page 249)
½ cup extra-virgin olive oil
2 tablespoons balsamic vinegar
2 cloves garlic, thinly sliced
2 tablespoons thyme
½ cup golden raisins
8 ounces sweet Italian sausage, removed from
    its casings
8 ounces cremini mushrooms, trimmed and
    quartered

2 cups cherry tomatoes, halved
2 cups White Chicken Stock (page 245) or
    low-sodium, store-bought chicken broth
1 cup juice from canned tomatoes
1 tablespoon sliced basil
Salt
Freshly ground black pepper
About ½ cup canola oil
1 small head radicchio, thinly sliced

Put the quail in a baking dish or other shallow vessel. Dress with the extra-virgin olive oil, balsamic vinegar, one third of the garlic, and 1 tablespoon of the thyme. Toss to coat the quail with the marinade, cover, and let marinate in the refrigerator for at least 8 hours, or up to 24 hours.

When ready to cook the dish, put the raisins in a bowl and cover with hot water. Let plump for 10 minutes, then drain.

Heat a wide, deep, heavy-bottomed pot over medium heat. Add the sausage and cook until browned and the fat has rendered, approximately 8 minutes. Drain or spoon all but 2 tablespoons of the sausage fat from the pot, leaving the sausage in the pot. Add the mushrooms and the remaining garlic and cook until the garlic is lightly browned and the mushrooms have softened, approximately 5 minutes. Add the raisins, tomatoes, chicken stock, and tomato juice, bring to a boil, lower the heat, and simmer until the mixture has thickened to a stew, approximately 10 minutes, smashing the tomatoes as they cook. Stir in the remaining 1 tablespoon thyme and the basil, and season with salt and pepper. Remove the pan from the heat, cover, and set aside.

Preheat the oven to 400°F.

Remove 4 of the quail from the marinade, wipe off any solids, and pat the quail dry. Heat a skillet over medium-high heat. Season the quail with salt and pepper and drizzle each quail with about 1 tablespoon canola oil. Put the quail in the skillet, breast side down, without crowding, and cook until lightly browned and golden, approximately 5 minutes. Turn over and transfer to a roasting pan. Repeat with the remaining 4 quail. Once all of the quail have been browned, transfer the roasting pan to the oven and roast until cooked through, 2 to 3 minutes. (To check for doneness, use a sharp, thin-bladed knife to nick the back of 1 quail and ensure the flesh has turned from dark red to pink.)

To serve, spoon some stew onto one side of each of 4 dinner plates. Make a nest of radicchio in the center of each plate, and put 2 quail on the other side of the nest.

CHICKEN LIVER TARTINE
with Port Wine Sauce, Warm Onion Salad, and Grilled Bread

SERVES 4

In old cultures where families bought, or still buy, whole birds, there's always the question of what to do with the livers. I like to serve my chicken livers on grilled or toasted bread—a tartine if you will—in this open-faced answer to liver and onions with fancy gravy. This is a perfect lunch dish, or, when served with some scrambled eggs, a great breakfast.

Incidentally, you no longer need to buy a chicken to get the livers. Most supermarkets sell them in little plastic containers in the poultry section.

4 tablespoons (½ stick) butter

½ medium red onion, thinly sliced

½ medium white onion, thinly sliced

2 medium leeks, white and very light green parts only, thinly sliced

2 medium shallots, thinly sliced

6 scallions, white and green parts, thinly sliced on the diagonal

⅓ cup sliced parsley

2 tablespoons chopped thyme

Salt

Freshly ground black pepper

1 tablespoon extra-virgin olive oil

2 cups flour

1 pound chicken livers (about 8 pieces), trimmed

2 tablespoons canola oil

1 cup ruby port wine

2 tablespoons Veal Demi-Glace (page 246), or store-bought veal demi-glace, or 6 tablespoons Dark Chicken Stock (page 245) reduced to 2 tablespoons over high heat

1 tablespoon plus 1 teaspoon White Chicken Stock (page 245), low-sodium, store-bought chicken broth, or water

4 slices country or peasant bread, ½ inch thick, grilled or toasted

Heat 2 tablespoons of the butter in a wide, deep, heavy-bottomed sauté pan over medium-high heat. Add the red and white onions, the leeks, shallots, and scallions, and cook until well wilted and slightly browned, approximately 8 minutes. Add the parsley and thyme, season with salt and pepper, and drizzle with extra-virgin olive oil. Remove the pan from the heat and keep the onion salad warm.

Put the flour in a bowl and season with salt and pepper. Add the livers to the bowl and toss to coat them with the flour.

Heat the canola oil in a sauté pan set over medium-high heat. Remove the chicken livers from the bowl, shaking off any excess flour, and add them to the pan. Sauté until lightly browned on all sides, approximately 5 minutes. Add the port to the pan and cook, scraping up any flavorful bits stuck to the bottom of the pan. Add the veal demi-glace and chicken stock, bring to a boil, and cook until the liquids have reduced to a thick sauce, approximately 3 minutes. Remove the pan from the heat and stir in the remaining 2 tablespoons butter.

To serve, put 1 slice of toast in the center of each of 4 plates. Top with some onion salad and then the livers. Spoon some sauce over each serving.

DUCK BREASTS
with Roasted Fall Root Salad and Truffle Vinaigrette

SERVES 4

This is a dish to enjoy when fall has settled in and there's a chill in the air. The salad of frisée and half-mashed root vegetables is an irreverent, rustic accompaniment that should become a versatile addition to your repertoire. Serve it alongside roasted beef or chicken as well.

1 large Yukon Gold potato, peeled and cut into 8 equal wedges

3 large carrots, peeled and cut crosswise into 3 pieces each

1 large beet, peeled and cut into 8 equal wedges

½ cup plus 2 tablespoons extra-virgin olive oil

Salt

Freshly ground black pepper

4 Pekin (Long Island) duck breasts, 6 to 8 ounces each

2 medium shallots, 1 minced, 1 thinly sliced

2 teaspoons white truffle oil

1 tablespoon sherry vinegar

1 tablespoon red wine vinegar

1 head frisée lettuce, ends trimmed, white and yellow parts only, separated into leaves

¼ cup parsley

Preheat the oven to 375°F

Put the potato in a small baking dish, the carrots in another, and the beet in a third. Drizzle each vegetable with 2 tablespoons extra-virgin olive oil and season with salt and pepper. Cover each baking dish with aluminum foil and roast until soft to a knife-tip, approximately 30 minutes for the carrots and potato and 45 minutes for the beet.

Heat a large, ovenproof skillet, preferably cast-iron, over medium heat. Score the duck skin a few times with a very sharp knife, and season the duck breasts with salt and pepper. Add the breasts to the pan, skin side down, and cook until the fat has rendered from the skin and the skin has turned nicely brown and crispy, approximately 15 minutes. Drain the fat from the pan and discard. Transfer the duck breasts to the oven and cook for approximately 7 minutes for medium rare, or longer for more well-done.

When the duck breasts are done, transfer them to a cutting board and let rest for 5 minutes.

Make the vinaigrette: Put the minced shallot, truffle oil, sherry and red wine vinegars, and remaining ¼ cup extra-virgin olive oil in a bowl and whisk together. Season with salt and pepper. Set aside.

Make a salad by gently fork-crushing the warm roasted vegetables and transferring them to a bowl. Add the frisée, sliced shallot, and parsley, drizzle with the vinaigrette, and gently toss. Season with salt and pepper.

Slice the duck breasts and fan them out on 4 dinner plates. Pile some salad next to the duck, and drizzle any extra vinaigrette around the plate. Serve.

DUCK BREASTS
with Radishes, Anchovy, and Orange

SERVES 4

Laurence Edelman, The Red Cat's sous-chef, made this for me one day. When he told me the ingredients, I thought I must have misunderstood him: duck, radishes, anchovy, and orange. What was he thinking? But once I tasted it I found it to be such a unique, wonderful, and totally unexpected combination of ingredients that I knew I wanted to put it in the book. The seemingly disparate flavors all play smartly off the duck and each other—the salty anchovy against the peppery radish, with the bright orange and herbaceous parsley livening the whole affair.

4 Pekin (Long Island) duck breasts,
　6 to 8 ounces each
Salt
Freshly ground black pepper
2 tablespoons butter
12 French breakfast radishes, quartered or
　halved lengthwise, depending on size

8 anchovy fillets, mashed to a paste with
　1 teaspoon Dijon mustard
1 tablespoon lemon juice
¼ cup sliced parsley
1 orange, separated into segments (see
　grapefruit instructions, page 123)
½ cup celery leaves
Extra-virgin olive oil, for drizzling

Preheat the oven to 350°F

　Heat a large, ovenproof skillet, preferably cast-iron, over medium heat. Score the duck skin a few times with a very sharp knife, and season the duck breasts with salt and pepper. Add the breasts to the pan, skin side down, and cook until the fat has rendered from the skin and the skin has turned nicely brown and crispy, approximately 15 minutes. Drain the fat from the pan and discard. Transfer to the oven and cook for approximately 7 minutes for medium rare, or longer for more well done.

　When the duck breasts are done, transfer them to a cutting board and let rest for 5 minutes.

　While the duck is cooking, melt the butter in a heavy-bottomed sauté pan. Add the radishes and sauté until lightly browned, approximately 4 minutes. Add the anchovy paste and mix well with a spoon to coat the radishes with the paste. Season with salt and pepper. Add the lemon juice and parsley, taste, and adjust the seasoning with salt and pepper.

　Slice the duck breasts into thin slices. Spoon some radishes onto each of 4 dinner plates. Arrange the slices of 1 duck breast around the radishes on each plate. Garnish with the orange segments and celery leaves. Drizzle with olive oil and sprinkle with salt. Serve.

TURKEY SCHNITZEL
with Orzo Mac and Cheese and Black Mushroom Puree

SERVES 4

When we were testing recipes for this book, Harold Dieterle, the former sous-chef of The Harrison, had a special way of referring to dishes that were especially rich or decadent. "That is so dirty!" he would exclaim, a big, happy grin on his face. Well, it doesn't get any dirtier than this, at least not in this book. This is unparalleled by all (except maybe the baked fontina appetizer): breaded, fried turkey; creamy mac and cheese (made with orzo for a change of pace); and a savory mushroom sauce. Not only is this shamelessly over the top, the kind of thing that will have people moaning with pleasure at the dinner table, but it's also stunning: The white pasta and black sauce stand in stark contrast to one another. If you make this, your friends and family will remember it always.

10 tablespoons (1 stick plus 2 tablespoons)
    butter, plus more if necessary
1 small shallot, minced
Salt
Freshly ground black pepper
1 cup black trumpet mushrooms
4 cups Dark Chicken Stock (page 245) or
    store-bought dark chicken broth
1 tablespoon extra-virgin olive oil
4 turkey tenderloins (sometimes sold as
    "turkey tenders"), 3 to 4 ounces each
3 cups plus 3 tablespoons flour

4 eggs
4 cups dried bread crumbs, preferably
    Japanese panko, crushed by hand or ground
    into medium-fine crumbs
3 tablespoons chopped thyme
1½ cups orzo
3 cups milk
4 ounces Gruyère cheese, grated (1 cup)
4 ounces Fontina cheese, grated (1 cup)
4 ounces Parmigiano-Reggiano cheese, grated
    (1 cup)

Make the black trumpet sauce: Melt 2 tablespoons of the butter in a medium heavy-bottomed saucepan. Add the shallot, season with salt and pepper, and sauté until softened but not browned. Add the mushrooms and cook until they begin to soften and brown slightly, approximately 2 minutes. Add the stock, bring to a boil, then lower the heat and simmer until slightly thickened, approximately 3 minutes. Transfer the contents of the pan to a blender and puree to make a black sauce. Taste and season with salt and pepper, and drizzle with the extra-virgin olive oil. Return to the pan and keep warm, or let cool, cover, and refrigerate for up to 8 hours. Gently reheat before proceeding.

Place 1 piece of turkey between two pieces of plastic wrap. Use a meat tenderizer or the bottom of a heavy pan to pound it to a thickness of ⅛ inch. Set aside and repeat with the remaining turkey slices.

Put 3 cups of the flour in a shallow dish and the eggs in another dish. Lightly beat the eggs. Put the bread crumbs in a third dish, add the thyme, and season with salt and pepper. Dredge the turkey pieces in the flour, shaking off any excess, then dip in the egg, and dredge in the bread crumbs, pressing down to coat the pieces with the crumbs. The turkey can be prepared to this point, loosely covered with plastic wrap, and refrigerated for up to 2 hours. Let come to room temperature before proceeding.

Make the macaroni and cheese: Bring a large pot of salted water to a boil. Add the orzo and cook until al dente, approximately 6 minutes. Drain and set aside.

Put 6 tablespoons of the butter in a large, heavy-bottomed pot and melt it over medium-high heat. Whisk in the remaining 3 tablespoons flour, a little at a time, and cook, whisking constantly, for approximately 3 minutes, without letting it brown. Add the milk in small increments, whisking to prevent lumps from forming. Add the Gruyère, Fontina, and Parmigiano-Reggiano, a handful at a time, whisking to form a thick, creamy sauce. Add the orzo to the pot, stir it in, and season with salt and pepper. Remove the pot from the heat and set aside, covered, to keep warm.

Heat the remaining 2 tablespoons butter in a sauté pan set over medium-high heat. One by one, cook the turkey pieces until nicely browned, approximately 3 minutes per side. Transfer to a plate as you finish cooking the other pieces. Add more butter to the pan between batches, if necessary. Should the butter become dark and murky, carefully wipe out the pan before adding any more butter.

To serve, spoon some sauce onto each of 4 dinner plates. Spoon some orzo mac and cheese onto each plate and lean a schnitzel against it.

MEATS & GAME

TUSCAN PORK LOIN

with Greens and Pecorino

GRILLED PORK CHOPS

with Port Wine Sauce and Creamed Red Onions

SAVORY PORK SAUSAGE

with Clams and Garlic

CALF'S LIVER AU POIVRE

with Melted Tomato and Sage Sauce

SAUTÉED VEAL CUTLETS

with Eggs, Parsley and Onion Salad, and Lemon

OSSO BUCO

with Saffron Couscous and Escarole

VEAL CHOPS

with Eggplant Puree and Balsamic

CRISPY FRIED RABBIT

with Herbs, Lemon, and Rémoulade

PRIME NEW YORK SHELL STEAKS

with Yukon Golds, Fennel, Aïoli, and Cabernet

ROASTED RIB STEAKS

with Barolo and Braised Celery

BRAISED SHORT RIBS

with Semolina Pearls, Fall Roots, and Mushrooms

ROASTED LEG OF LAMB

with Red Onions and Sour Cherries

CURRIED LAMB CHOPS

with Orzo, Spinach, Lemon, and Egg

ROASTED VENISON

with Pancetta, Radicchio, and Balsamic

To me, the appeal of meat and game is twofold. First, there's the primal, carnivorous satisfaction of the texture and taste of the meat itself; whether it's beef, pork, veal, lamb, or venison, there's a certain type of appetite that only some kind of meat will satisfy.

As with dark poultry, the other big attraction meat holds for me is its undeniably delicious fat. There's nothing like the soul-satisfying flavor of, say, charred pork fat—which tastes almost like bacon—or the mouthfeel of a well-marbled steak. Cooking other ingredients in rendered fat is a province of cooking with meat; you don't, for example, sear a piece of delicate flounder in a pan, then sweat your vegetables in the fat left behind . . . because there isn't any fat left behind. But fry up some bacon and you had better cook some eggs or potatoes or mushrooms or greens in the fat; it would be practically sacrilegious not to.

Largely because of that fat, meats can stand up to certain cooking techniques, flavors, and textures that would overwhelm most fish and fowl. Slow braising, for example, is ideal for tough, fatty cuts such as osso buco or short ribs, and these meats partner well with accompaniments such as creamed red onions, saffron couscous, or a Barolo reduction. I do throw in a delicate dish here and there—like the pork loin with greens and Pecorino, which is essentially a salad—but for the most part, I serve meats with elements that you wouldn't, or couldn't, use in many other contexts.

Meats also tend to bring out the traditionalist in me, leading me to more conventional pastures than seafood and poultry do. I find myself drawn to classic preparations such as a roasted leg of lamb or pork loin, a grilled steak or pork chop, and braised osso buco. Where I get creative is in the accompaniments, riffing on things like the risotto Milanese you'd serve with that osso buco, or the potatoes you expect with a steak. That said, there are times when there's nothing like simplicity; on a hot summer afternoon, a perfectly grilled steak with just a squeeze of lemon and a drizzle of olive oil can be just as inspired a dish as venison on a blustery fall evening.

TUSCAN PORK LOIN
with Greens and Pecorino

SERVES 4

On a clear, breezy spring or summer day, this is what I want to eat: an uncomplicated main-course salad of tender, juicy roasted pork, bitter greens, and slivers of salty cheese, with some fruity virgin olive oil and the zing of lemon juice pulling it all together. You can adapt it to incorporate your own favorite spring and summer ingredients, such as cranberry beans, black olives, and shaved raw asparagus.

2 pounds pork loin

½ cup plus 2 tablespoons lemon juice

½ cup plus 3 tablespoons extra-virgin olive oil

3 cloves garlic, coarsely chopped

3 branches rosemary

Salt

Freshly ground black pepper

1 small bunch arugula

1 small head frisée, ends trimmed, white and yellow parts only

1 baby artichoke

8 ounces fava beans in the pod, peeled (see Note)

1 teaspoon sliced mint

1 teaspoon sliced parsley

1½ ounces Pecorino, shaved into shards with a vegetable peeler

Put the pork in a baking dish or other shallow vessel. Add ¼ cup plus 2 tablespoons of the lemon juice, 3 tablespoons of the oil, the garlic, and the rosemary branches, and toss to coat the pork. Cover and refrigerate overnight.

Preheat the oven to 400°F.

Set a roasting pan over two stovetop burners and heat the pan over medium-high heat. Remove the pork from its marinade, brushing off any solids. Season the pork with salt and pepper, add it to the pan, and cook, turning the pork as needed, until a light brown crust forms on all sides, approximately 8 minutes. Transfer the pan to the oven and roast until an instant-read thermometer inserted to the center of the pork reads 145°F, approximately 40 minutes more. Remove the pan from the oven. Transfer the pork to a plate, tent with foil to keep warm, and let rest for 10 minutes. (During this time, the internal temperature should rise to 150 to 155°F.)

While the pork is resting, make a salad by putting the arugula and frisée in a bowl. Trim the artichoke by cutting off the top third with a heavy kitchen knife, then trimming the stem to 1 inch. Peel the stem to remove the bitter green exterior, then shave the artichoke on a mandoline (or slice very thin with a knife) and add the slices to the bowl. Add the fava beans, remaining ¼ cup lemon juice, remaining ½ cup oil, the mint, and parsley, and toss.

Slice the pork and divide among 4 plates. Top with the salad, then with some shaved cheese.

NOTE TO THE COOK Peel fava beans by removing the tough outer pod, then carefully remove the skin that envelops each bean. Eight ounces fava beans in the pods yield about ¼ cup beans.

GRILLED PORK CHOPS
with Port Wine Sauce and Creamed Red Onions

SERVES 4

There's nothing new about a pork chop, but a grilled pork chop is always wonderful, and the accompaniments here create a perfect marriage. When the cream from the onions seeps into the sauce of port wine and veal stock infused with porcini mushrooms, rosemary, and thyme, it's a beautiful and delicious thing.

4 bone-in pork chops, approximately 10 ounces each

About 2 tablespoons extra-virgin olive oil

2 tablespoons chopped thyme, plus 2 sprigs thyme

2 tablespoons chopped rosemary, plus 1 sprig rosemary

2 tablespoons canola oil

2 medium shallots, thinly sliced

1¼ teaspoons crushed dried porcini mushrooms

½ cup ruby port

2 cups Veal Stock (page 246) or low-sodium, store-bought beef broth

1 tablespoon butter

Salt

Freshly ground black pepper

Creamed Red Onions (recipe follows)

¼ cup coarsely chopped black olives, such as Gaeta or Niçoise

Rub the pork chops with the extra-virgin olive oil to coat, then season with the chopped thyme and chopped rosemary. Put on a plate in a single layer, cover loosely with plastic wrap, and refrigerate overnight.

When ready to proceed, preheat a gas grill to high, or prepare a charcoal grill for grilling, letting the coals burn until covered with white ash.

To make the sauce, pour the canola oil into a medium, heavy-bottomed saucepan and heat over medium heat. Add the shallots and sauté until softened but not browned, approximately 4 minutes. Add the porcinis, thyme sprigs, and rosemary sprig; stir; and cook until the mushrooms begin to stick onto the bottom of the pot, approximately 30 seconds. Add the port and stir to loosen the mushrooms. Bring to a boil, lower the heat, and simmer until the port is reduced by half, approximately 2 minutes. Add the stock, bring to a boil, then lower the heat and simmer until reduced to ½ to ¾ cup of nicely thickened sauce, 6 to 8 minutes. Strain the sauce and discard the solids. Whisk the butter into the sauce, season with salt and pepper, cover to keep warm, and set aside.

Season the pork with salt and pepper and grill until nicely charred on both sides and cooked through, approximately 8 minutes per side.

To serve, spoon some creamed red onions onto each plate and set a pork chop alongside. Top each chop with 1 tablespoon chopped olives, spreading them over the surface of the chop. Spoon some sauce around the chop.

Creamed Red Onions

Serve this rich side dish with just about any grilled meats or game.

4 small red onions, sliced into ¼-inch-thick
    rings
Canola oil, for brushing onion slices
Salt
Freshly ground black pepper

¼ cup dry sherry
1 cup White Chicken Stock (page 245) or
    low-sodium, store-bought chicken broth
1 cup cream

Preheat a gas grill to high, or prepare a charcoal grill for grilling, letting the coals burn until covered with white ash.

Brush the onion slices with oil and season with salt and pepper. Place on the grill and grill until nicely charred and softened, approximately 3 minutes per side. Remove from the grill and separate into rings.

Heat a sauté pan over low heat (or over the grates of a grill). Add the onions and cook for 1 minute. Add the sherry, raise the heat, and boil until the sherry has reduced by half, approximately 4 minutes. Add the stock and boil until reduced and the onions are just coated with stock, approximately 6 minutes. Add the cream and cook until reduced and the onions are just coated with cream, approximately 5 minutes. Taste and adjust the seasoning with salt and pepper. The onions can be cooled, covered, and refrigerated for up to 4 hours. Reheat gently before serving.

SAVORY PORK SAUSAGE
with Clams and Garlic

SERVES 4

I got the inspiration for this dish from the Portuguese community of my native Rhode Island, specifically from a dish called *Porco a Alentejana*, which combines juicy pork and salty clams. My version puts the pork in a homemade sausage, which is shaped into a knife-and-fork-worthy "burger," and then set atop the lusty, garlicky broth. Make sure you have some bread around to mop up all the sauce.

1½ pounds ground pork

1 teaspoon sliced sage

1 clove garlic, minced

Salt

Freshly ground black pepper

½ cup dry white wine

1¼ pounds littleneck clams, scrubbed

1½ ounces bacon (about 1½ strips), finely
   diced

½ medium onion, finely diced

Pinch of crushed red pepper flakes

1 tablespoon finely diced roasted red pepper
   (see page 244)

¾ cup Dark Chicken Stock (page 245) or
   store-bought dark chicken broth

5 canned peeled tomatoes, crushed by hand,
   with their juice

1 tablespoon canola oil

¼ teaspoon chopped oregano

½ teaspoon sliced cilantro

2 tablespoons sliced parsley

1 tablespoon butter

Put the pork in a bowl and add the sage, half of the garlic, 1 teaspoon salt, and ½ teaspoon pepper. Knead to incorporate, then divide into 4 portions, shaping each one into a 1-inch-thick patty. Set on a plate, cover with plastic wrap, and refrigerate until ready to cook, but no longer than 48 hours.

When ready to cook, let the patties come to room temperature and preheat the oven to 400°F.

Pour the wine into a large, heavy-bottomed pot and heat it over medium-high heat. Add the clams, cover, and steam until the clams open, approximately 3 minutes. Discard any clams that have not opened. Strain the cooking liquid through a fine-mesh strainer set over a bowl and set the liquid aside. When the clams are cool enough to handle, remove the top half of each clam's shell and discard it.

Put the bacon in a heavy-bottomed pot and cook over medium heat until it renders enough fat to coat the bottom of the pot, approximately 3 minutes. Add the onion and remaining garlic, and sauté for 2 minutes. Add the red pepper flakes, roasted pepper, stock, tomatoes, and reserved clam cooking liquid, and simmer the stew for 8 minutes.

Meanwhile, pour the oil into a wide, deep, ovenproof skillet, preferably cast-iron, and heat it over medium-high heat. Season the patties with salt and pepper and brown them on one side for 2 minutes. Turn them over and transfer to the oven until cooked through, approximately 10 minutes.

Stir the oregano, cilantro, parsley, and butter into the stew. Rest the clams on top of the stew for 30 seconds to reheat them.

Divide the clam stew among 4 shallow bowls, top each with a pork sausage, and serve.

CALF'S LIVER AU POIVRE
with Melted Tomato and Sage Sauce

SERVES 4

If you grew up in an Italian-American household, then there's a fair chance you learned to love calf's liver early. There are a lot of people this applies to. I know this for a fact, because when I wanted to put a calf's liver dish on the opening menu at The Red Cat, my partner Danny objected. "Who's going to order calf's liver?" was his perfectly reasonable question. Well, I went ahead and put it on the menu, and it surprised even me how well it sold. It was good to know that I wasn't the only one out there with fond memories of this much-maligned bit of offal. The key to great calf's liver is to not overcook it, and to serve it with something a little acidic and a little sweet.

The sauce here is a real old-school, Northern Italian red sauce that gets its deep flavor from browned bacon and garlic.

Serve this with the broccoli rabe on page 193.

1 cup balsamic vinegar

½ cup diced bacon (from 2 ounces slab or thick-cut bacon)

2 cloves garlic, thinly sliced

1 28-ounce can whole peeled tomatoes, with their juice

1 teaspoon sliced sage

¼ teaspoon crushed red pepper flakes

4 pieces calf's liver, ¾ inch thick, 1½ to 2 pounds total

1 tablespoon freshly cracked black pepper

2 tablespoons canola oil

Pour the vinegar into a small, heavy-bottomed saucepan and heat over high heat. Bring to a boil, lower the heat, and simmer until reduced to ¼ cup, approximately 3 minutes. (The reduction can be cooled, transferred to an airtight container, and kept at room temperature for up to 2 weeks. Reheat gently before proceeding.)

To make the sauce, put the bacon in a medium, heavy-bottomed saucepan, set over low heat, and cook until it browns and renders enough fat to coat the pan, approximately 5 minutes. Add the garlic, raise the heat to medium, and sauté until lightly browned, approximately 4 minutes. Add the tomatoes, bring the liquid to a simmer, lower the heat, and simmer until reduced by half, approximately 5 minutes. Add the sage and red pepper flakes.

Meanwhile, season the calf's liver with the black pepper. Heat the oil in a wide, deep, heavy-bottomed sauté pan over medium-high heat. Add the liver and sear well, approximately 5 minutes, then turn over, lower the heat to medium-high, and sear on the other side for approximately 2 minutes for medium rare. (As the liver is done, its exterior color will darken upward from where the liver meets the pan. It is cooked to medium rare when the entire exterior has darkened.)

To serve, put 1 slice of liver on each of 4 dinner plates, spoon some sauce over the top, and finish by drizzling the balsamic reduction around the dish.

SAUTÉED VEAL CUTLETS
with Eggs, Parsley and Onion Salad, and Lemon

SERVES 4

This amped-up, but not terribly complicated, version of veal scallopini breads pounded-out veal slices with a mixture of bread crumbs, thyme, Parmesan cheese, and garlic, then tops the cooked veal with a fried egg and a parsley-and-onion salad. To really get the full effect, don't overcook the egg yolk: You want the hot yolk to run out over the veal, enriching the entire dish. It's just as decadent as it sounds, but the lemon wedges invite diners to cut the richness to suit their own taste.

½ small onion, diced

½ cup sliced parsley

2 teaspoons drained capers

4 canned anchovy fillets, finely sliced

1 teaspoon extra-virgin olive oil

Salt

Freshly ground black pepper

¾ cup flour

6 eggs

¾ cup bread crumbs, preferably Japanese panko

½ cup grated Parmigiano-Reggiano

1 tablespoon chopped thyme

1 small clove garlic, finely chopped

4 pieces veal scallopini, 4 ounces each

4 tablespoons (½ stick) butter

2 tablespoons canola oil

1 lemon, cut into 8 wedges

Put the onion, parsley, capers, anchovies, and extra-virgin olive oil in a small bowl. Season with salt and pepper, stir to combine, and set aside.

Pour the flour out onto a plate and spread to an even thickness. Break 2 of the eggs into a wide, shallow bowl and lightly beat them.

Put the bread crumbs, cheese, thyme, and garlic in a bowl. Season with salt and pepper and stir to incorporate the ingredients, then spread the mixture out on another plate.

One by one, put the veal pieces between two pieces of plastic wrap and, using a meat mallet or heavy skillet, pound to a thickness of ¼ inch.

Season the veal with salt and pepper. Dredge in the flour, then dip in the eggs, letting any excess egg run off, then press into the bread-crumb mixture, making sure the mixture adheres.

Melt 2 tablespoons of the butter in a wide, deep sauté pan over medium-high heat. Add 2 scallopini and cook until golden brown, approximately 3 minutes. Turn over and cook until golden brown on the other side, another 3 minutes. Transfer each scallopini to its own dinner plate, melt the remaining 2 tablespoons butter in the pan, and repeat with the remaining 2 scallopini.

While the last 2 scallopini are cooking, heat the canola oil in a wide, deep sauté pan over medium-high heat. Break the remaining 4 eggs into the pan, being careful not to let them run together, and fry them until the whites are set but the yolks are still runny, approximately 3 minutes.

To serve, top the veal on each plate with a fried egg. Top the egg with some of the parsley and onion salad. Put 2 lemon wedges on each plate for squeezing over the dish at the table.

OSSO BUCO
with Saffron Couscous and Escarole

SERVES 4

Osso buco is one of the great big classics of the Italian kitchen. The name means "hole in the bone," but that's beside the point. All you need to know is that an osso buco is a humungous veal shank, braised to the point that the meat falls apart when prodded gently with a fork, and served most famously with risotto a la Milanese, or saffron risotto. My version makes a saffron couscous instead, which cooks much more quickly. I also add a little sautéed escarole for extra texture and color.

4 osso buco, 12 to 16 ounces each, tied around the equator with kitchen twine

Salt

Freshly ground black pepper

¼ cup plus 2 tablespoons flour

½ cup plus 2 tablespoons olive oil

1 large carrot, peeled and coarsely chopped

½ onion, coarsely chopped

2 stalks celery, coarsely chopped

2 cloves garlic, 1 chopped and 1 sliced

1 beefsteak tomato, coarsely chopped

6 sprigs thyme

2 cups dry white wine

3 cups White Chicken Stock (page 245) or low-sodium, store-bought chicken broth

3 cups Veal Stock (page 246) or low-sodium, store-bought beef broth

1 large head escarole, trimmed to the pale green portion and quartered

2 teaspoons saffron threads

2 cups Israeli couscous (available in some supermarkets and specialty grocers)

⅓ cup grated Parmigiano-Reggiano

2 tablespoons butter

1 tablespoon sliced parsley

Preheat the oven to 375°F.

Season the osso buco with salt and pepper, dredge them in the flour, and set aside on a plate.

Heat ½ cup of the oil in a large, heavy-bottomed pot or Dutch oven. Add the osso buco and brown on all sides, approximately 7 minutes per side. Don't be shy—let them develop a nice dark crust. Transfer to a plate and set aside. Pour off all but about ¼ cup of fat from the pot.

Add the carrot, onion, celery, and chopped garlic, and cook until lightly browned. Add the tomato, thyme, wine, chicken stock, and veal stock, and bring to a boil. Return the osso buco to the pot and bring the liquid to a simmer. Cover the pot and transfer to the oven. Braise until the meat is fork-tender and pulls away from the bone with the tug of a fork, approximately 2 hours.

As the meat braises, periodically check on it to be sure the liquid isn't boiling aggressively; it should be at the mildest of simmers. If it's bubbling violently, reduce the temperature by 25 degrees; if it isn't bubbling at all, raise it by 25.

During the final 10 minutes of the osso buco's cooking, heat the remaining 2 tablespoons oil in a sauté pan. Add the sliced garlic and cook for 1 minute. Add the escarole and cook until wilted, approximately 3 minutes. Season with salt and pepper and set aside.

Bring 3 cups of salted water to a boil. Add the saffron and couscous and cook until al dente, approximately 5 minutes. Drain and add to the pan with the escarole. Stir in the cheese and butter. Set aside.

Transfer the osso buco to a plate and tent with foil to keep warm. Strain the sauce through a fine-mesh strainer set over a pot. Bring it to a simmer over high heat, then lower the heat and simmer until reduced and nicely thickened, 5 to 10 minutes, skimming off any fat with a spoon.

Put 1 osso buco on each of 4 dinner plates, spoon some couscous and 1 piece of escarole along-side, and drizzle with the reduced braising liquid. Garnish with some parsley and serve.

VEAL CHOPS
with Eggplant Puree and Balsamic

SERVES 4

This is a clean and not-too-rich summertime dish based on the contrast between the char-grilled exterior of the veal chop and the luscious eggplant puree, a colorful mixture featuring red and yellow peppers and flecks of parsley and basil. The whole thing is really picked up by the balsamic reduction, proving once again how versatile this quick sauce can be.

4 veal chops, about 14 ounces each	Salt
5 tablespoons olive oil	Freshly ground black pepper
2 cloves garlic, sliced, plus 1/2 clove garlic, minced	1/2 medium red bell pepper
	1 medium yellow bell pepper
Grated zest of 1/2 lemon	1 small shallot, minced
1 tablespoon chopped thyme	1/4 cup sliced parsley
1 cup balsamic vinegar	2 teaspoons sliced basil
2 medium eggplants, about 1 1/4 pounds each, halved lengthwise	1/4 cup extra-virgin olive oil

Put the chops in a glass baking dish or other shallow vessel. Drizzle with 2 tablespoons of the olive oil and scatter the sliced garlic, lemon zest, and thyme over them. Turn to coat with the marinade, cover, and refrigerate overnight.

Pour the vinegar into a small, heavy-bottomed saucepan and heat over high heat. Bring to a boil, lower the heat, and simmer until reduced to 1/4 cup, approximately 3 minutes. (The reduction can be cooled, transferred to an airtight container, and kept at room temperature for up to 2 weeks. Reheat gently before proceeding. This can also be done in a small saucepan on the grill; see next step.)

Preheat a gas grill to high, or prepare a charcoal grill for grilling, letting the coals burn until covered with white ash.

Score the cut sides of the eggplants with a sharp, thin-bladed knife. Rub the cut sides with 2 tablespoons of the olive oil. Season with salt and pepper and wrap individually in aluminum foil, snugly, but not too tightly. Place on the grill, close the cover, and cook until the eggplants are golden and soft to a knife-tip, 10 to 15 minutes.

Transfer the eggplants to a cutting board, remove and discard the foil, and let the eggplants cool.

While the eggplants are cooling, grill the peppers: Rub the peppers with the remaining tablespoon olive oil and place on the grill. Grill, turning as necessary, until the peppers are softened but not blackened, approximately 5 minutes. Transfer the peppers to a cutting board and let cool.

Remove the veal chops from the marinade and brush off any marinade solids. Season with salt and pepper and grill until cooked through, with nice grill marks, approximately 7 minutes per side.

Meanwhile, when the eggplants are cool enough to work with, scoop out the flesh, gathering it on a cutting board. Coarsely chop it with a knife, and transfer to a bowl. Seed and finely dice the peppers and add them to the bowl. Add the minced garlic, shallot, parsley, basil, and extra-virgin olive oil to the bowl and stir to integrate the ingredients. Season with salt and pepper.

To serve, put a chop on each of 4 dinner plates and put some eggplant puree next to it. Drizzle some balsamic reduction around the plate.

NOTE TO THE COOK You can omit the balsamic reduction and finish by drizzling with extra-virgin olive oil and serving with lemon wedges alongside.

CRISPY FRIED RABBIT
with Herbs, Lemon, and Rémoulade

SERVES 4

The epitome of my "just a little different" philosophy, this is fried chicken, only made with rabbit. The succulence of the rabbit is enough to add interest and surprise to one of the most familiar dishes in America, especially when you toss some lemon slices into the oil and fry them into tart, crispy chips. I also love adding herbs to fried foods such as French fries and fritto misto. Whenever you have a pot of hot oil going, toss in some sage leaves, rosemary branches, or other herb sprigs, draining them on paper towels and seasoning them just as you do the principal ingredient. In the case of rosemary, I crumble the leaves over whatever I'm serving and discard the branches.

Can you make this with chicken? Absolutely—you could substitute two three-pound chickens for the rabbits and it would be delicious. But try it with rabbit at least once.

2 rabbits, approximately 3 pounds each,
   cut into 8 pieces each by your butcher
About 2 cups buttermilk
8 eggs
6 cups flour
1 cup cornstarch
½ cup salt, plus more for seasoning
¼ cup garlic powder

¼ cup onion powder
¼ cup sliced sage
2 tablespoons cayenne
2 tablespoons Hungarian sweet paprika
1 tablespoon plus 1 teaspoon celery seed
Canola oil, for frying
3 lemons, very thinly sliced
Celery Root Rémoulade (recipe follows)

Put the rabbit pieces in a bowl. Pour the buttermilk over them. Cover and refrigerate for 24 hours.

Put the eggs in a bowl, and lightly beat them. In another bowl, stir together the flour, the cornstarch, the ½ cup salt, the garlic powder, onion powder, sage, cayenne, paprika, and celery seed.

One by one, remove the rabbit pieces from the buttermilk, letting any excess liquid run off. Coat them with the flour mixture, then dip in the eggs, then roll in the flour mixture again to coat.

Pour oil into a wide, deep-sided pot to a depth of 6 inches and bring to a temperature of 375°F over medium heat. Line 2 plates with paper towels.

Carefully add the rabbit pieces to the pot in small batches and fry until golden and crispy, approximately 12 minutes. Use tongs or a slotted spoon to transfer the rabbit to one paper-towel-lined plate. Season immediately with salt.

Let the oil return to a temperature of 350°F and repeat with another batch of rabbit. Continue to repeat until all of the rabbit has been fried. Add the lemon slices during the final 2 minutes of frying of the final batch of rabbit. Transfer the fried lemon slices to their own paper-towel-lined plate so the slices drain directly on the paper towels and not into the rabbit. Season them with salt as well.

To serve, set the rabbit out on a platter, scatter the lemon slices over it, and pass the rémoulade alongside for spooning or dipping.

Celery Root Rémoulade

MAKES ABOUT 2½ CUPS

This is awesome with fried potatoes, fish, shellfish, pâté, or chilled, poached seafood. The grated celery root imparts a deep celery flavor and makes the sauce extra creamy.

2 cups mayonnaise

1 tablespoon Dijon mustard

1 clove garlic, minced

1 teaspoon hot sauce

2 tablespoons red wine vinegar

1 teaspoon sliced parsley

1 teaspoon finely chopped chives

1 teaspoon sliced tarragon

½ cup shredded celery root

Salt

Freshly ground black pepper

Put the mayonnaise, mustard, garlic, hot sauce, vinegar, parsley, chives, tarragon, and celery root in a bowl and mix together. Season with salt and pepper to taste. The rémoulade can be covered and refrigerated for up to 2 to 3 days.

PRIME NEW YORK SHELL STEAKS
with Yukon Golds, Fennel, Aïoli, and Cabernet

SERVES 4

When you're going to cook a steak, you have two options: Just grill it up and go conventional with baked potatoes, a tomato and onion salad, creamed spinach, and the like. And there's nothing wrong with that. In fact, sometimes it can hit the spot like nothing else. Or you can try something special, such as this recipe, which rethinks steak and potatoes, adding tomato and fennel to the plate and tossing the vegetables with a garlic mayonnaise (aïoli).

4 prime New York shell steaks, about
    14 ounces each, preferably center cut
¼ cup chopped rosemary
Salt
Freshly ground black pepper
2 tablespoons olive oil
2 medium shallots, thinly sliced
5 black peppercorns

1 sprig thyme
2 cups Cabernet Sauvignon or other full-bodied
    wine
2 cups Veal Stock (page 246) or low-sodium,
    store-bought beef broth
1 tablespoon butter
Aïoli-Dressed Fennel, Potato, and Tomato
    (recipe follows)

Preheat a gas grill to high, or prepare a charcoal grill for grilling, letting the coals burn until covered with white ash.

Season the steaks on both sides with rosemary, salt, and pepper. Set aside while you make the sauce.

Pour the olive oil into a medium, heavy-bottomed saucepan. Add the shallots and sauté until softened but not browned, approximately 2 minutes. Add the peppercorns, thyme sprig, and wine, and bring to a boil over high heat. Lower the heat and simmer until reduced by two thirds to three fourths, approximately 6 minutes. Add the stock, bring to a boil, then lower the heat and simmer until reduced to ½ cup to ¾ cup liquid, approximately 6 minutes. Strain through a fine-mesh strainer set over a bowl, discard the solids, whisk in the butter, and season with salt and pepper. Set aside and keep warm.

Grill the steaks for about 6 minutes per side or until the internal temperature is 125°F for a moist, juicy medium rare. Allow the steaks to rest at room temperature for 10 minutes. (During this time the temperature will rise to approximately 130°F.)

To serve, put 1 steak on each of 4 large dinner plates. Arrange the vegetables alongside and spoon some sauce over and around the steak.

Aïoli-Dressed Fennel, Potato, and Tomato

SERVES 4 AS A SIDE DISH

Serve this warm potato salad with grilled and roasted meats and fish.

1 egg yolk

1 teaspoon lemon juice, plus more to taste

3 cloves garlic, smashed and peeled

1 cup extra-virgin olive oil

Salt

Freshly ground black pepper

3 medium Yukon Gold potatoes, cut into ½-inch dice

2 plum tomatoes, seeded and cut into ½-inch dice

2 bulbs fennel, trimmed and cut into ½-inch dice

¼ cup olive oil

Make the aïoli by putting the egg yolk, lemon juice, and garlic in a blender and starting the motor. Slowly add the extra-virgin olive oil in a thin stream to form a thick and creamy emulsion. Season with salt, pepper, and more lemon juice, if needed. Cover, and refrigerate for up to 2 days.

Preheat the oven to 400°F.

Bring a medium pot of salted water to a boil over high heat. Add the potato dice and boil until a sharp, thin-bladed knife easily pierces to the center of a piece of potato, approximately 5 minutes. Drain the potatoes and put into a large bowl.

Put the tomatoes and fennel in a bowl, drizzle with the olive oil, and season with salt and pepper. Transfer to a baking dish in a single layer, cover with foil, and roast until softened but not browned, approximately 20 minutes.

Add the fennel and tomatoes to the bowl with the potatoes. Add the aïoli and stir gently to coat the vegetables with the aïoli. Serve warm.

ROASTED RIB STEAKS
with Barolo and Braised Celery

SERVES 4

Steak on the bone doesn't just mean a porterhouse. These rib-eyes get extra flavor from the bone, and the meat is sturdy enough to get along with one of the biggest Italian wines, Barolo. Braised celery makes this taken-for-granted vegetable a side dish in its own right, and you might be surprised at how well it stands up for itself, even in this brawny company.

2 double-cut rib-eye steaks on the bone, about 30 ounces each

2 tablespoons sugar

1 tablespoon plus 1 teaspoon finely ground red pepper flakes (grind them in a coffee or spice grinder) or cayenne

Salt

Freshly ground black pepper

2 medium shallots, thinly sliced

10 black peppercorns

2 cups Barolo wine

¼ cup red wine vinegar

2 cups Veal Stock (page 246) or low-sodium, store-bought beef broth

4 sprigs thyme

1 tablespoon butter

Braised Celery (recipe follows)

Rub the steaks all over with the sugar and ground red pepper flakes, and season generously with salt and black pepper. Let rest at room temperature for 20 minutes to 2 hours.

Preheat a gas grill to high, or prepare a charcoal grill for grilling, letting the coals burn until covered with white ash.

To make the sauce, put the shallots, peppercorns, wine, and vinegar in a heavy-bottomed saucepan and bring to a boil over medium heat, cooking until reduced by two thirds, approximately 7 minutes. Add the veal stock and thyme, and simmer for about 20 minutes, or until the sauce coats the back of a spoon. Strain through a fine-mesh strainer set over a bowl. Whisk in the butter and season with salt and pepper. Set aside and keep warm.

Grill the steaks for about 10 minutes per side, or until the internal temperature is 125°F, for a moist, juicy medium rare. Allow the steaks to rest at room temperature for 10 minutes. (During this time the temperature will rise to approximately 130°F.)

To serve, slice the steaks and divide among 4 dinner plates. Spoon some sauce over and around the steaks and place some braised celery alongside.

Braised Celery

I love this with braised and roasted meats.

1¼ cups White Chicken Stock (page 245) or
    low-sodium, store-bought chicken broth
1 head celery, cleaned and cut into 3-inch
    batons

1 tablespoon butter
1 tablespoon extra-virgin olive oil
Salt
Freshly ground black pepper

Preheat the oven to 400°F.

Pour the stock into a medium, heavy-bottomed pot or Dutch oven and bring to a gentle simmer over medium heat. Add the celery to the pot, cover with foil, and braise in the oven until the celery is soft to the touch, approximately 25 minutes.

Drain off all but a few tablespoons of liquid, swirl in the butter and oil, and season with salt and pepper. Serve.

BRAISED SHORT RIBS

with Semolina Pearls, Fall Roots, and Mushrooms

SERVES 4

Short ribs fall into that popular category of meats that are tough, but that soften up during a long, slow braising. There's no room for weakness alongside a short rib; meek accompaniments simply don't stand a chance of being noticed. So, I pair these ribs with root vegetables, button mushrooms, and Israeli couscous, which bring a nice toothsome quality to the plate. Braising a short rib does require patience: First, you need to really sear the meat on all sides, so get the pan nice and hot and don't be afraid to let the meat get really dark; this is what provides the rich color and a lot of the flavor of the sauce. Second, once you've got the pan in the oven, check on it periodically to be sure the liquid is just barely simmering, so that the meat becomes super-tender rather than seizing up.

½ cup plus 2 tablespoons canola oil

4 pounds bone-in short ribs, about 8 ribs

Salt

Freshly ground black pepper

1 large carrot, peeled and coarsely chopped

½ onion, coarsely chopped

2 stalks celery, coarsely chopped

2 cloves garlic, coarsely chopped

2 sprigs rosemary

2 sprigs thyme, plus 1 tablespoon chopped thyme

2 cups robust red wine, such as Shiraz or Zinfandel

6 cups White Chicken Stock (page 245) or low-sodium, store-bought chicken broth

2 cups Veal Stock (page 246) or low-sodium, store-bought beef broth

1 beefsteak tomato, coarsely chopped

1 cup Israeli couscous

1 tablespoon extra-virgin olive oil

5 ounces cipollini onions

5 ounces baby carrots, trimmed and peeled

5 ounces baby golden beets, trimmed (if using larger beets, peel and halve or quarter them)

5 ounces baby white turnips, trimmed (if using larger turnips, peel and halve or quarter them)

5 ounces button mushrooms, larger ones halved

1 tablespoon butter, at room temperature

2 tablespoons sliced parsley

Preheat the oven to 375°F.

Pour ¼ cup of the canola oil into a heavy-bottomed roasting pan and heat it on two stovetop burners over high heat. Season the ribs with salt and pepper, carefully add them to the pan without crowding, and sear on all sides, approximately 7 minutes per side. Don't be shy—go ahead and let them develop a nice dark crust.

Transfer the ribs to a plate and pour off and discard all but 2 tablespoons of fat from the pan. Add the carrot, chopped onion, celery, and garlic, and cook until softened but not browned, approximately 4 minutes. Add the sprigs of rosemary and thyme and the wine, bring to a boil, and boil until reduced by half, approximately 5 minutes. Add the chicken stock, veal stock, and tomato. Season lightly with salt and pepper, and bring to a boil. Return the ribs to the pan. (If the liquid does not cover the ribs, add more chicken or veal stock, or water.) Cover with foil and braise in the oven for 2 hours, or until the meat is tender and pulls away from the bone with the tug of a fork. As the ribs braise, periodically check on them to be sure the liquid isn't boiling aggressively; it should be at the mildest of simmers. If it's bubbling violently, reduce the temperature by 25 degrees; if it isn't bubbling at all, raise it by 25.

Meanwhile, bring a small pot of salted water to a boil. Add the couscous and boil until al dente, approximately 8 minutes. Drain, toss with the extra-virgin olive oil, and set aside.

After the ribs have been braising for approximately 1 hour and 15 minutes, cook the vegetables: Heat 2 tablespoons of the canola oil in a wide, deep, heavy-bottomed sauté pan over medium-high heat. Add the cipollini onions and baby carrots and sauté until cooked through and tender to a knife-tip, approximately 12 minutes. Transfer the onions and carrots to a bowl, pour the oil out of the pan, and add 2 tablespoons fresh canola oil. Heat over medium-high heat, add the beets and turnips, and sauté until tender to a knife-tip, approximately 10 minutes. Transfer to the bowl with the onions and carrots. Replace the oil as before with 2 tablespoons fresh oil, and heat over medium-high heat. Add the mushrooms and sauté until just softened, approximately 5 minutes. Add the mushrooms to the bowl with the other vegetables and set aside.

When the ribs are done, use tongs or a slotted spoon to set them aside. Pour the braising liquid through a fine-mesh strainer set over a bowl and discard the solids. Transfer the reserved cooked vegetables to a pot, add just enough braising liquid to make a nice, stew-like sauce (about 1½ cups liquid), and stir in the couscous. Stir in the chopped thyme and butter and season to taste with salt and pepper.

Spoon some of the couscous stew over each of 4 plates, making sure to get a good mix of vegetables in each spoonful. Top with the ribs, garnish with parsley, and serve.

NOTE TO THE COOK Israeli couscous isn't really a grain; it's pearls of semolina that resemble couscous, so I refer to it as "semolina pearls" in many of my recipes.

ROASTED LEG OF LAMB
with Red Onions and Sour Cherries

SERVES 8

Most people swear by the combination of lamb and rosemary, or if they go for the jelly, lamb and mint. But I find that the sweetness of basil is the perfect counterpoint to the gamy flavor of lamb.

1 leg of lamb, bone in, 10 to 12 pounds

¼ cup plus 2 tablespoons extra-virgin olive oil

1 cup chopped basil

⅓ cup freshly ground black pepper, plus more to taste

Salt

4 medium red onions

½ cup Cabernet Sauvignon or other full-bodied red wine

¼ cup balsamic vinegar

1 cup Veal Stock (page 246) or low-sodium, store-bought beef broth

1 tablespoon butter

¾ cup dried sour cherries, soaked in hot water for 10 minutes and drained

Rub the lamb leg all over with ¼ cup of the oil, then coat with the basil and pepper. Let marinate in the refrigerator, covered with plastic wrap, for at least 2 hours or up to 24 hours.

Preheat the oven to 400°F.

Season the lamb all over with salt; set, fat side up, on a rack in a shallow roasting pan. Roast for 30 minutes, then lower the oven temperature to 350°F and continue to roast until an instant-read thermometer inserted to the thickest part of the lamb reads 120°F to 125°F for medium rare, another 90 minutes to 2 hours.

Transfer the lamb to a cutting board, tent with foil to keep it warm, and let rest for 20 minutes. Reserve the pan and its juices. Do not turn off the oven.

Meanwhile, peel the onions, cut off both ends, and slice each onion in half at the equator into 2 thick rings. (If using large onions, cut each into three or four 1-inch-thick rings.) Place the rings flat on a baking dish, drizzle with the remaining 2 tablespoons oil, season with salt and pepper, and roast until soft and caramelized, approximately 30 minutes.

While the onions are roasting, make the sauce: Skim any fat from the lamb's roasting pan. Set the pan over two burners, add the red wine and balsamic, bring to a simmer over high heat, and reduce by half, approximately 4 minutes, stirring and scraping up any browned bits from the bottom of the pan. Pour in the stock, bring to a simmer, and simmer until nicely thickened, 5 to 8 minutes. Remove from the heat. Stir in the butter and the sour cherries, pour in any accumulated juices from the resting lamb, and season with salt and pepper.

To serve, slice the lamb lengthwise against the grain until you reach the bone, then rotate the leg and repeat. Arrange the slices on dinner plates. Set a red onion slice alongside and spoon some sauce over and around the lamb.

CURRIED LAMB CHOPS
with Orzo, Spinach, Lemon, and Egg

SERVES 4

Lamb chops, marinated in curry and grilled until blackened, are paired with an orzo sauce inspired by the Greek *avgolemono* soup, which features chicken stock, egg, and lemon. Here, the egg is scrambled, creating yellow ribbons like those you'd find in fried rice. The flavors get along great, especially when the lamb drippings find their way into the pasta. But the real beauty of this dish is the most primal thing on the plate: the charred lamb fat.

3 tablespoons Dijon mustard

2 tablespoons honey

1 tablespoon curry powder

½ teaspoon cayenne

4½ tablespoons lemon juice

1 teaspoon red wine vinegar

2 cloves garlic, chopped

1 cup canola oil

2 half-racks of lamb, approximately 2 pounds
    total weight, cut into 4 double chops

Salt

1⅓ cups orzo

Freshly ground black pepper

3 tablespoons butter

2 eggs, beaten

1 cup sliced spinach leaves

2 tablespoons sliced parsley

¾ cup White Chicken Stock (page 245) or
    low-sodium, store-bought chicken broth

Put the mustard, honey, curry, cayenne, 3 tablespoons of the lemon juice, the vinegar, and chopped garlic in a nonreactive baking dish or other shallow dish, and slowly whisk in 1 cup of the canola oil to make an emulsified marinade. Put the lamb in the dish and turn to coat. Cover and refrigerate for at least 24 hours or up to 48 hours.

When ready to cook and serve, preheat a gas grill to high, or prepare a charcoal grill for grilling, letting the coals burn until covered with white ash.

Bring a pot of salted water to a boil. Add the orzo and cook until al dente, approximately 8 minutes. Drain and set aside.

Remove the chops from the marinade, brushing off any marinade solids. Season the chops with salt and pepper and grill them until nicely charred and cooked through, 5 to 6 minutes per side for medium rare, or a bit longer for more well-done. Set the chops aside to rest for 5 minutes while you finish the orzo.

Heat 1½ tablespoons of the butter in a heavy-bottomed sauté pan over medium-high heat. Add the eggs and cook, stirring, until well-done. Transfer the eggs to a plate or bowl. Put the remaining 1½ tablespoons butter in a heavy-bottomed pot and melt it over medium-high heat. Add the orzo, spinach, parsley, scrambled eggs, the remaining 1½ tablespoons lemon juice, and the chicken stock and cook, stirring, until all the ingredients are warm, approximately 2 minutes.

To serve, mound some orzo in the center of each plate and lean a double chop against it.

ROASTED VENISON
with Pancetta, Radicchio, and Balsamic

SERVES 4

This staggeringly efficient recipe lets you make the sauce and the vegetable in the roasting pan the venison was cooked in, and to do so while the venison is resting. Bitter radicchio and sour balsamic vinegar make a satisfying and complete pair, and the delicious fat from the venison drippings, butter, and pancetta doesn't hurt, either.

1 venison loin, 1½ pounds
Salt
Freshly ground black pepper
2 tablespoons canola oil
2 ounces pancetta, finely diced

1 large head radicchio, thinly sliced
¼ cup balsamic vinegar
1½ cups Veal Stock (page 246) or low-sodium, store-bought beef broth
2 tablespoons butter

Preheat the oven to 450°F.

Season the venison with salt and pepper. Set a roasting pan over two stovetop burners, add the oil, and heat the pan over medium-high heat. Add the venison and sear it on both sides, 2 to 3 minutes per side. Transfer the pan to the oven and roast the venison for 8 minutes. Turn the venison over and roast for approximately 7 minutes longer for rare. (An instant-read thermometer inserted to the center of the rack will read 120°F to 125°F.) Transfer the venison to a cutting board and tent it with foil to keep it warm. Let rest for 10 minutes while you make the sauce. (During this time the temperature will rise to approximately 130°F.)

Pour any drippings from the roasting pan into a small bowl.

Place the roasting pan over two burners over medium heat on the stovetop. Add the pancetta and cook until it browns and renders enough fat to coat the bottom of the pan, approximately 5 minutes. Add the radicchio and cook, stirring, just until wilted, approximately 1 minute. Add the vinegar and cook, scraping to loosen any flavorful bits stuck onto the bottom of the pan, until nearly evaporated, approximately 1 minute. Add the stock, bring to a boil, then lower the heat and simmer until reduced to about 1 cup liquid, approximately 5 minutes. Remove from the heat and stir in the venison drippings and butter until the butter is melted. Season with salt and pepper.

Spoon some radicchio and sauce onto the bottom of 4 dinner plates. Cut the venison into chops and put 2 chops on top of the radicchio on each plate. Serve.

VEGETABLES

SPAGHETTI SQUASH
à la Red Cat

SWEET-AND-SOUR BABY ONIONS

RED-HOT RAPINI

BRAISED ARTICHOKE HEARTS
alla Romagna

WHITE MUSHROOMS
Roasted with Anchovies

CHANTERELLES
with Capers

GREEN BEANS
Stewed with Tomatoes, Almonds, and Ricotta Salata

GRILLED RADICCHIO AND PANCETTA
with Balsamic

WHITE BEANS
with Pancetta and Peas

POTATOES
with Anchovies, Capers, and Olive Oil

ROASTED YELLOW TURNIPS, YUKONS, AND FENNEL
with Gorgonzola

BAKED ACORN SQUASH

CAULIFLOWER GRATIN

MISSION FIGS
with Mint, Red Onion, Honey, and Balsamic

SPICED FRENCH FRIES

BEETS
with Blue Cheese and Walnuts

For me, vegetable dishes are a matter of ancestral pride. Italians have a word for them, *contorni*, and it's rare to sit down to a true Italian feast without at least one or two side dishes, maybe a starch and something green, or some beets or mushrooms. It says a lot about the Italian sensibility. Because the preparations are so elemental, the cooks can turn out more food dishes, and the people at the table get to sample a variety of flavors, deciding for themselves how much of each one to eat.

These dishes also do double duty extremely well: You can serve a vegetable dish one day as an accompaniment to, say, roast pork, and then polish off leftovers the next day with fresh bread and some stuff foraged from the fridge, such as some mozzarella and prosciutto, perhaps.

The recipes in this chapter were all designed in this spirit. I encourage you to call on them wherever and whenever you crave their flavors. Not only are they versatile at home, but at least half the recipes in this chapter are also terrific condiments for picnics. Because they can be served at room temperature, they offer that precious ease of preparation, and they travel well. Any contorni worth its salt will also make a great antipasti (starter).

Side-dish requirements change based on what the main course is; they're influenced by whether you're serving fish, poultry, or meat, and by what kind of sauce and accompaniments you already have on the plate. Accordingly, each of the dishes in this chapter comes with my suggestions for when to serve it.

SPAGHETTI SQUASH
à la Red Cat

SERVES 4

Spaghetti squash has got to be one of the coolest vegetables: Roast it, then scrape it with a fork, and it creates pasta-like strands, more like angel hair than spaghetti—but you get the idea. The best thing about it is that, like its namesake pasta, you can do just about anything with it, such as tossing it with pancetta and peas, butter and Parmesan, or Brussels sprouts and turnips. At The Red Cat, Chef Bill McDaniel dresses spaghetti squash with a simple, colorful sauce of butter, zucchini, and red bell pepper.

Serve this with fish or poultry.

2 large spaghetti squash, about
   2 pounds each
4 tablespoons extra-virgin olive oil
Salt
Freshly ground black pepper
8 tablespoons (1 stick) butter
2 tablespoons drained capers

Skin of ½ small zucchini, removed in strips
   with a vegetable peeler and diced (¼ cup)
¼ cup diced red bell pepper
⅓ cup lemon juice
¼ cup sliced parsley
1 small plum tomato, peeled, seeded, and diced
   (see page 244)

Preheat the oven to 400°F.

Cut both squash in half lengthwise and scoop out all of the seeds. Rub the squash inside and out with 3 tablespoons of the oil and season with salt and pepper.

Put the squash, cut side down, on a cookie sheet and cover with foil. Roast until the rind is slightly soft, or gives with a little pressure, approximately 20 minutes.

Remove the squash from the oven, uncover, and set aside for a few minutes. As soon as they are cool enough to handle, scrape the meat out with a fork, gathering it in a bowl and keeping it warm.

Heat a wide, heavy-bottomed sauté pan over medium-high heat. Melt the butter and cook until it turns brown, approximately 5 minutes. Add the capers, zucchini, and bell pepper to stop the cooking. Stir in the lemon juice, the remaining tablespoon extra-virgin olive oil, and the parsley, and season with salt and pepper.

In a large mixing bowl, toss the squash with the butter sauce and diced tomato. Serve.

SWEET-AND-SOUR BABY ONIONS

SERVES 4

Sweet cipollini onions, their sugars enhanced by caramelizing, are cooked with balsamic vinegar until it reduces, coating the onions with an intensely flavored glaze. The result is especially good with roasted or cured meats, pâté, and poultry. You can serve this dish hot, but it's really best to let the onions marinate overnight in the refrigerator, and then serve at room temperature.

For a great condiment, cut these up and put them in a sandwich.

¼ cup canola oil

1½ pounds cipollini onions, peeled

⅔ cup balsamic vinegar

Salt

Freshly ground black pepper

Preheat the oven to 400°F.

Heat the oil in a wide, deep, heavy-bottomed, ovenproof sauté pan over medium-high heat. Add the onions and sauté until they begin to brown, 5 to 6 minutes. Add the vinegar, season with salt and pepper, and bring the vinegar to a boil. Transfer the pan to the oven and cook until the vinegar is reduced to a glaze, stirring twice, and the onions have softened completely, offering no resistance to a knife-tip, approximately 5 minutes.

Remove the pan from the oven and let cool. If you have time, transfer the onions to an airtight container and refrigerate overnight. Serve at room temperature.

RED-HOT RAPINI

SERVES 4

Rapini is the true Italian name for the bitter broccoli (known here as rabe) traditionally sautéed with garlic in olive oil and often liberally seasoned with crushed red pepper flakes. Rather than the two-step process of boiling, then sautéing the rabe, this method sautés and then steams it in the same pan with a little bit of stock. Not only is this easier, but it also keeps the broccoli's flavor in the pan rather than letting it seep out into the blanching liquid.

This is one of the real go-to sides at The Red Cat. I can't think of anything I wouldn't serve it with.

2 tablespoons extra-virgin olive oil

1 tablespoon canola oil

4 cloves garlic, thinly sliced

2 shallots, finely diced

2 bunches broccoli rabe, about 2 pounds total weight, bottom ½ inch of stems trimmed

¼ cup White Chicken Stock (page 245), low-sodium, store-bought chicken broth, or water

Salt

Freshly ground black pepper

Generous pinch of crushed red pepper flakes

2 tablespoons butter

Pour 1 tablespoon of the olive oil and the canola oil into a deep-sided sauté pan with a cover. Add the garlic and shallots and sauté until lightly golden, approximately 3 minutes. Add the broccoli rabe and stir to incorporate for 1 minute, then add the stock and stir. Reduce the heat, cover, and cook until the liquid is almost gone and the broccoli rabe is crisp-tender, approximately 8 minutes. Remove the cover and season with salt, pepper, and red pepper flakes. Stir in the butter and remaining tablespoon olive oil and serve.

BRAISED ARTICHOKE HEARTS
alla Romagna

SERVES 4

You've never tasted artichokes like this: braised in oil infused by mint, garlic, and lemon. The braising liquid is something you should keep in mind for salad dressings, herbed mayonnaise, and vegetable aïoli.

I serve these with just about anything: fish, poultry, meat, or other vegetables.

3 cups extra-virgin olive oil, plus more if needed

3 cups canola oil, plus more if needed

4 sprigs mint

4 sprigs thyme

2 cloves garlic, crushed and peeled

1 teaspoon crushed red pepper flakes

2 lemons

4 large artichokes

Pour both of the oils into a medium, heavy-bottomed pot and heat over medium heat. Add the mint, thyme, garlic, and red pepper flakes to the pot and let them infuse the oil as it warms. Continue to heat the oil until hot but not simmering.

Meanwhile, halve 1 of the lemons. Fill a large bowl with cold water and squeeze half the lemon into the water, catching any seeds in your hand. Thinly slice the remaining 1½ lemons and add them to the oil.

Prepare the artichokes: Cut off the top third of the artichokes with a heavy kitchen knife, then trim the stems to 1 inch. Peel the remaining portion of stem to remove the bitter green exterior. As the artichokes are trimmed, place them in the lemon water to keep them from turning brown.

Remove the artichokes from the water, pat them dry with paper towels, and add them to the oil. If the oil doesn't completely cover the artichokes, add equal amounts of extra-virgin olive oil and canola oil until it does. Cover the pot and slowly cook the artichokes until soft to a knife-tip, approximately 1 hour. Use tongs or a slotted spoon to transfer the artichokes to a plate or platter. When cool enough to handle, remove all the leaves and then the hairy choke using a tablespoon. Let cool to room temperature. (The artichoke hearts can be covered and refrigerated for up to 2 days.)

WHITE MUSHROOMS
Roasted with Anchovies

SERVES 4

Most of the time, white button mushrooms don't get much respect in the kitchen, but I find them to have a nice, full mouthfeel, and I love the way they soak up other flavors. Roasted with garlic and anchovies, and finished with extra-virgin olive oil and parsley, they become a complex side dish with very little work.

Serve these with just about anything; they're especially good with eggs in the morning, with polenta as a meal, or alongside roasted chicken.

1½ pounds white button mushrooms, trimmed

2 cloves garlic, thinly sliced

6 anchovy fillets, coarsely chopped

4 tablespoons extra-virgin olive oil

Salt

Freshly ground black pepper

¼ cup sliced parsley

Preheat the broiler.

Put the mushrooms, garlic, and anchovies in a bowl. Toss with 1 tablespoon of the oil and season with salt and pepper. Toss and then spread out in a single layer on a cookie sheet. Broil for 5 minutes, then shake the pan to ensure even cooking and broil until dry, approximately 5 more minutes. Remove the sheet from the oven, transfer the mushrooms to a bowl, drizzle with the remaining 3 tablespoons oil, and scatter the parsley on top. Toss and serve.

CHANTERELLES
with Capers

Chanterelles and capers are a great combination that you almost never see. I myself happened upon it: When making a dish of striped bass with chanterelles one night, it occurred to me to add some capers. Their saltiness got along surprisingly well with the earthy, elegant mushrooms. Rather than slowly cooking and softening the mushrooms, the idea here is to sear them quickly in a very hot pan—the browned exterior adds another flavor component—then toss them with butter and capers. The result has the element of surprise: delicate-looking chanterelles that pack a big punch.

Serve this with just about anything you'd eat mushrooms with, including fish and roast chicken.

2 tablespoons canola oil

2 pounds fresh chanterelle mushrooms, torn by hand into uniform pieces

7 large shallots, thinly sliced into rings

Salt

Freshly ground black pepper

1 tablespoon butter

2 tablespoons drained capers

Heat 1 tablespoon of the canola oil in a large, heavy-bottomed pan over high heat. Add half of the mushrooms and half of the shallots in one layer to sear them evenly, making sure they brown nicely. After a few moments, stir and continue to sauté for about 5 minutes. Season with salt and pepper, add half of the butter and half of the capers, and stir to incorporate. Transfer to a serving bowl, wipe out the pan, and repeat with the remaining ingredients, adding the finished mushrooms to the bowl with the others. Serve hot or at room temperature.

GREEN BEANS

Stewed with Tomatoes, Almonds, and Ricotta Salata

SERVES 4

This dish comes straight from my memory of family dinners: beans stewed in tomato broth until they're so soft you can cut them with a fork, then tossed with almonds, along with a pinch of pepper flakes to spice things up. It's not the most beautiful dish, and it sounds a little weird. All I can tell you is it's delicious, packed with contrasting flavors and textures. The two types of cheese pull all the elements together.

The amount of liquid may seem excessive, but a lot of it evaporates over the long cooking time; starting with a lot ensures the dish remains juicy when it's done.

In addition to eating this with roast pork and polenta, I like it as a warm salad with bread.

½ cup roasted whole almonds

3 tablespoons olive oil

6 cloves garlic, thinly sliced

1 medium onion, finely chopped

1 28-ounce can whole peeled tomatoes, crushed by hand, with their juice

10 ounces green beans, trimmed

1 cup White Chicken Stock (page 245), low-sodium, store-bought chicken broth, or water

Salt

Freshly ground black pepper

2 tablespoons grated Pecorino Romano cheese

Pinch of crushed red pepper flakes

¼ cup crumbled ricotta salata

Put the almonds in a wide, deep skillet and toast over medium-high heat until fragrant, approximately 5 minutes. Set aside.

Heat the oil in a heavy-bottomed sauté pan over medium-high heat. Add the garlic and onion and sauté until softened but not browned, approximately 4 minutes. Add the tomatoes, green beans, and stock. Stir, bring to a simmer, lower the heat, cover, and stew for 1 hour. Add the almonds, season with salt and pepper, and continue to stew, covered, until the beans are very soft to the bite, 30 minutes to 1 hour more. Stir in the Pecorino and red pepper flakes and adjust the seasoning with salt, if necessary.

Preheat the oven to 400°F.

Transfer the mixture to a baking dish, top with the ricotta salata, and bake just until the cheese melts, approximately 4 minutes. Remove the dish from the oven and serve.

NOTE TO THE COOK You can substitute goat cheese or fresh or smoked mozzarella for the ricotta salata.

GRILLED RADICCHIO AND PANCETTA
with Balsamic

SERVES 4

Wrapping bitter radicchio wedges in thin slices of pancetta helps hold them together on the grill. It also imparts tremendous flavor as the fat cooks out of the pancetta and right into the vegetable. The vinegar offers essential contrast to the radicchio, giving the dish a much-needed acidic lift. This is one preparation that is decidedly *not* friendly to substitutions; it has to be made with balsamic vinegar for its unique intensity and sweetness. In case you're wondering where this came from, I was inspired by the components of a bacon, lettuce, and tomato sandwich.

Serve this with grilled or roasted meats.

2 heads radicchio
1 pound thinly sliced pancetta, well chilled
   (about 30 slices)

¼ cup extra-virgin olive oil
3 tablespoons balsamic vinegar

Preheat a gas grill to high, or prepare a charcoal grill for grilling, letting the coals burn until covered with white ash.

Cut each head of radicchio in half through the root. Cut each half into 3 wedges; each about ¾ inch thick, to make 12 wedges, leaving each wedge attached at the root to hold it together.

Unroll each pancetta slice so that it resembles a bacon slice and wrap it around the radicchio, using 2 or 3 overlapping slices per wedge to completely encase the vegetable, and gently squeeze it together to seal the radicchio within. Grill until the pancetta is crisp and the radicchio is wilted and the ends are a little charred, approximately 4 minutes per side.

Transfer the radicchio to a serving platter and drizzle with the oil and vinegar. Serve hot.

NOTE TO THE COOK You can also cook this under the broiler.

WHITE BEANS

with Pancetta and Peas

SERVES 4

White beans are one of the kitchen's universal donors; they go just as well with poultry and meat as they do with a variety of fish. Here, they're complemented by sautéed pancetta, sweet peas, and—most dramatically—caramelized fennel, which gives the whole dish a pleasing, springy flavor.

Serve this with white-fleshed fish, roast chicken, and game.

8 ounces dried white beans, preferably Great Northern or cannellini (about 1 cup)

2 tablespoons extra-virgin olive oil

Salt

2/3 cup defrosted frozen peas, or shelled fresh peas

4 ounces pancetta, finely diced

1/2 small bulb fennel, finely diced

2 cloves garlic, thinly sliced

1/2 cup grated Parmigiano-Reggiano

1 tablespoon butter

2 tablespoons sliced parsley

Freshly ground black pepper

Soak the white beans overnight in enough cold water to cover by 4 inches.

Drain the beans and put them in a heavy-bottomed pot. Add 3 cups cold water and the extra-virgin olive oil, and season with salt. Bring to a simmer, cover, and continue to simmer until the beans are tender, 40 to 50 minutes. There should be approximately 1/4 cup of liquid left in the pot; reserve it and the beans in separate bowls to keep the beans from becoming soggy.

If using fresh peas, while the beans are simmering, bring a small pot of salted water to a boil over high heat. Add the peas and cook for 2 minutes. Drain and refresh under cold running water to stop the cooking and set the color. Drain again and set aside.

Rinse out and dry the pot you used to cook the beans. Put the pancetta in the pot and cook over medium heat until the fat is rendered and the pancetta is crispy, approximately 5 minutes. Transfer to a bowl and set aside.

Add the fennel to the pot with the pancetta fat and sauté slowly over medium heat until nicely caramelized, approximately 25 minutes. Transfer to a bowl using a slotted spoon, leaving behind as much fat as possible.

Add the garlic to the pot and sauté until lightly browned, approximately 5 minutes. Add the beans and their liquid, pancetta, fennel, peas, cheese, butter, and parsley. Season with salt and pepper and cook for a minute or two, stirring, until all of the ingredients are warm and the flavors are integrated. Transfer to a bowl and serve.

POTATOES
with Anchovies, Capers, and Olive Oil

SERVES 4

It's hard to go wrong with pan-fried potatoes, which are a pretty fine all-purpose side dish. Add anchovies and capers, and the potatoes drink up their flavors, becoming something else altogether—an intensely rustic blend of starch and salt, earth and sea.

Serve this with fish dishes and grilled or roasted beef.

1½ pounds Red Bliss potatoes (about 6 medium), cut into ¼-inch coins or thicker

¼ cup plus 2 tablespoons extra-virgin olive oil

Salt

Freshly ground black pepper

4 anchovy fillets, minced

2 tablespoons drained capers

¼ teaspoon crushed red pepper flakes

¼ cup sliced parsley

2 teaspoons chopped oregano

Preheat the oven to 450°F.

Put the potatoes in a bowl, drizzle with ¼ cup of the oil, and season with salt and pepper. Spread out on a cookie sheet in a single layer and roast until tender to a knife-tip, golden, blistered, and slightly crisp, approximately 15 minutes.

Meanwhile, heat the remaining 2 tablespoons oil in a sauté pan over low heat. Add the anchovies and mash with a wooden spoon to dissolve. Raise the heat, add the capers, and season with pepper and the red pepper flakes.

When the potatoes are done, add them to the pan with the anchovies and capers and toss well. Add the parsley and oregano and season with salt and pepper. Transfer to a serving bowl and serve at once.

ROASTED YELLOW TURNIPS, YUKONS, AND FENNEL
with Gorgonzola

SERVES 4

I personally think that the too-often-maligned, uncelebrated yellow turnips are the coolest vegetable in the market. They have a totally unique texture and flavor and when they're in season, from September to April, I use them as often as possible. One of my favorite at-home meals is shaved yellow turnips with penne, butter, and black pepper.

This side dish is meant for the fall, when turnips and potatoes are among the limited seasonal offerings. Be especially careful to cut the vegetables the same size, so they cook at the same rate. Serve this with duck and venison.

1¼ pounds Yukon Gold potatoes, peeled and cut into 1-inch dice

1 pound yellow turnips, peeled and cut into 1-inch dice

1 large bulb fennel, about 1 pound, cored and cut into 1-inch dice

8 cloves garlic

2 tablespoons extra-virgin olive oil

1 tablespoon chopped thyme

Salt

Freshly ground black pepper

2 to 3 tablespoons balsamic vinegar

2 Bosc pears, cut into 1-inch dice

4 ounces Gorgonzola cheese

Preheat the oven to 475°F.

Put the potatoes, turnips, fennel, and garlic in a bowl. Drizzle the oil over the vegetables, scatter the thyme over them, and season with salt and pepper. Toss well.

Turn the contents of the bowl out into a large baking dish and roast for about 45 minutes, or until the vegetables are golden and tender to a knife-tip.

Meanwhile, pour the balsamic vinegar into a saucepan and reduce over medium heat until thickened to a syrupy consistency, approximately 3 minutes. Set aside.

When the vegetables are done, fold in the pears, crumble the cheese on top, and return the baking dish to the oven for 3 minutes. When the cheese is melted, remove the dish from the oven and drizzle with the balsamic vinegar glaze. Serve.

BAKED ACORN SQUASH

SERVES 4

In the fall, there's no better side dish than squash. Pureed, mashed, or diced, its natural sweetness and fiery orange color are irresistible. One of the easiest ways to cook squash is also one of the best ways of coaxing out all its flavor: Simply baking squash halves that are dressed with butter, sugar, and herbs is all it takes to yield a formidable side. You could make this with other squash, but the size and ridges of an acorn are ideal for both portioning and presentation.

This goes great with poultry and game, and it's a natural for Thanksgiving dinner.

2 acorn squash, about 1½ pounds each, halved
    and seeded
4 tablespoons (½ stick) butter
Salt

Freshly ground black pepper
2 tablespoons light brown sugar
2 tablespoons chopped thyme or rosemary

Preheat the oven to 350°F.

Cut a small slice off the skin side of each squash half so it can lie flat on a cookie sheet. Arrange the halves on a sheet without crowding and put 1 tablespoon of the butter in each cavity. Season with salt, pepper, the brown sugar, and the thyme.

Roast until tender to a sharp, thin-bladed knife, 35 to 45 minutes. Serve hot.

NOTE TO THE COOK For a delicious snack or garnish, rinse and dry the squash seeds and roast them in a 375°F oven until lightly golden, approximately 5 minutes. Salt them and serve them instead of nuts at your next cocktail party, or sprinkle them over salads.

CAULIFLOWER GRATIN

SERVES 4

This is a somewhat funkier alternative to potato gratin, with a cool presentation to boot: it's served right in the pan. But this isn't just a textural change. Cauliflower is a more nuanced choice than potato, with a slightly musky flavor. Roasting the cauliflower is a necessary step that removes its moisture, thereby preventing the gratin from becoming watery. Serve this with roast chicken or beef. You can also toss cooked pasta in the sauce before baking it.

1 head cauliflower, separated into small to medium florets
2 tablespoons canola oil
Salt
Freshly ground black pepper
2 tablespoons butter

1 clove garlic, minced
$\frac{1}{4}$ cup plus 2 tablespoons dried bread crumbs (preferably Japanese panko)
$\frac{1}{4}$ cup plus 3 tablespoons grated Parmigiano-Reggiano cheese
2 cups cream

Preheat the oven to 350°F.

Put the cauliflower in a bowl and drizzle with the oil. Season with salt and pepper, spread out on a cookie sheet, and roast until tender to a knife-tip, approximately 15 minutes. Remove from the oven and set aside.

Meanwhile, melt the butter in a heavy-bottomed sauté pan over medium-high heat. Add the garlic and cook for 30 seconds. Add the bread crumbs and cook, tossing frequently, until lightly golden. Remove the pan from the heat, toss in 3 tablespoons of the cheese, and season with salt and pepper. Set aside.

Turn the oven up to 400°F.

Pour the cream into an 8-inch, heavy-bottomed, ovenproof sauté pan and bring to a boil over high heat. Continue to boil until reduced to $\frac{1}{2}$ cup, approximately 8 minutes. Fold in the remaining $\frac{1}{4}$ cup cheese and the cauliflower. Top evenly with the bread crumbs. Transfer to the oven and bake until the crumbs turn golden brown, approximately 5 minutes.

Remove the pan from the oven and serve the gratin right from the pan at the table.

MISSION FIGS
with Mint, Red Onion, Honey, and Balsamic

SERVES 4

This side dish is all about playing off the plump, juicy quality of fresh figs with four very distinct ingredients: mint, onion, honey, and balsamic vinegar. It's a salad-like side that, if the ingredients were chopped, would be a delicious relish. It's good with cured meat, roasted or grilled lamb, and as a relish on a crostini. You can also serve it as an actual salad with crumbled Gorgonzola on top.

2 tablespoons honey

2 tablespoons balsamic vinegar

1/3 cup extra-virgin olive oil

1 1/2 pounds Mission figs, halved or quartered
   depending on size

1/2 medium red onion, very thinly sliced

1/4 cup sliced mint

1/4 cup sliced parsley

Salt

Freshly ground black pepper

Put the honey, balsamic vinegar, and oil in a bowl and stir them together. Add the figs, onion, mint, and parsley. Season with salt and pepper and toss. Serve.

SPICED FRENCH FRIES

SERVES 4

Anyone can make a French fry, but the difference between an everyday fry and a great fry is profound. The secret is in the management of starch and temperature. I like to use russet potatoes, soaking them in cold water, cutting them while cold, and blanching them from a cold state in low-temperature oil before frying in hot oil to crisp and brown them. To be honest, you probably won't make a perfect batch the first time you make this recipe, but if you pay close attention, your fry-making acumen will increase exponentially before you know it.

8 Idaho potatoes, approximately 8 ounces each

About 1 gallon canola oil

1 tablespoon salt

¾ teaspoon curry powder

Heaping ¼ teaspoon cayenne

Peel the potatoes, put them in a large bowl, cover with cold water, and refrigerate overnight. Drain and cut into fries measuring 4 inches long by ¼ inch thick, then return them to the bowl. Set the bowl under cold running water and rinse until all excess starch is removed and the water runs clear, approximately 20 minutes. Drain.

Pour oil into a heavy-bottomed pot to a depth of 8 inches, and heat the oil to 200°F. Blanch the fries in batches in the oil for 10 minutes, then use a slotted spoon to transfer them to a cookie sheet to cool. Straighten them out and chill them in the refrigerator for at least 2 hours, or up to 2 days. (Let the oil cool, then strain it and reserve it for the next step. Store it in an airtight container in a cool, dark, dry place.)

In a small bowl, combine the salt, curry powder, and cayenne. Set aside.

When ready to cook and serve the fries, pour the reserved oil into a heavy-bottomed pot to a depth of 8 inches, and heat the oil to 350°F.

Line a plate with paper towels. Carefully lower the fries into the oil in small batches, so they do not stick together, and make sure they stay submerged in the oil the whole time. (Do not overcrowd, or the oil can overflow, and the fries will not cook evenly.) Fry until golden crisp, approximately 5 minutes. Remove the fries from the oil using a slotted spoon or a wire oil basket and transfer to the paper-towel-lined plate. Season with some of the spice mixture. Repeat with the remaining fries and spice mixture, letting the oil come back up to 350°F before each batch.

Serve hot.

NOTE TO THE COOK The spice mixture is also great rubbed into chicken or meat before cooking.

BEETS
with Blue Cheese and Walnuts
SERVES 4

I'll be the first one to say it: The combination of beets, blue cheese, and walnuts is nothing new; it's been around as the basis of a salad for years. But leave out the greens, and it becomes a powerful all-purpose dish, especially good with grilled and roasted meats. A few small decisions make it come alive, like seeking out Maytag cheese, which actually crumbles rather than gobbing up on you, and seasoning the walnuts with brown sugar and cayenne.

4 large red beets	1/2 medium red onion, thinly sliced
1 tablespoon butter	1 tablespoon sliced parsley
1/2 cup walnut halves	2 tablespoons extra-virgin olive oil
1 tablespoon plus 1 teaspoon light brown sugar	1 tablespoon aged sherry vinegar
Pinch of cayenne	Freshly ground black pepper
Salt	2 tablespoons crumbled Maytag blue cheese

Preheat the oven to 350°F.

Wrap the beets in foil, set on a cookie sheet, and roast until a sharp, thin-bladed knife easily pierces to their center, approximately 2 hours. Remove from the oven and let cool. Do not turn off the oven.

While the beets are cooling, put the butter and walnuts in an ovenproof sauté pan and put in the oven for a minute to melt the butter. Season with the brown sugar, cayenne, and salt, toss, and return to the oven for 5 minutes to toast and flavor the walnuts. Remove from the oven and set aside. When cool enough to work with, coarsely chop the walnuts.

Remove the beets from their skins and cut into 1-inch wedges.

Transfer the beets to a bowl. Add the onion, parsley, oil, and vinegar. Gently toss, season with salt and pepper, transfer to a serving plate, and scatter the walnuts and cheese over the top.

DESSERTS

RISOTTO FRITTERS

BAKED GORGONZOLA-STUFFED PEAR

APPLE TARTE TATIN

STRAWBERRY-RHUBARB CRISP

SUMMER JERSEY PEACH MELBA SUNDAE

BRÛLÉED RICE PUDDING
with Raspberries

VANILLA PANNA COTTA
with Tangerine Sauce and Pomegranate Seeds

AFFOGATO

DEVIL'S FOOD CAKE
with Chocolate Sauce and Dark Chocolate Sorbet

ROCKY ROAD SUNDAE

CRÈME FRAÎCHE ICE CREAM SANDWICH
with Hot Fudge Sauce

STRAWBERRY GRANITA SUNDAE

ICE CREAMS AND SORBETS

TANGERINE SORBET

CHOCOLATE SORBET

YOGURT SORBET

PROSECCO SORBET

MALTED MILK CHOCOLATE ICE CREAM

VANILLA ICE CREAM

CARAMEL ICE CREAM

BLUEBERRY ICE CREAM

BANANA ICE CREAM

I have nothing but respect for those who have mastered the pastry arts. If you're adept at making flowers or blowing shapes out of molten sugar, then my hat's off to you. If you can cut ribbons from chocolate and get them to stand up like Stonehenge on top of a cake, then I'm impressed.

But, personally, I'm less technical when it comes to dessert. I'm really just looking for something that tastes good. Now, I'd rather it be pretty to look at than the other way around, but as a cook, I gravitate toward the most straightforward preparations possible. There's an old line that chefs are surgeons—improvisers who do whatever it takes to get each dish out of the kitchen, responding with creativity to unexpected twists and turns—while pastry chefs are pharmacists, following tried and true formulas over and over again, with no deviation whatsoever. Looked at in those terms, I try to bring a savory mindset to the world of sweetness, with more forgiving recipes and preparations.

This chapter keeps true to my pastry preferences with a selection of desserts ranging from the elemental (sundaes) to the slightly more ambitious (Devil's Food Cake with Chocolate Sauce and Dark Chocolate Sorbet). None of them requires any more skill or experience than most of the savory dishes in the book, so even if you're something of a pastry-phobe, you should have no trouble navigating most of these recipes

to great success. There are a number of recipes for ice cream, sorbet, and granita at the end of the chapter. They're not just there for show; making these dessert staples from scratch is easy, and there's nothing—I mean *nothing*—like having homemade ice cream in the freezer. It's better than anything you can buy.

I'd like to acknowledge The Red Cat's pastry chefs past (Rebecca Mason) and present (Jeff Gerace), for sharing a few of their recipes with me, and in turn with you. The flavors and techniques in this chapter are, as in the rest of the book, a hodgepodge of American, Italian, and French influences, sometimes on the same plate, as in a Brûléed Rice Pudding made with Italian Arborio rice.

Like the savory stuff, desserts are seasonal. With that in mind, there's something for every time of year in these pages, including rhubarb and strawberry for the late spring and early summer, peaches and raspberries for the mid- to late summer, apples and pears for the fall, and citrus and chocolate for the winter. Same goes for the ice creams and sorbets, which include everything from sparkling wine and berry flavors to chocolate and caramel. There are also a few anytime desserts such as the Affogato and the Risotto Fritters.

One more thing: All of these desserts can be made—or substantially prepared—ahead of time, often a day or more in advance, so they're all good choices for entertaining.

RISOTTO FRITTERS

SERVES 4

You can serve these crunchy, fried risotto cakes—inspired by the savory ones Italians use as a vehicle for leftovers—with just about any ice cream you like, or on their own for post-meal snacking. This risotto is a "quickie" version, made by adding all of the liquid at the beginning and simply simmering the rice as you would regular white or brown rice. Since the batter needs to rise for at least an hour, make it and the sugar coating ahead of time, then just fry and dust when the dinner is finished.

Fine sea salt

$\frac{1}{2}$ cup Arborio rice

1 cup milk

1 package dry yeast (2$\frac{1}{4}$ teaspoons)

1$\frac{1}{4}$ cups flour

1 cup plus 1 tablespoon sugar

1 teaspoon ground cinnamon

$\frac{1}{4}$ teaspoon ground cardamom

Canola oil, for frying

Put 3 cups water and a pinch of sea salt in a medium, heavy-bottomed saucepan and bring to a boil over high heat. Add the rice, lower the heat, and simmer until cooked, 15 to 20 minutes. Carefully pour off any excess water and spread the rice out on a parchment- or wax-paper-lined cookie sheet to cool.

Pour the milk into a small saucepan and heat over medium heat until just warm to the touch. Turn off the heat, whisk in the yeast, and let sit for 5 minutes.

Put the flour, 1 tablespoon of the sugar, and $\frac{1}{2}$ teaspoon salt in a bowl and whisk together, then whisk in the milk and fold in the rice. Let rise for 1 hour, or until double in volume; if it seems to be rising too quickly during that time, punch it down.

While the rice mixture is rising, make a sugar coating for the fritters: Put the remaining 1 cup sugar, the cinnamon, cardamom, and $\frac{1}{4}$ teaspoon salt in a bowl and mix well.

When ready to serve, pour the oil into a pot to a depth of 4 inches, and heat the oil to 350°F. Line a plate with paper towels. Carefully scoop the batter into the oil using a quarter-cup measure filled only halfway. Cook only a small batch of scoops at a time so they do not stick together, and fry until golden brown, approximately 6 minutes, making sure the fritters stay submerged in the oil the whole time. (Do not crowd, or the oil can overflow, and the fritters will not cook evenly.) Remove the fritters from the oil using a slotted spoon and transfer to the paper-towel-lined plate to drain. Blot any grease on top of the fritters with a paper towel.

Toss the fritters in the sugar coating, transfer to a serving bowl, and serve warm.

BAKED GORGONZOLA-STUFFED PEAR

SERVES 4

Like a cheese course with its traditional fresh and dried fruit accompaniments, this dessert straddles the worlds of sweet and savory. For a sit-down dinner or special occasion, you could even serve it in place of a cheese course, as a sort of pre-dessert.

2 ripe Bartlett pears, halved lengthwise and
    cored with a melon baller

6 ounces Gorgonzola or Roquefort cheese,
    softened
2 tablespoons honey

Preheat the oven to 350°F.

    Cut a bit off the rounded side of each pear half so the halves can lie flat without wobbling or tipping over. Arrange the pear halves in a baking dish, cored side up. Divide the cheese among the scooped-out cavities. Bake in the oven until the pears are warmed and the cheese is melted and bubbling, 7 to 8 minutes.

    Transfer 1 pear-half to each of 4 dessert plates and drizzle with honey. Serve hot.

APPLE TARTE TATIN

SERVES 8

Tarte Tatin is a classic French pastry, and the original upside-down dessert. Rather than making a tart in a tart dish and arranging fruit on top of it, the fruit (apples) is arranged in the well of a sauté pan, baked with the pastry on top, and the whole thing is turned upside down. This is delicious with Vanilla Ice Cream (page 238) or Caramel Ice Cream (page 238).

1¼ cups flour, plus extra for rolling
½ cup (1 stick) plus 4½ tablespoons butter, chilled
1 teaspoon fine sea salt

¾ cup sugar
1 vanilla bean, split, seeds scraped
5 baking apples, peeled, cored, and cut into 8 equal wedges

Put the flour and ½ cup plus 1 tablespoon of the butter in a stand mixer fitted with the paddle attachment and mix on low speed until they come together into pea-size pieces. Add ¼ cup water and the salt and continue to mix just until the mixture comes together in a ball. (Add 1 or 2 additional tablespoons of water, if necessary, to help the mixture come together in a ball.) Transfer to a bowl, cover with plastic wrap, and refrigerate for 30 minutes.

Roll out the pastry dough on a lightly floured surface into a circle 11 inches in diameter (if using a pan smaller than 10 inches to cook the caramel and apples, then make the circle slightly smaller) and about ⅛ inch thick. Prick it all over with a fork. Transfer to a cookie sheet and refrigerate.

Preheat the oven to 350°F.

In a heavy 10-inch sauté or cast-iron pan, heat the sugar, the remaining 3½ tablespoons butter, and the scraped vanilla seeds and pod over medium heat until the sugar turns amber, 8 to 10 minutes. Remove the pan from the heat, use tongs to remove and discard the vanilla pod, and arrange the apple wedges in a circular pattern in the pan, starting at the outside edge and working your way in toward the center. Pack them in very tightly; they will shrink as they bake.

Lay the pastry over the apples, tucking in any excess dough. Bake in the oven until the pastry becomes nicely golden, approximately 30 minutes. Remove the tart from the oven and let it rest for about 15 minutes.

Carefully and quickly invert the tart onto a serving plate or platter, cut into individual servings, and serve warm.

NOTE TO THE COOK You can use store-bought puff pastry in place of the dough here.

STRAWBERRY-RHUBARB CRISP

SERVES 6 TO 8

This is an early-summer dessert that—like the best summer cooking—doesn't ask you to spend too much time in the kitchen. You just toss some rhubarb and strawberries with sugar, lemon, and honey, top them with dough, and bake. You can serve it with Vanilla Ice Cream (page 238), with whipped cream, or all by itself. You can also make single-serving portions in eight-ounce ceramic baking dishes, baking them for approximately twenty minutes.

2 cups rolled oats

1 cup light brown sugar

3/4 cup flour

1 teaspoon salt

8 tablespoons (1 stick) butter, melted

4 pints fresh strawberries, hulled and cut in half

1 cup sliced rhubarb

3/4 cup granulated sugar

2 tablespoons honey

1 tablespoon lemon juice

Center a rack in the oven and set a large baking sheet on the bottom rack to catch any spills. Preheat the oven to 400°F.

Put the oats, brown sugar, flour, and salt in a medium bowl. Add the melted butter and toss until the ingredients are evenly moistened; then pinch the topping into large crumbs.

Put the strawberries, rhubarb, granulated sugar, honey, and lemon juice in a large bowl and stir together. Spread the mixture into a 10-inch deep-dish pie plate. Scatter the crumbs over the top, all the way to the edge. Bake for about 30 minutes, or until the rhubarb mixture is tender to a knife-tip, the filling is bubbling, and the topping is golden.

Remove the plate from the oven and let rest for 15 minutes. Serve the crisp warm.

SUMMER JERSEY PEACH MELBA SUNDAE

SERVES 4

I'm always looking for ways to change up a classic, but I also believe that when you see perfection, you don't mess around with it. Peach Melba, a sundae of vanilla ice cream, raspberry sauce, and peaches, was created by Auguste Escoffier himself for the Australian opera singer Nellie Melba. I tried to do something different with it countless times, but nothing was as good as the original. So I surrender: Here's my recipe for a classic that never fails to please.

3 cups raspberries

2 tablespoons kirsch

½ cup powdered sugar

2 strips lemon zest, removed with a vegetable peeler, with no pith

1½ tablespoons lemon juice

4 peaches, whole, plus 2 peaches, finely diced

1⅔ cups white wine, preferably Chablis

2¼ cups granulated sugar

1 vanilla bean, split, seeds scraped

2 cups Vanilla Ice Cream (page 238) or store-bought vanilla ice cream

Almond Sablés (recipe follows), or store-bought madeleines or amaretti cookies

Whipped cream (optional)

Make the raspberry sauce: Put 1 cup of the raspberries, the kirsch, powdered sugar, lemon zest, and lemon juice in a food processor fitted with the steel blade. Process to a smooth consistency. Strain through a fine-mesh strainer set over a bowl, pressing down with a rubber spatula to extract as much sauce as possible. Discard the solids. Cover and chill the sauce for at least 2 hours, or up to 24 hours.

Bring a pot of water to a simmer over high heat. Add the 4 whole peaches and cook for about 30 seconds. Remove with a slotted spoon, set aside, and when cool enough to handle, remove the skins with the aid of a paring knife. Discard the skins and set the peeled peaches aside.

Put the wine, granulated sugar, vanilla bean and seeds, and 1¾ cups water in a medium, heavy-bottomed pot and bring to a boil over high heat. Lower the heat so the mixture is simmering, add the peeled peaches, cover, and poach until the peaches are soft, approximately 15 minutes, fewer if the peaches are very ripe. Remove the peaches from the poaching liquid with a slotted spoon and, when cool enough to handle, quarter them.

To make the sundaes, put some raspberry sauce in the bottom of 4 bowls or sundae glasses. Add 1 scoop of ice cream, a few raspberries, 2 peach quarters, 3 or 4 cookies, some diced peaches, another scoop of ice cream, a few more raspberries, 2 more peach quarters, and more cookies and diced peaches. Top with more raspberry sauce and whipped cream, if desired.

Almond Sablés

You can enjoy these cookies on their own, in other sundaes, or with coffee or espresso drinks.

6 tablespoons butter, at room temperature

½ cup plus 1 tablespoon sugar

¼ cup plus 2 tablespoons almond flour (see Note)

Pinch of fine sea salt

¼ cup plus 2 tablespoons all-purpose flour, plus extra for rolling

1 cup sliced blanched almonds

Put the butter and sugar in a bowl and beat together with a wooden spoon until smooth. Beat in the almond flour, salt, and all-purpose flour. Fold in the almonds, cover, and refrigerate for at least 1 hour, or overnight.

Preheat the oven to 350°F.

Roll out the dough on a lightly floured surface to a thickness of ½ inch and cut into 1-inch squares. Arrange the squares on a nonstick baking sheet and bake until golden brown, approximately 8 minutes. Cool on a wire rack.

NOTE TO THE COOK You can buy almond flour from health food stores, specialty grocers, and baking supply shops. (Also, see Mail-Order Sources, page 249.) Or you can make your own. To make 1 cup almond flour, put 2 cups sliced almonds in a food processor fitted with the steel blade. Pulse to a fine powder, but do not overwork or it will turn into a pasty, butter-like mixture. Store almond flour at room temperature in an airtight container in a cool, dark, dry place.

BRÛLÉED RICE PUDDING
with Raspberries

SERVES 4

Rice pudding meets crème brûlée in this summertime dessert. A pudding is made from Arborio rice (yes, the same one used for risotto), then divided among single-serve dishes. Berries are embedded in it, and then it's covered with sugar, which is melted under the broiler. It's just as complex and delicious as it sounds.

⅓ cup Arborio rice

⅓ cup sugar, plus more for brûléeing

3 cups milk

½ vanilla bean, split, seeds scraped

Pinch of fine sea salt

2 egg yolks

½ cup cream

¾ cup raspberries

Put the rice, sugar, 1 cup of the milk, the vanilla bean and seeds, and salt into a large, heavy-bottomed saucepan. Bring to a simmer over low-medium heat, stirring constantly so the rice doesn't scorch or stick to the bottom of the pot. When the milk has reduced by half, add another cup of milk and continue cooking and stirring until that has reduced by half. Add the remaining cup of milk and continue cooking and stirring until it has reduced by half and the mixture is nicely thick. Remove the pot from the heat and stir in the egg yolks. Transfer to a clean bowl, cover the surface with plastic wrap, and refrigerate the pudding until cold, 2 to 3 hours.

Remove the vanilla bean from the rice pudding. Whip the cream to stiff peaks and fold into the pudding. The mixture can be covered and refrigerated for up to 2 hours.

Preheat the broiler.

Divide the pudding mixture among four ovenproof 6-ounce serving dishes. Embed some raspberries into each serving. Sprinkle a thin layer of sugar on the surface of the puddings. Set the serving dishes in a roasting pan and fill the pan with warm tap water halfway up the sides of the serving dishes. Broil until the sugar is caramelized and hard, 1 to 2 minutes. Carefully remove the dishes from the pan and serve immediately.

VANILLA PANNA COTTA
with Tangerine Sauce and Pomegranate Seeds

SERVES 4

Even if I weren't of Italian descent, I think I'd love panna cotta, the creamy dessert that has fascinated diners for generations. Unlike other cream-based desserts such as crème brûlée or flan, it's not made with custard; rather than using eggs as a binding element, it uses just enough gelatin to hold it together. Because it's so creamy, panna cotta is a wonderful foil for intense flavors; no matter what you pair it with—even such vibrant stuff as tangerine sauce and pomegranate seeds—you never lose the flavor or rich texture of the panna cotta itself.

2 teaspoons powdered gelatin

2 tablespoons warm water

1 cup milk

1½ cups cream

¼ cup plus 2 tablespoons sugar

1 vanilla bean, split, seeds scraped

6 tangerines

⅛ teaspoon cornstarch

Seeds of 1 pomegranate

Put the gelatin in a bowl, add the warm water, and let bloom for 3 to 4 minutes.

Put the milk, cream, ¼ cup of the sugar, and half the vanilla bean and all of the seeds in a pot and bring to a boil over high heat. Remove the pot from the heat. Whisk in the bloomed gelatin and strain through a fine-mesh strainer set over a bowl. Divide the mixture among four 6-ounce ramekins. Let cool, then refrigerate until set, 4 to 6 hours, or overnight if possible.

Juice 5 of the tangerines and strain the juice. Reserve 1 cup. Segment the remaining tangerine (see page 123), and set the segments aside.

Make the tangerine sauce: Put the remaining 2 tablespoons sugar, the remaining ½ vanilla bean, and the reserved tangerine juice in a saucepan and bring to a boil over high heat. Stir in the cornstarch until dissolved and continue to cook for 1 minute. Strain through a fine-mesh strainer set over a bowl. Let cool to room temperature, then cover and chill in the refrigerator until cold, at least 2 hours.

When ready to serve, dip the ramekins into a bowl of warm water for 5 seconds to loosen them, then invert onto plates, tapping gently until the panna cotta comes out. Top with some sauce and scatter some pomegranate seeds and tangerine segments around the plate. Serve.

AFFOGATO

SERVES 4

This dessert is a variation of the Italian classic that features a scoop of vanilla ice cream topped with a shot of hot, freshly made espresso. The espresso cools, melting just a bit of the ice cream on contact to create the ultimate combination of coffee and cream. This version adds amaretti cookies—Italian macaroons made with almonds—to the mix, working them into the ice cream.

1¼ cups sliced almonds

1½ teaspoons cornstarch

¾ cup powdered sugar

2 egg whites

⅓ cup plus 1 tablespoon granulated sugar

½ teaspoon vanilla extract

1 tablespoon amaretto liqueur

Pinch of fine sea salt

⅓ cup demerara sugar (see Note)

1 pint Vanilla Ice Cream (page 238) or
    store-bought vanilla ice cream

4 shots espresso

Preheat the oven to 400°F.

Put the almonds on a cookie sheet and toast in the oven until toasted and fragrant, approximately 4 minutes. Let cool, then transfer to the bowl of a food processor fitted with the steel blade. Add the cornstarch and powdered sugar and pulse to a fine mixture.

Lower the oven temperature to 300°F.

Put the egg whites in the bowl of a stand mixer fitted with the whisk attachment and whip on medium speed until frothy. Increase the speed slightly and slowly add the granulated sugar. Whip until stiff peaks form. Add the vanilla, amaretto, and salt, then fold in the almond mixture by hand with a rubber spatula. Transfer to a pastry bag fitted with the plain tip and pipe 1½-inch-round cookies onto a nonstick or parchment-paper-lined cookie sheet. Sprinkle with demerara sugar.

Bake for 20 minutes, then lower the temperature to 200°F and bake until crunchy, about 30 more minutes. Remove the amaretti from the oven and let cool. Chop the cookies into ⅛- to ¼-inch pieces.

Put the ice cream in a bowl. Add the amaretti and use a rubber spatula to stir the amaretti into the ice cream. (If using store-bought ice cream, you may need to let it soften in the refrigerator or on the counter for 15 minutes.) The cookies need not be fully incorporated, just worked into the ice cream a bit.

To make the desserts, put 3 scoops of amaretti cookie ice cream into each of 4 bowls. Pull 4 shots of espresso and pour 1 shot over each serving.

NOTES TO THE COOK Demerara sugar is partially refined, naturally light brown sugar that's used to finish pastries. It dissolves completely, which is essential in the preparation of the cookies here. If you can't find it, you can substitute turbinado or superfine sugar.

You can substitute store-bought amaretti cookies for the homemade ones here.

DEVIL'S FOOD CAKE

with Chocolate Sauce and Dark Chocolate Sorbet

SERVES 8

A deconstructed devil's food cake, this dessert is all about chocolate complementing itself: chocolate cake (actually, it's mocha, comprising cocoa and coffee), a sauce of semisweet and bittersweet chocolate moderated by a touch of vanilla, and chocolate sorbet on the side. It sounds unbelievably rich, but thanks to the careful balancing of different levels of sweetness and bitterness, it all adds up to be a surprisingly understated, elegant affair.

1½ tablespoons butter, melted, plus extra for
    greasing muffin cups

½ cup flour, plus extra to flour muffin cups

¾ cup sugar

6 tablespoons unsweetened cocoa powder
    (preferably Valrhona)

¾ teaspoon baking soda

¼ teaspoon baking powder

1 egg

1 egg yolk

½ cup buttermilk

¼ cup warm brewed coffee

½ teaspoon vanilla extract

Chocolate Sauce (page 229)

1 pint Chocolate Sorbet (page 235) or
    store-bought chocolate sorbet

Preheat the oven to 375°F.

Make the cakes: Butter and flour 8 muffin cups. In a large bowl, whisk the sugar with the cocoa, flour, baking soda, and baking powder. In another bowl, whisk together the egg, egg yolk, buttermilk, coffee, and melted butter. Whisk the egg mixture into the dry ingredients.

Pour the batter into the cups and bake until a toothpick inserted to the center of a cake comes out clean, approximately 15 minutes. Let cool slightly, then invert the cakes onto a wire rack to cool completely.

To serve, place an inverted cake onto each of 8 plates, drizzle with chocolate sauce, and set a scoop of chocolate sorbet alongside.

ROCKY ROAD SUNDAE

SERVES 4

Another of the sundaes in perpetual rotation at The Red Cat, this one deconstructs the classic rocky road ice cream, assembling all of the ingredients—walnuts, chocolate, marshmallows, and of course ice cream—into one sundae. Not surprisingly, they work as well this way as they do in a carton of ice cream, especially since we candy the walnuts and add a chocolate sauce and blondies to the mix.

1 cup walnuts

½ egg white, lightly beaten

1½ teaspoons vanilla extract

2 tablespoons light brown sugar

4 tablespoons (½ stick) butter

1 cup (packed) dark brown sugar

1 egg

1 cup flour

½ teaspoon baking powder

⅛ teaspoon baking soda

½ teaspoon fine sea salt

2 pints Caramel Ice Cream (page 239) or store-bought caramel ice cream

2 dozen small store-bought, gourmet marshmallows

Chocolate Sauce (recipe follows)

Preheat the oven to 300°F.

Make the candied walnuts: Toss the walnuts with the egg white and ½ teaspoon of the vanilla extract in a large bowl. Sprinkle the light brown sugar over the nuts and toss to coat. Spread the nuts on a cookie sheet in a single layer and bake until dry, 30 to 40 minutes, shaking the pan periodically to ensure even cooking. Remove from the oven and set aside to cool. Once cool, lightly crush them.

Raise the oven temperature to 350°F.

Make the blondies: Put the butter and dark brown sugar in a medium saucepan and melt them together over medium heat. Remove the pan from the heat and stir in the egg with a wooden spoon. Stir in the remaining teaspoon vanilla, followed by the flour, baking powder, baking soda, and salt.

Spray a 9 by 9-inch baking pan with nonstick spray, or use a nonstick pan. Pour the batter evenly into the pan and bake until a toothpick inserted to the center of the blondies comes out clean, approximately 16 minutes. (They will look a little underbaked, but that is when they are best.) Remove from the oven and set aside to cool. When cool, cut into ½-inch cubes.

To serve, layer the sundae components in bowls or sundae glasses: Start with 2 scoops of caramel ice cream, then top them with blondie cubes, some crushed nuts, and marshmallows. Top with chocolate sauce and serve.

Chocolate Sauce

MAKES ABOUT 1 CUP

1 tablespoon light corn syrup

4 ounces semisweet chocolate (preferably
   Valrhona 70%, Guanaja), coarsely chopped

1 ounce bittersweet (not unsweetened)
   chocolate (preferably Valrhona 61%, Extra
   Bitter), coarsely chopped

1 teaspoon vanilla extract

Pour the corn syrup and ⅓ cup water into a medium, heavy-bottomed saucepan and bring to a simmer over medium heat. Lower the heat to low and stir in the chocolates until they are melted and the sauce is smooth. You should have about 1 cup of sauce. Remove the pan from the heat and let cool until warm but not hot. Stir in the vanilla extract.

CRÈME FRAÎCHE ICE CREAM SANDWICH
with Hot Fudge Sauce

SERVES 6

I like to bring a little kitchen whimsy to my desserts, and this one is an adult play on an ice cream sandwich. No element here is taken for granted: The cakes are a compelling combination of chocolate and almonds, the filling is flavored by the tanginess of crème fraîche, and the sorbet is made from an unexpected source: yogurt. This recipe takes a bit of work, but it's divided into steps so you can attack it at your own pace.

CHOCOLATE ALMOND CAKES

1 cup semisweet chocolate (preferably Valrhona 70%, Guanaja), coarsely chopped

3 tablespoons butter, at room temperature

3 egg yolks

4 egg whites

½ cup sugar

½ cup almond flour (see Note, page 221)

1 tablespoon cocoa powder

1 tablespoon cornstarch

Preheat the oven to 325°F.

Put the chocolate and butter in the top of a double boiler set over simmering water and stir with a rubber spatula to help them melt together.

Put the egg yolks and ¼ cup plus 2 tablespoons water in a bowl and whisk until soft peaks form and the eggs increase in volume by approximately three times. Whisk the yolks into the chocolate.

Put the egg whites and sugar into the bowl of a stand mixer fitted with the whisk attachment and whip until soft peaks form. Remove the bowl from the mixer. Sift together the almond flour, cocoa powder, and cornstarch and fold them into the egg whites.

Fold the egg-white mixture into the chocolate mixture. Line a 9- by 13-inch cookie sheet with a 1-inch rim with parchment paper. Spread the batter out on the lined cookie sheet and bake until set, approximately 15 minutes. Remove the sheet from the oven, trim the overbaked, crusty edges, and cut into 2 rectangles of equal size. Freeze for at least 2 hours, or until firm.

CRÈME FRAÎCHE FILLING

6 egg yolks

1½ cups sugar

6 egg whites

2 cups crème fraiche

⅔ cup cream

ASSEMBLY

1 pint Yogurt Sorbet (page 236)

Hot Fudge Sauce (recipe follows)

Put the yolks and ½ cup sugar in the top of a double boiler set over simmering water and cook, whisking, until pale ribbons form, approximately 4 minutes. Remove the pot from the heat and transfer the mixture to the bowl of a stand mixer. Fit the mixer with the whisk attachment and whip until cool, approximately 10 minutes. Remove the bowl from the mixer and set aside.

Put the egg whites and the remaining 1 cup sugar in the pot of a double boiler set over simmering water and cook, whisking, until soft peaks form, approximately 5 minutes. Remove the pot from the heat and fold the egg-white mixture into the egg-yolk mixture.

Put the crème fraîche and cream in a bowl and whip until soft peaks form. Fold into the egg and sugar mixture.

Remove the cakes from the freezer. Put the filling in between the cakes, sandwich, and cut into 6 sandwiches. Freeze until ready to serve.

To serve, put 1 ice cream sandwich on each of 6 plates. Put a scoop of sorbet alongside, and drizzle hot fudge sauce over and around the sandwich.

Hot Fudge Sauce

MAKES ABOUT 1 CUP

¼ cup plus 2 tablespoons cream
½ tablespoon vegetable oil
1½ tablespoons light corn syrup

4 ounces bittersweet (not unsweetened) chocolate (preferably Valrhona 61%, Extra Bitter), coarsely chopped
2 tablespoons milk

Put ¼ cup of the cream, the vegetable oil, and corn syrup in a medium, heavy-bottomed saucepan and bring to a boil over high heat. Remove the pan from the heat and whisk in the chocolate until it melts. Whisk in the remaining 2 tablespoons cream and the milk. Keep warm in a double boiler set over simmering water until ready to serve.

The sauce can be cooled, transferred to an airtight container, and refrigerated for up to 3 days. Reheat before serving.

STRAWBERRY GRANITA SUNDAE

SERVES 4

The textural contrasts in this sundae—more of a layered parfait, really—are as stark as they come: shaved strawberry granita and an airy, fluffy anise mousse. It's cool, creamy, and crunchy, and it's ideal for summer entertaining because both components can be made in advance and assembled in seconds.

¾ cup slivered almonds

½ tablespoon anise seed

1 cup cream, plus more if needed

⅓ teaspoon powdered gelatin

1 tablespoon warm water

Heaping ⅓ cup sugar

4 egg yolks

1 pint Strawberry Granita (recipe follows)

Put the almonds in a pan and toast over high heat until toasted and fragrant, approximately 4 minutes. Remove from the heat and let cool. Coarsely chop the almonds in a food processor or transfer to a cutting board and chop by hand with a chef's knife. Set aside.

Put the anise seed in a pan and toast over high heat until lightly toasted and fragrant, approximately 2 minutes. Transfer to a cutting board and coarsely chop it.

Pour the cream into a small saucepan and add the anise seed. Bring to a boil, then remove from the heat and let steep for 20 minutes. Strain through a fine-mesh strainer set over a heat-proof measuring cup. You should have 1 cup of infused cream; if you don't, add enough cream to achieve that volume. Refrigerate until very cold, at least 4 hours or overnight.

Put the gelatin in a small bowl, add the 1 tablespoon warm water, and let bloom for 3 to 4 minutes.

Put the sugar in a small saucepan, add ¼ cup water, and cook until the mixture reaches a temperature of 220°F. Add the softened gelatin. Put the yolks in the bowl of a stand mixer fitted with the whisk attachment. With the motor running on high speed, slowly pour the sugar mixture down the side of the mixing bowl. Whip until the eggs and sugar are cool.

Meanwhile, whip the cooled cream by hand in a bowl with a whisk until soft peaks form.

Remove the bowl from the stand mixer and fold the whipped cream into the egg mixture.

To serve, put a layer of granita in the bottom of each of four 6- to 8-ounce bowls or sundae glasses. Top with a layer of anise mousse. Sprinkle with chopped almonds. Repeat with granita, mousse, and almonds, and finish with one last layer of granita and a few more almonds. Serve immediately.

Strawberry Granita

MAKES ABOUT 1 QUART

½ cup sugar

2½ tablespoons corn syrup

2 pints strawberries

Pinch of fine sea salt

Few drops of lemon juice

Put the sugar, ½ cup water, and corn syrup in a small saucepan and bring to a boil over high heat. Remove the pan from the heat and set aside to cool.

Puree the strawberries with the sugar syrup in a blender or a food processor fitted with the steel blade. Add the salt and lemon juice (just enough to brighten the taste of the berries, but not to taste like lemon). Strain the mixture through a fine-mesh strainer over a nonreactive baking dish and freeze the mixture until icy around the edges, approximately 1 hour. Scrape with a fork. Repeat the freezing and scraping twice. Let freeze for at least 2 hours, or overnight.

To serve, scrape with a fork one last time, then divide among 4 bowls.

ICE CREAMS AND SORBETS

There was a time, not that long ago, when making your own sorbets and ice creams was a pretty big deal, involving rock salt and hand-cranked machines. Today, there are a lot of affordable, compact, and easy-to-use ice-cream machines on the market that make it a pretty small commitment of time and effort.

TANGERINE SORBET

MAKES ABOUT 1 QUART

3¾ cups tangerine juice (from 16 to
    20 tangerines)
Juice of 1½ lemons

¾ cup sugar, plus more if necessary
Pinch of fine sea salt

Mix all of the ingredients together in a bowl, and taste. If the mixture doesn't seem sweet enough, add some more sugar.

   Freeze in an ice-cream maker according to the manufacturer's instructions.

CHOCOLATE SORBET

MAKES ABOUT 1 QUART

2 cups plus 3 tablespoons sugar
¾ cup cocoa powder (preferably Valrhona)

7 ounces bittersweet (not unsweetened)
    chocolate (preferably Valrhona 61%, Extra
    Bitter), coarsely chopped

Put the sugar and 2¾ cups water in a medium saucepan and bring to a boil over high heat. Whisk in the cocoa powder and return to a simmer. Remove from the heat and whisk in the chocolate. Mix with a hand blender, or process briefly in a blender; strain through a fine-mesh strainer set over a bowl; and let cool. Transfer to an ice-cream maker and freeze according to the manufacturer's instructions.

YOGURT SORBET

1 quart plain yogurt   2¼ cups sugar

Line a fine-mesh strainer with cheesecloth, set over a bowl, and pour the yogurt into the strainer. Refrigerate the setup overnight, to remove the excess water from the yogurt.

Put the sugar and 2 cups water into a small saucepan and cook, stirring, until the sugar dissolves into a syrup. Let cool, transfer to an airtight container, and refrigerate until cold.

Stir together the drained yogurt and sugar syrup and freeze in an ice-cream maker according to the manufacturer's instructions.

PROSECCO SORBET

MAKES ABOUT 1 QUART

1⅓ cups sugar   ½ bottle (375 ml) of prosecco
1 bay leaf   Few drops of lemon juice
1 sage leaf   Pinch of fine sea salt
½ ripe peach

Put the sugar, 1¾ cups water, bay leaf, and sage leaf into a pot and bring to a boil over high heat. Remove the pot from the heat and remove the bay and sage leaves with tongs or a slotted spoon. Let the mixture cool. You should have 1¼ cups syrup; measure it and discard any extra.

Puree the peach in a blender or a food processor fitted with the steel blade. Transfer to a bowl and add the syrup, prosecco, lemon juice, and salt. Strain through a fine-mesh strainer set over a bowl, transfer to an ice-cream maker, and freeze according to the manufacturer's instructions.

MALTED MILK CHOCOLATE ICE CREAM

MAKES ABOUT 1 QUART

5¼ ounces high-quality milk chocolate, chopped

2 ounces bittersweet (not unsweetened) chocolate (preferably Valrhona 61%, Extra Bitter), coarsely chopped

Heaping ¼ cup malted milk powder

1½ cups cream

⅓ cup plus 1 tablespoon sugar

Pinch of fine sea salt

1½ cups half-and-half

3 egg yolks

Put the milk chocolate and bittersweet chocolate in the top of a double boiler set over simmering water to melt. Stir in the malted milk powder.

Put the cream, sugar, salt, and half-and-half in a medium saucepan and bring to a boil over medium-high heat. Whisk the egg yolks in a heat-proof medium bowl. Slowly add half of the hot liquid to the yolks, whisking constantly, then return the entire mixture to the saucepan. Pour in the melted chocolate and stir over medium heat until the mixture just begins to thicken, approximately 4 minutes. Strain through a fine-mesh strainer set over a bowl and let the mixture cool. (To speed the cooling, you can set the bowl in the refrigerator, or in another bowl filled halfway with ice.)

Freeze in an ice-cream maker according to the manufacturer's instructions.

VANILLA ICE CREAM

MAKES ABOUT 1 QUART

1½ cups milk

1½ cups cream

¾ cup sugar

1 vanilla bean, split, seeds scraped

Pinch of fine sea salt

8 egg yolks

Put the milk, cream, sugar, vanilla seeds and pod, and salt in a medium saucepan and bring to a boil over medium-high heat. Whisk the egg yolks in a heat-proof medium bowl. Slowly add half of the hot liquid to the yolks, whisking constantly, then return the entire mixture to the saucepan. Stir over medium heat until the mixture just begins to thicken, approximately 4 minutes. Strain through a fine-mesh strainer set over a bowl and let the mixture cool. (To speed the cooling, you can set the bowl in the refrigerator, or in another bowl filled halfway with ice.)

Freeze in an ice-cream maker according to the manufacturer's instructions.

CARAMEL ICE CREAM

MAKES ABOUT 1 QUART

2 cups milk

2 cups cream

1 cup sugar

10 egg yolks

Pinch of fine sea salt

Put the milk and cream in a medium saucepan and heat over medium heat, but do not boil.

In a large saucepan, cook the sugar and 1 cup water over medium heat to a dark, amber caramel, approximately 5 minutes. Pour in the hot milk mixture, being very careful, as the hot caramel will sizzle and spit. Bring the mixture to a boil to dissolve all of the sugar.

Whisk the egg yolks in a medium bowl. Slowly add half of the hot caramel mixture to the yolks, whisking constantly, then return the entire mixture to the saucepan. Add the salt. Stir over low heat until the mixture thickens enough to coat the back of the spoon, approximately 7 minutes. Strain through a fine-mesh strainer set over a bowl and let the mixture cool. (To speed the cooling, you can set the bowl in the refrigerator, or in another bowl filled halfway with ice.)

Freeze in an ice-cream maker according to the manufacturer's instructions.

BLUEBERRY ICE CREAM

MAKES ABOUT 1 QUART

1$\frac{1}{2}$ cups milk

1$\frac{1}{2}$ cups cream

1$\frac{1}{4}$ cups sugar

Fine sea salt

8 egg yolks

$\frac{1}{4}$ teaspoon coriander seed, crushed and wrapped in cheesecloth

2 coins peeled fresh ginger, about 1 inch in diameter and $\frac{1}{8}$ inch thick

1 pint blueberries

$\frac{1}{2}$ lemon

Put the milk, cream, $\frac{1}{2}$ cup of the sugar, and a pinch of salt in a medium saucepan and bring to a boil over medium-high heat. Whisk the egg yolks in a medium bowl. Slowly add half of the hot liquid to the yolks, whisking constantly, then return the entire mixture to the saucepan. Stir over medium heat until the mixture just begins to thicken, approximately 4 minutes. Strain through a fine-mesh strainer set over a bowl and let the mixture cool. (To speed the cooling, you can set the bowl in the refrigerator, or in another bowl filled halfway with ice.)

Meanwhile, put the remaining $\frac{3}{4}$ cup sugar, 1 cup of water, the coriander, and ginger in a small saucepan, bring to a boil, and pour into a heat-proof bowl over the blueberries. Cover with plastic wrap and let steep until the mixture cools to room temperature, approximately 15 minutes.

When the custard is cool and the berries are cool, put $\frac{1}{2}$ cup of the blueberries in a bowl with $\frac{1}{4}$ cup of the blueberry poaching syrup. Mix with a hand blender, or in a blender. Whisk into the ice-cream base. Strain the rest of the blueberries. Discard the ginger and coriander. Fold the blueberries into the pureed base and add a pinch of salt and some lemon juice to taste (you should use just less than the juice of $\frac{1}{2}$ lemon). Discard the rest of the blueberry poaching syrup, or save for another use, such as flavoring drinks.

Freeze in an ice-cream maker according to the manufacturer's instructions.

BANANA ICE CREAM

MAKES ABOUT 1 QUART

1½ cups milk

1½ cups cream

1 vanilla bean, seeds scraped, pod reserved
   for another use

¾ cup sugar

Pinch of fine sea salt

8 egg yolks

⅔ cup mashed ripe banana (from 1½ to
   2 bananas)

Put the milk, cream, vanilla seeds, sugar, and salt in a medium saucepan and bring to a boil over medium-high heat. Whisk the egg yolks in a heat-proof medium bowl. Slowly add half of the hot liquid to the yolks, whisking constantly, then return the entire mixture to the saucepan. Stir over medium heat until the mixture just begins to thicken, approximately 4 minutes. Strain through a fine-mesh strainer set over a bowl and let the mixture cool. (To speed the cooling, you can set the bowl in the refrigerator, or in another bowl filled halfway with ice.)

Transfer the mixture to a blender, in batches if necessary, and blend in the bananas.

Freeze in an ice-cream maker according to the manufacturer's instructions.

STOCKS & BASIC TECHNIQUES

PEELING AND SEEDING TOMATOES

To peel tomatoes, bring enough water to generously cover the tomatoes to a boil in a pot set over high heat. Fill a large bowl halfway with ice water.

Remove the core from the top of the tomatoes (where the stem meets the flesh) with a paring knife, and score the bottom of each tomato with a shallow X. Submerge the tomatoes in boiling water and cook until the peel begins to pull away from the flesh, approximately 15 seconds. Use tongs or a slotted spoon to transfer the tomatoes to the ice water to stop the cooking. Once cooled, remove the skins by pulling them off by hand, or with the aid of a paring knife.

To seed a tomato, simply cut off the top $\frac{1}{2}$ inch and gently squeeze out the seeds. If peeling tomatoes, seed them after peeling.

ROASTING PEPPERS

To roast peppers, grill them over an open flame, or impale them on a long meat fork and cook them in the flame of a gas stove, turning them, until blackened and blistered all over. Immediately transfer them to a heat-proof bowl and cover tightly with plastic wrap. Let steam in their own heat for 5 minutes. Remove the plastic and, when cool enough to handle, peel the peppers, then halve and seed them and slice as desired.

WHITE CHICKEN STOCK

MAKES ABOUT 2 QUARTS

5 to 6 pounds chicken bones (or skinless
   chicken parts, such as thighs or wings)
1 large carrot, peeled and cut into large pieces
1 large onion, peeled and halved

2 stalks celery, cut into large pieces
1 bay leaf
3 sprigs thyme

Rinse the bones well under cold running water and transfer to a stockpot. Cover with about 4 quarts cold water. Gradually bring the water to a simmer over medium heat and let simmer for 10 minutes. Drain the chicken bones to remove any impurities, such as fat and blood. Cover again with about 4 quarts cold water, or enough to cover the solids by at least 1 inch. Add the carrot, onion, celery, bay leaf, and thyme. Gradually bring the water to a simmer over medium heat and let simmer for 4 to 6 hours, periodically skimming any fat or impurities with a spoon. (If the water falls below the level of the solids, add enough to cover them by 1 inch.) Strain.

   The stock can be used right away or cooled, transferred to an airtight container, and refrigerated for up to 3 days or frozen for up to 2 months.

DARK CHICKEN STOCK

MAKES ABOUT 2 QUARTS

5 to 6 pounds chicken bones
¼ cup olive oil
1 large carrot, peeled and cut into large pieces
1 large onion, peeled and halved
1 stalk celery, cut into large pieces

1 bay leaf
3 sprigs thyme
2 large beefsteak tomatoes, halved
4 quarts White Chicken Stock (recipe above)

Preheat the oven to 350°F.

   Put the chicken bones in a roasting pan and roast until golden brown, approximately 40 minutes, shaking the pan periodically to ensure even roasting. Remove from the oven and set aside.

   Pour the oil into a stockpot and heat it over medium heat. Add the carrot, onion, and celery and cook until softened but not browned, approximately 4 minutes. Add the bay leaf, thyme, tomatoes, chicken bones, and stock. Bring to a simmer and continue to simmer for 6 hours, periodically skimming any fat or impurities with a spoon. (If the liquid falls below the level of the solids, add enough water to cover them by 1 inch.) Strain.

   The stock can be used right away or cooled, transferred to an airtight container, and refrigerated for up to 3 days or frozen for up to 2 months.

VEAL STOCK (AKA BEEF STOCK) AND VEAL DEMI-GLACE

MAKES ABOUT 2 QUARTS STOCK OR 2 CUPS DEMI-GLACE

1 large onion, cut into ¼-inch rings, plus
   1 large onion, peeled and halved
4 tablespoons canola oil
Salt
Freshly ground black pepper
1 large carrot, peeled and cut into large pieces
3 stalks celery, cut crosswise into large pieces

2 heaping tablespoons tomato paste
5 pounds veal knuckle or shank bones,
   split in half
2 cups dry white wine
1 large beefsteak tomato, quartered
3 sprigs thyme

Preheat a gas grill to high, or prepare a charcoal grill for grilling, letting the coals burn until covered with white ash.

Brush the onion halves with 2 tablespoons of the oil, season with salt and pepper, and grill until the cut sides are completely charred, about 3 minutes. Remove from the grill and set aside. (Alternatively, you can blacken the onion halves on an indoor gas grill, or by impaling the onions on a fork and cooking them in the flame of a gas jet on the stovetop.)

Heat the remaining 2 tablespoons oil in a heavy-bottomed stockpot over medium heat. Add the carrot, celery, and sliced onion, and cook until softened but not browned, approximately 4 minutes. Add the tomato paste, grilled onions, and veal bones, and stir to coat the other ingredients with the paste. Add the wine and cook until it reduces completely, approximately 6 minutes. Add the tomato and thyme and 4 quarts cold water, or enough to cover the solids by at least 1 inch, and bring to a simmer. Continue to simmer for 8 to 10 hours, periodically skimming any fat or impurities with a spoon. (If the water falls below the level of the solids, add enough to cover them by 1 inch.) Strain.

To make veal demi-glace, simmer the strained stock until it coats a wooden spoon and is reduced to about 2 cups.

The stock, or demi-glace, can be used right away or cooled, transferred to an airtight container, and refrigerated for up to 3 days or frozen for up to 2 months.

SHELLFISH STOCK

MAKES ABOUT 2 QUARTS

2 tablespoons olive oil

1 large onion, coarsely chopped

2 stalks celery, coarsely chopped

1 medium bulb fennel, coarsely chopped

1 bay leaf

1 teaspoon fennel seeds

8 ounces littleneck clams, scrubbed

8 ounces mussels, scrubbed and debearded

1 cup dry white wine

Pinch of saffron threads

Heat the oil in a heavy-bottomed stockpot. Add the onion, celery, and fennel and cook until softened but not browned, approximately 4 minutes. Add the bay leaf and fennel seeds, then the clams and mussels. Add the wine and 4 quarts cold water, or enough to cover the solids by at least 1 inch.

Bring to a simmer and simmer for 1½ hours, periodically skimming any fat or impurities with a spoon. (If the water falls below the level of the solids, add enough to cover them by 1 inch.) Strain and finish with a pinch of saffron.

Use the stock right away, or cool, cover, and refrigerate for up to 2 days, or freeze for up to 2 months.

MAIL-ORDER SOURCES

D'ARTAGNAN
Duck and duck products, game birds,
poultry, and smoked and cured meats
800-327-8246, ext. 0
www.dartagnan.com

JAMISON FARM
Lamb and lamb products
800-237-5262
www.jamisonfarm.com

KALUSTYAN'S
Beans, honeys, legumes, nut flours, oils, salts,
spices, and vinegars
800-352-3451
www.kalustyans.com

LOBSTER PLACE
Fish and shellfish from New York City
212-255-5672
www.lobsterplace.com

NUESKE'S
My favorite bacon
800-382-2266
www.nueskemeats.com

NIMAN RANCH
Beef, pork, lamb, and double-smoked bacon
866-808-0340
www.nimanranch.com

PIKE PLACE FISH
Fish and shellfish from Seattle
800-542-7732
www.pikeplacefish.com

SALUMERIA BIELLESE
French and Italian charcuterie
212-736-7376
www.salumeriabiellese.com

ACKNOWLEDGMENTS

Thanks, you guys:

Pam Krauss, of Potter, who shared our vision and let us go with it, and Rica Allannic, the new editor on the block, who brought it all home and, believe or not, knows where every comma in the book is and why we decided to leave it there.

Andrew Friedman, my coauthor, who said "We gotta do a book" every time he came to dinner at The Red Cat until he got his way; I'm glad he did.

David Sawyer, our photographer, for venturing into the land of cookbooks with us; and to his wife and agent, Mara Singer, for not beating us up too much on the deal.

Harold Dieterle, TV superstar in the making, for helping us test the recipes every other Wednesday. It'll be cool to say we knew you when.

Bill McDaniel, executive chef of The Red Cat, for helping us prepare for recipe testing each week, and more than that—for being such an excellent captain of the first ship I ever owned.

Tucker—no, not Carlson—Amy Tucker, my former assistant, who helped us in the kitchen during the early days of testing.

At Potter, Jane Treuhaft, Mark McCauslin, Linnea Knollmueller, and Amy Corley, for all their help in turning a manuscript into a book.

Denise Canter, for selecting the perfect props for the photographs.

Joey Campanaro, longtime friend, colleague, and chef, for being one of my favorite kitchen collaborators, contributing some of the recipes to the book, and shepherding the food for the photo shoot.

Mike Price and Laurence Edelman, for cooking the food we shot for the book.

Janis Donnaud, my agent, for believing there was a book here, and helping us get it to the right people.

Alicia Nosenzo and Connor Coffey, our first managers (Alicia's moved on to a larger job in the company; Connor's just moved on)—the place would not be what it is if you hadn't been there.

Phil Baltz, the only publicist I have ever had. Keep up the good work. And please return my phone call.

All the journalists, editors, and producers who helped put The Red Cat (and my other restaurants) on the map—thanks for spreading the word.

Mom and Dad—for everything.

Danny Abrams, for being a great business partner, the yin to my yang, and the more sensible one of the pair, unless you count the time he cut the buckles off his Gucci loafers.

Billy, Bob, Paul, and Bob, for your endless support over the years.

Everybody who works or has worked with us over the years in all my restaurants. This is a team sport, and you've helped us get to the "show" and maintain a winning record.

Pam Norwood, for her unwavering and everlasting support since I arrived in New York. Asante sana.

Pooty, Surfcino, and G-Man, mates for life.

All of our loyal patrons—you know who you are—who trekked all the way over to Tenth Avenue before it was fashionable to do so, and who make it fun to come to work every day.

New York City—I came here for what I said would be a maximum two-year look-see. That was twelve years ago. I ain't going nowhere.

INDEX